Death Rites
and Hawaiian Royalty

Death Rites and Hawaiian Royalty

Funerary Practices in the Kamehameha and Kalākaua Dynasties, 1819–1953

RALPH THOMAS KAM

McFarland & Company, Inc., Publishers
Jefferson, North Carolina

LIBRARY OF CONGRESS CATALOGUING-IN-PUBLICATION DATA

Names: Kam, Ralph Thomas, author.
Title: Death rites and Hawaiian royalty : funerary practices in the Kamehameha and Kalākaua dynasties, 1819–1953 / Ralph Thomas Kam.
Other titles: Funerary practices in the Kamehameha and Kalākaua dynasties, 1819–1953
Description: Jefferson, North Carolina : McFarland & Company, Inc., Publishers, 2017 | Includes bibliographical references and index.
Identifiers: LCCN 2017036997 | ISBN 9781476668468 (softcover : acid free paper) ∞
Subjects: LCSH: Hawaiians—Funeral customs and rites. | Hawaiians—Kings and rulers—Biography. | Funeral rites and ceremonies—Hawaii—History. | Hawaiians—Social life and customs—History.
Classification: LCC DU624.65 .K34128 2017 | DDC 393/.930996909041—dc23
LC record available at https://lccn.loc.gov/2017036997

BRITISH LIBRARY CATALOGUING DATA ARE AVAILABLE

ISBN (print) 978-1-4766-6846-8
ISBN (ebook) 978-1-4766-2861-5

© 2017 Ralph Thomas Kam. All rights reserved

No part of this book may be reproduced or transmitted in any form or by any means, electronic or mechanical, including photocopying or recording, or by any information storage and retrieval system, without permission in writing from the publisher.

On the cover: Poola (stevedores) pull the catafalque of King David Kalākaua in 1891 (courtesy Hawaii State Archives)

Printed in the United States of America

McFarland & Company, Inc., Publishers
  Box 611, Jefferson, North Carolina 28640
    www.mcfarlandpub.com

In memory of my grandmother
Anna Lau Kam,
whose death first introduced me
to Western funerals,
and to my uncle Ernest Kam,
who maintained the Chinese traditional
bai san observances for his father

Acknowledgments

Special thanks go to the staff of the Hawaii State Archives, Archives of the Hawaiian Historical Society, Bishop Museum Archives, Department of Accounting and General Services Land Survey Office, Department of Accounting and General Services Bureau of Conveyances, and Hawaiian Mission Children's Society Library.

Table of Contents

Acknowledgments	vi
Preface	1
Introduction	3
Death of Kamehameha the Great	7
Death of Likelike and Traditional Hawaii Mourning Practices	8
An Early Model	9
Lying in State	13
Funerals	13
Processions	14
Royal Deaths After the Overthrow	14
1. Royal Deaths	**17**
Royal Deaths During the Kamehameha Dynasty	17

Kamehameha the Great (1819) *17*; Kauwai (1823) *18*; Keōpūolani (1823) *21*; George Cox Keʻeaumoku (1824) *25*; Kaumualiʻi (1824) *28*; Kamehameha II and Kamāmalu (1824) *31*; Kalanimoku (1827) *36*; Nāmāhana (1829) *36*; Kamanele (1831) *38*; Keaweaweʻulaokalani I (1832) *38*; Queen Kaʻahumanu, Kuhina Nui (1832) *38*; David Kamehameha (1835) *40*; John Young (1835) *41*; Nāhiʻenaʻena (1837) *41*; Kīnaʻu (1839) *44*; Kuini Liliha (1839) *46*; Hoapili (1840) *47*; Chiefess Kapiʻolani (1841) *47*; Keaweaweʻulaokalani II (1842) *48*; Hoapili Wahine (1842) *48*; Haʻalilio (1845) *48*; Kekāuluohi (1845) *50*; William Pitt Leleiohoku, Kaʻiminaʻauao and Moses Kekuaiwa (1848) *51*; Kealiʻiahonui (1849) *53*; Kaʻōanaʻeha (1850) *55*; Kekauʻōnohi (1851) *55*; James Young Kanehoa (1851) *56*; James Kaliokalani (1852) and Polly Paʻaʻāina (1853) *57*; Kamehameha III (1854) *58*; Abner Pākī (1855) *63*; Kōnia (1857) *64*; Keoni Ana (1857) *65*; Joshua Kaeo (1858) *66*;

Thomas Charles Byde Rooke (1858) *66*; John William Pitt
Kīna'u (1859) *68*; Bennet Nāmākēhā (1860) *69*; Abigail
Maheha (1861) *70*; Jane Lahilahi Young (1862) *72*; Prince of
Hawai'i (1862) *72*; Keolaokalani Pākī Bishop (1863) *74*; King
Kamehameha IV (1863) *74*; Robert Crichton Wyllie (1865) *79*;
Princess Victoria Kamāmalu (1866) *80*; Grace Kama'iku'i
(1866) *82*; Kaisara (Caesar) Kapa'akea (1866) *83*; Mataio
Kekūanāo'a, Kuhina Nui (1868) *85*; High Chiefess Keohokā-
lole (1869) *87*; Queen Kalama (1870) *88*; Kamehameha V
(1872) *92*; Jane Loeau (1873) *94*; King William Charles
Lunalilo (1874) *95*

Royal Deaths During the Kalākaua Dynasty   98
Charles Kana'ina (1877) *99*; William Pitt Leleiohoku
Kalahoolewa (1877) *100*; Fanny Kekelaokalani Young (1880)
103; Peter Young Kaeo (1880) *104*; Ruth Keanolani Kanahoa-
hoa Ke'elikōlani (1883) *106*; Princess Victoria Kūhiō Kinoiki
Kekaulike (1884) *111*; Bernice Pauahi Bishop (1884) *112*;
Queen Emma (1885) *115*; Princess Miriam Likelike (1887)
121; Prince Edward Abel Keliiahonui (1887) *126*; King
David Kalākaua (1891) *127*; John Owen Dominis (1891)
136

Royal Deaths During the Provisional Government
and the Republic of Hawaii   138
Virginia Kapooloku Po'omaikelani (1895) *138*; Ka'iulani (1899)
139; Queen Kapi'olani (1899) *143*

Royal Deaths During the Territory of Hawaii   146
Albert Kūnuiākea (1903) *147*; Robert W. Wilcox (1903) *150*;
Mary Kūnuiākea (1904) *152*; David Kawānanakoa (1908) *152*;
Archibald Scott Cleghorn (1910) *156*; Charles Reed Bishop
(1915) *157*; Lili'uokalani (1917) *158*; Jonah Kūhiō Kalaniana'ole
(1922) *166*; Elizabeth Keka'aniau (1928) *170*; Elizabeth
Kahanu (1932) *171*; Abigail Wahi'ika'ahu'ula Campbell (1945)
172; David Kalākaua Kawānanakoa (1953) *175*

2. Burial Places   177
Fort Tomb   180
Tomb near Halekamani   180
Moku'ula Tomb   180
Royal Tomb at Pohukaina, Honolulu (1825)   181
Mauna 'Ala, Royal Mausoleum at Kawānanakoa, Nu'uanu, Honolulu   184
John Young Tomb *187*; Kamehameha Tomb (1887) *187*;
Wyllie Tomb (1904) *190*; Kalakaua Crypt (1910) *192*;

Kawānakoa Tomb at Mauna 'Ala *198*; *Lunalilo Mausoleum* (1875) *205*

3. Undertakers 209

Conclusion 215
Glossary 217
Chapter Notes 219
Bibliography 235
Index 237

Preface

The deaths of the *ali'i*, of high chiefs, in ancient Hawai'i had the most profound impact on their subjects. They tattooed the dates or locations of their chiefs' deaths on their bodies and named their children for the day of their death or funeral. Despite the importance of the deaths, relatively little is recorded in Western history. This volume seeks to record in a comprehensive manner the obsequies of the Kamehameha and Kalākaua dynasties that drew thousands and tens of thousands of subjects to pay homage to their chiefs. Taken from journals, Hawaiian and English language newspaper articles and broadsides, *Death Rites and Hawaiian Royalty* chronicles the changing customs surrounding the death of the chiefs following the introduction of Western funerary practices. To a people with one of the most expressive modes of honoring their dead rulers, the Western obsequies provided a new layer of custom to an already complex form. Instead of replacing funerary traditions, the Western style of lying in state, processions, funerals and burials brought a new level of extravagance befitting royalty. The continued complexity of royal obsequies supports the observation by David E. Stannard in the *Puritan Way of Death* that "in traditional societies the individual is of such importance that his or her life is imaginatively extended through prolonged mourning or multiple burial rituals."[1] The obsequies for the rulers of the Kingdom of Hawai'i, some revered as gods, exemplify the impact of the royal Hawaiian way of death on the people of Hawaii.

Introduction

Hala i kea la hoʻi ʻole mai.
Gone on the road from which there is no returning.[1]
—Hawaiian proverb

From *iwi* (bones) hidden at night to mile-long extravagant funeral processions, the practices surrounding the death of royalty in Hawaiʻi took a radical shift after the visit of Captain James Cook initiated permanent contact with the West. But traditional indigenous observances also continued, despite efforts by missionaries to suppress them. The royal Hawaiian way of death formed the contested ground between the traditional activities surrounding the death of a chief and the newly introduced Western practices.

Ironically reports of the treatment of the British explorer's corpse and its dissection after his death at Kaʻawaloa on the island of Hawaiʻi graphically introduced the world to the traditional Hawaiian post-mortem customs. Bishop Museum retains a funerary artifact of the time. Item 1217 is described in a catalog of its holdings as "large wooden trough in which the bodies of the alii were dissected. The intestines and flesh were burned or cast into the sea; the bones were carefully cleaned and hidden in some cave."[2] But the post-mortem treatment of Cook would soon be a fleeting custom. The royal Hawaiian way of death went from the secreting of bones to hidden burial caves in the dark of night to the ostentatious displays of funeral parades and burial chapels. As with the rapid adoption of Western ways of war, dress, and architecture, Hawaiian *aliʻi*, or royalty, also chose to use the royal customs of the West regarding death rituals: lying in state, funerals, processions and burials in conspicuous locations. Despite the adoption of Western practices, some traditions survived through the last royal burial in the twentieth century.

Accounts of the death of Captain James Cook introduced the world to the funerary practices for Hawaiian royalty, practices that would disappear within a couple of decades (courtesy Hawaii State Archives [PP-70-1-039]).

The changes in funerary customs did not take place immediately following contact with the West and establishment of the Kingdom of Hawai'i, and at no point did all traditional practices cease. Several deaths of *ali'i* took place after contact with Western explorers but before the Western practices took root. Kameʻeiamoku, grandfather of Kuini Liliha and

Kameʻeiamoku, one of the twin advisors to Kamehameha, appears on the royal seal. He died in Lahaina, Maui, in 1802 (courtesy Hawaii State Archives [PP-17-10-019]).

one of the twin advisors to Kamehameha I who appear on the Hawaiian royal seal, died in Lahaina, Maui, in 1802. Keʻeaumoku Pāpaʻiahiahi, father of Kaʻahumanu, the favorite wife of Kamehameha, died in 1804. Namokuelua, the first wife of John Young, Kamehameha the Great's war companion, died the same year, on July 20, 1804. The brother of Kamehameha and grandfather of Queen Emma, Keliʻimaikai, died in 1809. A year later, in 1810, the other *haole* or foreign war companion of Kamehameha, Isaac Davis, died. Despite the high rank of the deceased, few accounts record the ceremonies attached to their deaths and burials, though one may assume that traditional practices continued. That certainly was the case in the treatment of the wife of Don Francisco de Paula Marin in 1811, which he described in his journal as "threw away the bones of Marin's wife."[3] Though Marin's term is not accurate, it is the same one used to describe for the burial of Keliʻimaikai, brother of Kamehameha I.

At least one element of traditional practices from that time has been preserved. A traditional funeral chant, or *kanikau*, written in 1804 by Kaʻahumanu for her father survives:

> Beloved art thou,
> And thou also,
> You two chiefs,
> The two high chiefs at Pueoʻula
> Kahaʻi, ruler of the island, Kahaʻi the chief,
> The sacred, heavenly emanation of Kāne.
> He is the heavenly thunder that rumbles on,
> That rolls away to the presence of Wākea.
> It roars in heaven for Kalanihonuakini,
> My chiefly father.
> A friend indeed is he.
> Beloved is he.
> I grieve for him till my breath is spent,
> I weep for my companion in the cold,
> My companion in the single embrace of the chill,
> Surrounded roundabout by the cold,
> The heavy cold without letup.
> There are two things that are warm as women,
> Where the chief can warm himself in the house,
> One of the two is fire and clothing,
> The other is the bosom of the companion,
> Here it is, here—here.[4]

Though the chant remains, few contemporaneous accounts exist. Yet, the chant's very survival points to what was important—the memory of the deceased and love expressed by his daughter. Even the funeral in 1810 of Westerner Isaac Davis, also known as High Chief ʻAikake, went unrecorded. The missionaries, chroniclers of many of the royal deaths, would not arrive for another decade after the death of Davis and the oral accounts of the funeral of the *haole*, or foreign, chief did not survive. The historic record is mostly absent regarding the funerals or burials of all of the previously mentioned chiefs, though the native Hawaiian historian, David Malo, did record the activities that followed the death of Pauli Kaoleioku, a son of Kamehameha the Great, the "chiefs and commoners were called and the wailing began."[5] For Kamehameha's son traditional practices are most likely to have occurred, but was Davis buried using Western practices? Intervening years have obscured any chance to know. Even the exact location of his final resting place, a graveyard for foreigners on the *makai*–ʻEwa side of King and Piʻikoi Streets, has been lost over time.

Death of Kamehameha the Great

The death of Kamehameha the Great marked one of the final displays of traditional funerary practices and displays for royalty. Within four years *aliʻi* would be introduced to the funeral practices of the New England missionaries and two years later to the display of coffins befitting royalty anywhere in the world.

Kamehameha himself most certainly participated in the traditional mourning practices that would occur after his own death. Ebenezer Townsend, Jr., owner of the *Neptune*, which anchored off the island of Hawaiʻi in 1798, wrote in his description of Kamehameha I: "two upper fore teeth gone, which added to the harshness of his countenance."[6]

Although no image of Kamehameha shows his missing teeth, an image by Jacques Arago shows a woman with two upper middle incisor teeth missing. Arago arrived aboard the French corvette *Uranie* on August 8, 1819, three months after the death of Kamehameha, so marks of mourning were still evident on his subjects and recorded in his drawings.

The funerary practices surrounding the death of Kamehameha I stand in marked contrast to the practices that followed in the coming century.

Left: **Drawing of Kamehameha the Great by Louis Choris. No portrait shows his missing teeth (courtesy Hawaii State Archives [PP-97-5-006]).** *Right:* **A portrait by Jacques Arago shows a woman with missing teeth following the death of Kamehameha I (courtesy Hawaii State Archives [REF VOY 2-003]).**

Death of Likelike and Traditional Hawaiian Mourning Practices

The death of Likelike (not to be confused by her namesake who was the sister of King David Kalākaua), the favorite wife of Kalanimoku, and daughter of high chief Kaikioʻewa, gave the recently arrived missionaries firsthand experience with the traditional mourning customs for *aliʻi*. Kalanimoku was considered by most early visitors as the equivalent of the prime minister under Kamehameha I. Elisha Loomis, in a letter to the American Board of Commissioners for Foreign Missions, the group that had sent the missionary companies, described Likelike as an "amiable and affectionate wife."[7] The death of the wife of Kalanimoku on March 4, 1821, days after the birth and death of her newborn child, featured the full range of traditional mourning practices. Hiram Bingham of the pioneer company of missionaries sent by the board recounted:

> On repeated visits to this house of mourning, for a few days, we had impressive lessons concerning the customs and tastes of the people. Some were cutting off each other's hair, close to the skin, on the sides of the head, leaving the rest long, and indulging in loud laughter. Some were lying on their faces, uttering loud wailing with tears, while others lay in a state of intoxication, suffering the time to pass unconsciously away. Some were burning semi-circular semi-cylindrical pieces of bark.[8]

Alphonse Pellion, another artist on the *Uranie*, had earlier depicted Likelike in a drawing with Kamāmalu and Keoua. Kamāmalu bore the semi-circular marks on her breasts. In the same drawing, Keoua, wife of Kuakini, governor of the island of Hawaiʻi, had the two sides of her head shorn.

The missionaries tried to convince Kalanimoku to replace the traditional practices with "an appropriate funeral service."[9] The entreaties of the missionaries eventually succeeded. Kalanimoku "consented to have a funeral sermon on the Sabbath, at his house, and listened with others, while some of the strange doctrines of 'Jesus and the resurrection,' were set forth as connected with the sin and death of mankind. He wished us to tell him, if his departed wife had gone to *heaven*."[10] The funeral sermon, given by Bingham in English, was "interpreted to Kolaimoku and the people."[11] Thus the missionaries were able to introduce to Hawaiian royalty a small portion of Western funerary practices—the funeral sermon. The introduction of other aspects would wait.

In January 1822, Elisha Loomis recorded in his journal the Western style burial for a Hawaiian youth. Loomis, also a member of the pioneer company, had arrived nearly two years earlier. On January 10, 1822, he wrote: "Today an interesting native boy died named John Pitt, who had

Introduction

Rikériki [Likelike], the favorite wife of Kalanimoku, (left) died shortly after the arrival of the pioneer missionary company in 1820. Kéohoua [Keoua], wife of Kuakini, (center) has the hair shorn from the sides of her head. Kamahamarou [Kamāmalu] (right) would later die in London with her husband, Kamehameha II. Drawing by Alphonse Pellion (courtesy Hawaii State Archives [REF VOY 2-005]).

been to America and could speak the English language with facility. He was interpreter for Boke."[12] The following day he recorded the burial of the assistant to the governor of O'ahu: "The native boy who died yesterday was buried today, in the manner customary in the U.S. The natives appear fond of imitating foreign customs."[13]

An Early Model

The death of Levi Parsons Bingham, the son of pioneer missionaries, Hiram and Sybil Bingham, on January 16, 1823, provided the first opportunity for *ali'i* to see firsthand Western funerary practices. Ironically, the missionaries had written in the *Sandwich Islands Mission Journal* less than a year earlier: "But our gratitude is due to God that our little number is graciously preserved & no inroads are yet made by death."[14] The child, born December 31, 1822, had lived just sixteen days. On Sunday, January 19, 1823, after the sermon at the chapel, "the king and principal chiefs and distinguished women, many of them in habiliments of mourning [...] assembled at the mission house."[15] The boy's coffin was taken in a procession to the chapel, where a funeral service took place, and from there to the nearby burial site. Given the close proximity of the three sites, the program featured obsequies almost in miniature. The *Missionary Herald at Home and Abroad* recorded the earnest wish of the missionaries regarding the child's funeral: "We hope the scenes and instructions of the day have made a favorable impression on the people."[16]

The royal funerals that followed, kept to the pattern of the Bingham child's funeral, only on a grander scale, usually displaying the following elements: lying in state, funeral, procession and burial. On the neighbor islands, like Kaua'i, however, traditional practices continued. Missionary Elizabeth Edwards Bishop recounted in her journal entry of November 21, 1823:

Portrait of Hiram and Sybil Bingham, parents of Levi Parsons Bingham, by Samuel F.B. Morse (courtesy Hawaii State Archives [PP-68-4-007]).

At early dawn we were awakened by the most doleful cries, and dismal moans. We immediately arose and ascertained the cause. A chief woman had died suddenly in a house but a step off. Around the door seated on the ground was a great number of chiefs and common people, beating their bodies, and making the most frantic gestures and uttering these doleful wailings. The friends of the deceased continued to assemble from different places in the neighbourhood. As they proceeded with slow and solemn step to the spot, some of the group arose to meet them. They would approach a few steps then stop, lift up their heads towards heaven, their arms thrown across their breasts and mourn as those who have no hope. Those who remained sitting answered with the same mournful sounds. So it has been through the day and our ears are almost deafened with their cries. [...] It is not uncommon when a chief dies for his friends to believe that some enemy has prayed him to death. A chief of some distinction told Mr. W. [Whitney] that the God must be very powerful to whom the man prayed to destroy this woman. When a chief dies his bones are preserved as objects of veneration. The manner of burying the dead is various according to circumstances. In many places it is the practice to deposit the bodies of deceased persons in the caves of high precipices which are difficult to access. Another way is to wrap he body in a large quantity of tapa, bind it with cords and bury it in such a posture as will best suit the size of the hole dug for the purpose. The universal

A marker for Levi Parsons Bingham and his brother stands in the Mission burying ground at Kawaiaha'o Church (photograph by author).

custom is to bury in the night in as private a manner as possible. When a person of distinction dies he is usually deposited in some house and covered with large stones over which tapas are spread and then the house is enclosed by a high wall. Another method to build a sepulcher of mud and stones over the grave. These are often white-washed and make a very decent appearance.[17]

Bishop, a member of the Second Company, arrived in Hawai'i on April 27, 1823, after a voyage of one hundred and fifty-eight days. She had sailed from New Haven, Connecticut, on the *Thames*. She gave birth to two children, Sereno Edwards Bishop, later a missionary in Hawai'i himself, and Jane Elizabeth Bishop.

On the island of Hawai'i, the obsequies for the father of Thomas Hopu on March 6, 1824, constituted one of the earliest opportunities for native Hawaiians there to observe Western practices. Hopu, a native Hawaiian who had attended the Cornwall School in Connecticut, returned to Hawai'i to help the First Company of missionaries. Artemas Bishop, husband of Elizabeth Bishop, and Asa Thurston reported to the board:

> Last evening the father of Thomas Hopu died. His head was silvered over with grey hairs of 80 years, an extreme old age for this country. We have reason to hope that the prayers and labors of Hopu with him, have blessed to his conversion, and that now he sleeps with Jesus. This afternoon the funeral was attended in the meeting house, where the corpse was brought in, enclosed in a decent coffin made by the hands of Hopu. Mr. T. addressed a large congregation from the words, "prepare to meet thy God." After service the interment took place, in the yard adjoining church where Hopu & his brother with their own hands let down the remains of their father, into his bed of rest, there to await the sound of the last trumpet. A short address & prayer closed the scene of the first Christian funeral ever witnessed in the island.[18]

Elizabeth Bishop, who five years earlier had witnessed the traditional Hawaiian obsequies on Kaua'i, would also serve as a role model for funerary practices on the Big Island. She died in Kailua, Kona, on February 21, 1828, the first adult of the mission to die in Hawai'i. Lucy Thurston, of the pioneer company, described the impact of Bishop's death and funeral:

> Then with deep love and respect we neatly dressed and enclosed our precious dead in a coffin. The natives in their transition state were delighted with this new order of things. A large concourse of chiefs and people assembled at our house, all habited in black with as much order and decency as I ever witnessed in my own country, the procession moved to the church, and from thence to the grave, where we committed the sacred deposit to the silent bosom of mother Earth. And we taught them to restrain their boisterous expressions of natural affection under the bereavement, and to bow with submission and thanksgiving to Him who is the Resurrection and the Life.[19]

The obsequies were seen by Hawaiians as a "new order of things."[20] Here the death of Bishop prompted "order and decency." Gone were the wailing and other demonstrations of grief as the missionaries "taught them to restrain their boisterous expressions." The rites included gathering at the residence of the deceased (lying in repose), procession to the church, an unrecorded, but assumed, service at the church (funeral), another procession to the grave and "deposit to the silent bosom of mother earth" (burial).

Future obsequies for royalty would include the same elements, conducted, of course, on a much grander scale.

Lying in State

The lying in state of the *ali'i* gave mourners one last chance to pay tribute to their chief. Although the practice of lying in state is defined as occurring in the main government building, as opposed to lying in repose at any other building, the term "lying in state" is used here regardless of location.

While the widespread lamentation that occurred after the death a member of royalty continued to take place, the practices surrounding Keōpūolani lying in state showed a marked departure from the excesses of the past, especially those that marked the passing of Kamehameha the Great. Decades later similar proactive restrictions were still needed as Kamehameha IV issued explicit orders to prevent the traditional Hawaiian practices following the death of Kamehameha III.

The lengthy lying in state often meant that the family of the departed would relocate to the Palace while the body remained there. A broadside reported the return to regular life for Princess Ka'iulani and Archibald Cleghorn after the death of Princess Likelike.

Funerals

Ostensibly a nation dedicated to Jehovah, the funerals of royalty had a Christian basis formed in a large part by the American missionaries sent to Hawai'i in 1819 by the American Board of Commissioners for Foreign Missions. The services included readings from the Bible translated by the missionaries, and hymns contained in the first book published in Hawai'i, a hymnal titled *Na Himeni Hawaii*, and subsequent hymnbooks.

Unlike the clergy who conducted the funerals for British royalty, the Protestant clergy conducting the funeral services for royalty in Hawai'i came from a country that had thrown off its ties to monarchy. Although the stone church at Kawaiaha'o is styled the Westminster Abbey of the Pacific because of its ties to Hawaiian royalty, the funerals held in its sanctuary differed significantly from their British counterparts. Even the earliest permanent English religious influence came not from the Church of England, but from William Ellis, a Nonconformist missionary sent originally to Tahiti by the London Missionary Society.

Processions

The Hawaiians have an adage: "*I lele no ka lupe i ke pola.* It is the tail that makes the kite fly. It is the number of followers that raises the prestige of the chief."[21] Besides allowing thousands to participate in honoring their fallen chief, the inherent hierarchy of royalty took its most visible form in the processions most often from the location where the bodies lay in state to the state funerals and from the religious services to the places of burial. The order of procession was a carefully crafted artifact, perfected half a world away. The Kingdom of Hawai'i had British royal funeral processions as a model for processions in Hawaii.

Besides being printed in newspapers, orders of procession were also printed on broadsides, large sheets printed on only one side, eliminating the width constraints of columns. The processions included a broad variety of participants: Undertakers, military bands, schools, Masonic organizations, militias, cavalry, and feather standards called *kāhili*.

The funerals, too, varied over time. They took place in thatched structures, in the coral church of Kawaiaha'o, at the homes of royalty and at Hale Ali'i, later called 'Iolani Palace. The ceremonies were conducted by American missionaries, and Anglican and Roman Catholic bishops.

Royal Deaths After the Overthrow

Even after the overthrow of the monarchy, respect for *ali'i* continued to be demonstrated in what were now termed state funerals. Governor Sanford Ballard Dole, once President Dole of the Republic of Hawai'i, and a minister under the Kingdom of Hawai'i, in his address to the first territorial legislature noted the deaths of two more members of a rapidly disappearing royal family:

> During the past year the Hawaiian community has twice been called upon to mourn the deaths of members of the last royal line of the monarchy: Her late Majesty, Queen Dowager Kapiolani, widow of His late Majesty, King Kalakaua, and Her late Royal Highness Princess Kaiulani, daughter of Her late Royal Highness Princess Likelike and the Honorable Archibald S. Cleghorn.
>
> State obsequies were tendered to the remains of both of these esteemed Aliis, and the mourning for them by all classes and nationalities was general and sincere.[22]

Strangely, the Territory of Hawai'i, part of the United States of America, a country whose very constitution eschews royal titles, paid homage to several descendants of Hawaiian chiefs and their spouses through the time of the Korean War.

Introduction 15

    The royal Hawaiian way of death evolved over one hundred and twenty-two years, from woven images containing royal bones and chaotic expressions of grieving to polished *koa* caskets with silver plates and gilded handles and carefully ordered and ranked processions. Still, the wailing, the vigil over the body with *kāhili*, and the funeral dirge persisted, a tribute to the power of traditional practices to survive the end of the *kapu* system and introduction of new forms of religion.

1

Royal Deaths

> Lele ka hāā.
> The spirit has flown away.[1]
> —Hawaiian proverb

Royal Deaths During the Kamehameha Dynasty

Kamehameha the Great (1819)

The death of Kamehameha the Great on May 8, 1819, and the funerary practices that followed include the most complete description of traditional practices related to the deaths of *aliʻi*. Kamehameha, the reputed son of Keōua, was born on the island of Hawaiʻi about 1758. Upon the death of his uncle, Kalaniopuʻu, Kamehameha started to consolidate the regions of the Big Island of Hawaiʻi, later fighting for control of neighboring Maui and Molokaʻi and then Oʻahu. When Kaumualiʻi ceded the Kingdom of Kauaʻi in 1810, all of the islands of the archipelago fell under the control of one chief. His death, therefore, surpassed that of all of the chiefs of the past. That death, on the day of Hoku by the Hawaiian lunar calendar, also provides a point of contrast with all the deaths that followed.

It would be the funeral practices following the death of Kamehameha that would have the greatest impact of the Western view of traditional practices. Even a half century after the death of the first Kamehameha, Western writers would continue to remember the event. Perhaps the best known of the authors to comment on the royal Hawaiian way of death was humorist Mark Twain, who described the death of Kamehameha in a serious account that contrasted the past practices with the contemporaneous funerary activities surrounding the death of Victoria Kamāmalu, great-granddaughter of the dynasty's progenitor. Twain wrote in *Roughing It*:

> Forty years ago it was the custom in the Islands to suspend all law for a certain number of days after the death of a royal personage; and then a saturnalia ensued which one may picture to himself after a fashion, but not in the full horror of the reality. The people shaved their heads, knocked out a tooth or two, plucked out an eye sometimes, cut, bruised, mutilated or burned their flesh, got drunk, burned each other's huts, maimed or murdered one another according to the caprice of the moment, and both sexes gave themselves up to brutal and unbridled licentiousness.[2]

Fortunately, native Hawaiian historian, Samuel Manaiakalani Kamakau, preserved the oral accounts of the obsequies surrounding the death of Hawaii's greatest king: "In the meantime when the land was defiled by the corpse of its ruling chief, it was considered in old days the proper thing for his heir to depart for another district for some days until the bones had been cleaned (ho'oma'ema'e ia), covered with basketwork (ka'ai ia), and placed within the tower ('anuu) of the heiau, as the corpses of chiefs were prepared in olden days for burial."[3]

When the son of Kamehameha I, Liholiho, departed from Kailua and arrived in Kawaihae "the voice of weeping and wailing arose and the sound of lamentation and general mourning, recalling their regret and reciting their love for their chief. It would be impossible to describe all their ways of expressing love and sorrow, even wishing to die with him. No nation on earth could have shown more grief and affection, and these manifestations of regret lasted many days."[4] Kalanimoku was among the individuals who wanted to be a death companion of Kamehameha, but he was prevented from carrying out his wish.[5]

Upon completion of the rituals, Ulumaheihei, also known as Hoapili, took the bones of Kamehameha and hid them as the king had instructed him.[6] The secreting of the bones prevented their desecration by enemies, who ofttimes would make fishhooks or arrowheads out of the bones. Thus the saying was repeated concerning Kamehameha the Great: "The morning star alone knows where Kamehameha's bones are guarded."[7]

Although he does not mention Kamehameha by name, David Malo wrote a chapter titled "Concerning Rituals During the Death of the Ali'i Nui" in his masterwork, *Ka Mo'olelo Hawai'i, Hawaiian Traditions*. He remarked on the difference accorded the high chief versus other chiefs: "If the ali'i nui who reigned died, then the rituals connected with his worship [death] were very different (ka 'oihana 'okoa loa kona ho'omana'ana). They were not like those of all other ali'i."[8]

Kauwai (1823)

The death of the youngest daughter of Kamehameha the Great, four years after her father, marked the first shift in royal funerary practices. For the missionaries, the Christian ceremony for Levi Parsons Bingham clearly had the desired effect, because just three days after the funeral, on the morning of January 22, 1823, "the little half-sister of the king and queen [Kamehameha II and Kamāmalu] called *Kauwai*, died of the dropsy," and the King asked "to have funeral services at the interment, in the same manner as on last Sabbath."

Kauwai was the last daughter of Kamehameha the Great, conceived by one of the wives known as *wahine pālama*, women set aside in a sacred enclosure. His daughter, whose full name was Kapapauai, was either the child of Manono or Kekāuluohi, both of whom he married in 1809 or 1810. Kamakau wrote in a newspaper article in 1868 that Kamehameha "took two young chiefesses to warm his old age. Ke-ka-ulu-ohi was the firstborn child of her mother Ka-heihei-malie and her father Ka-lei-mamahu; Manono's mother was Kaloloa-a-Kumu-koʻa and her father was Ke-kua-manoha. One of the two bore him his last child, a girl named Ka-papa-uai."[9] The missionary account, recorded before the orthography for the Hawaiian language had been standardized, called her Kauwai, which would have sounded the same as Ka-uai, a shortened form of Ka-papa-uai.

LYING IN STATE

The missionaries went to the "house of *Karaimoku*, where the corpse had been dressed for the grave, and laid into a decent coffin; and the king and principal chiefs, and distinguished women, were assembled, all habited in mourning, much in the same manner as the same number of respectable men and women in America, might be supposed to have appeared, on a similar occasion."[10]

FUNERAL

Hiram Bingham, the American missionary, whose loss had prompted the Western style funeral of Kauwai, performed the service. The *Missionary Herald* reported: "Probably not less than a thousand of the natives assembled in and about the house, and a sermon was preached by Mr. B. [Bingham] from Heb. ix, 27, 28, in the language of the country."[11] Hebrews 9:27–28, from the 1828 Hawaiian New Testament, read: "A ua hoomao-popoia ka make hookahi ana o na kanaka, a ma ia hope aku ka hoopai ana. Pela hoi o Kristo, a pau kona hoolilo hookahi ana ia ia iho i mohai e halihali aku i ka hewa o ka lehulehu, e ike hou ia oia me ka mohai ole, i ka lua o kona hiki ana mai, e ola'i ka poe e kiai ana ia ia."[12] Hebrews 9:27–28, from the Authorized (King James) Version, read: "And as it is appointed unto men once to die, but after this the judgment: So Christ was once offered to bear the sins of many; and unto them that look for him shall he appear the second time without sin unto salvation."[13]

PROCESSION

As with many of the funeral processions, the one for Kauwai had two parts. The first portion took her from the house of Kalanimoku where she was lying in state to the Chapel where the funeral service took place. "After a prayer was offered, a large procession, arranged by American consul, Mr. [John Coffin] Jones, moved to the chapel." After the service, "the procession returned to the fort."[14]

BURIAL

The Fort at Honolulu harbor was the location of the first interment of *aliʻi* remains after the introduction of Western practices. The fort had been started in 1816 to protect Honolulu harbor. Besides the armaments contained in the fort, it also included residences and storage. Given that burials often took place in the *hale pili,* or thatched houses, of close relatives, the burial in the fort seems quite appropriate. The *Missionary Herald* gives

Kauwai, sister of King Kamehameha II, was interred at the fort in Honolulu on January 19, 1823. The fort as it appeared in 1853 as depicted in the painting "View of the Honolulu Fort" by Paul Emmert (courtesy Hawaii State Archives).

no description of the burial itself, stating only that "the remains were decently interred."[15] The account does not indicate whether the body was buried or put in a tomb above the ground. Marin reported in his journal: "This day [January 24, 1823] they buried the daughter of Tameamea the old King with much state."[16] The fort may have become the de facto royal tomb on Oʻahu. Marin recorded in May 1823: "they buried in the fort the Indian [native Hawaiian] called Arapay [possibly Alapaʻi]."[17]

Keōpūolani (1823)

Though the rites for Kauwai demonstrated the rapid adoption of Western funerary practices by royalty, literally days after the first burial in the missionary graveyard, the death of the most sacred wife of Kamehameha, Keōpūolani, a year later, had the most profound effect on the practices following the death of royalty and marked a turning point from the traditional to the Western. Keōpūolani, whose name means "the gathering of the heavens or the clouds of heaven," was born in Pāhoehoe, Wailuku, Maui, in 1778. She was the daughter of Kiwalaʻo, King of Hawaiʻi, and Kekuiapoiwa, daughter of Keoua. Missionary Charles Stewart noted the significance of the service for Keōpūolani on future funerals: "This is the first Christian funeral of a high chief that has ever taken place in the islands; and will probably be a precedent for all future burials among the heads of the nation."[18] A joint letter from the missionaries noted in October 23, 1823: "Her peaceful death, & Christian burial truly creditable to her kindred occurred about 6 weeks since at Lahaina."[19]

Because of the request of Keōpūolani to restrict the excesses that followed the death of *aliʻi*, most of the traditional mourning practices ended in 1824. Kalanimoku had assured the missionaries, worried by past reports and their firsthand experience after the death of Likelike, "that Keopuolani had long before forbidden every heathen practice at her death; and that the people had received the strictest order against their former customs, *except wailing* [*italics* mine]."[20]

Kamakau recorded the active prevention of the custom of the death companion: "At her death, September 16, 1823, at Kaluaokiha in Lahaina, many persons in the back country came and offered themselves as her death companions (*moepuʻu*), but Hoa-pili refused them all, saying, 'It was the command of your lord that there should be no death companion, no wild mourning, because she had given herself to God.' There was indeed mourning and wailing but no wild demonstration, although Ka-lani-moku allowed liquor to flow like water. Blessed was Ke-opu-o-lani to put her faith in God and save so many innocent persons from death, those who owed nothing

1. Royal Deaths

Keōpūolani restricted traditional responses to her death to wailing. Plate in the 1828 edition of Charles S. Stewart's *Journal of a Residence in the Sandwich Islands, During the Years 1823, 1824, and 1825*.

to her and had not benefited from her wealth, but by old custom offered themselves to die with her."[21]

Notwithstanding her influence, not all traditional signs of mourning ended with her burial. English missionary, William Ellis, recorded the survival of a traditional custom just days after the interment of Keōpūolani. Queen Kamāmalu, also called by the longer form, Kamehamalu, was the half-sister and wife of King Kamehameha II, Liholiho, son of Keōpūolani. Although not as extreme as blinding an eye, knocking out their front teeth or burning patterns in their skin, Kamāmalu was continuing another practice to show respect. Ellis asked Kamāmalu the reason behind the obviously painful act of tattooing her tongue:

> Kamehamaru, queen of Riho Riho [...] gave me a fine answer to this effect, on the death of Keopuolani, her husband's mother. A few days after the interment, I went into a house where a number of chiefs were assembled for the purpose of having their tongues tattooed; and the artist was performing this operation on hers when I entered. [...] I remarked that I was sorry to see her following so useless a custom: and asked if it was not exceedingly painful? She answered, *He eha nui no, he nui roa ra kuu aroha!* Pain, great indeed; but greater my affection! After further remarks, I asked some others why they chose that method of showing their affectionate remembrance of the dead? They said, *Aore roa ia e naro!* That will never disappear, or be obliterated![22]

The tattooed remembrance would be an everyday reminder of the remembered individual. An Oʻahu chief displayed a prominent tattoo on his right

An Oʻahu chief had his arm tattooed with the death date of Kamehameha, part of the mourning ritual. He stands next to Keʻeaumoku, brother of Kaʻahumanu (courtesy Hawaii State Archives [REF VOY-2-014]).

forearm in English: "TAMAAHMAH | Died May 8 1819." So, too, the right forearm of a royal officer bore a similar tattoo.

Ellis recognized that not all traditional practices had ceased, but recorded that the most extreme forms had been eliminated: "Since the introduction of the gospel by Christian missionaries, or rather since the death of Keopuolani, in September, 1813 [should be 1823], all the wicked practices, and most of the ceremonies, usual on these occasions, have entirely ceased. Knocking out teeth is discontinued; wailing, cutting the hair, and marking the tongue are still practiced; but all the evil customs have been most strictly forbidden by the principal chiefs."[23]

Funeral procession of Keōpūolani included hundreds of mourners. Ships in the background fire salutes. From "Conversion et Mort de Keopuolani Rein des Iles Sandwich," 1825 (courtesy Hawaii State Archives [Paul Markham Kahn Collection, 3/22]).

Funeral

The funeral for Keōpūolani, mother of Kamehameha II, Kamehameha III and Princess Nāhiʻenaʻena took place not in Honolulu, but on Maui, when Lāhainā was the capital of the Kingdom of Hawaiʻi. The service took place under a large tree near the residence of Keōpūolani, the residence being too small for the numbers expected to attend. Kamakau reported concerning the presence of Kaheiheimālie: "In September, 1823, she heard in Hawaii of Ke-opu-o-lani's death and sailed at once to attend the burial ceremonies. The chiefs had all assembled at Lahaina, the body of the chiefess had been concealed, and Ulu-maheihei was in mourning."[24]

Procession

The published image of the funeral procession for Keōpūolani, in the *Memoir of Keopuolani*, shows just six *kāhili*, feather standards, around the bier. William Richards noted the hierarchy in the *Memoir of Keopuolani*:

> After service, a procession was formed, the prince [Kauikeaouli] and princess [Nahiʻenaʻena], and Hoapiri [Hoapili] and the king [Liholiho], and after them the chiefs *according to their rank* [*italics* mine]. The procession was led by the foreigners who were present, next to whom followed the missionaries in mourning dresses, and

directly preceding the corpse were the favorite attendants of the deceased. Following the chiefs was a large train of their attendants. All in the procession, amounting to about four hundred, were dressed in European style, except a few who fell in the rear after the procession first moved.[25]

The caption for the engraving gives further detail regarding the order of the procession, especially the ranking of the high chiefs immediately following the king: "Karaimoku and his brother Boki; King Taumuarii [Kaumuali'i] and Kaahumanu; Kuakini [the brother of Ka'ahumanu] and Kalakua [also known as Kaheiheimālie, sister of Ka'ahumanu]; Piia [also known as Nāmāhana, sister of Ka'ahumanu] and Wahinepio (third favorite wife of Kamehameha I and sister of Kalanimoku and Boki]; Kaikioeva [Kaikio'ewa, guardian of Kauikeaouli] and Keaveamahi [Keaweamahi]; and Naihi and Kapi'olani. Richards also pointed out the novelty of the event: "The path was thronged on every side, by thousands of people, who had never witnessed any thing of the kind before."[26]

BURIAL

In contrast to secreting of the bones of her husband, Kamehameha I, the burial of Keōpūolani took place in a known location amid great noise. Richards reported of the Western burial in a Western structure: "Minute guns were fired from the ships in the roads, and the bell continued tolling until the corpse was deposited in the place prepared for it, which was a new house built of stone and cemented with mud, designed as a tomb for the chiefs."[27]

George Cox Ke'eaumoku (1824)

The next royal obsequies, for George Cox Ke'eaumoku, displayed an early mixture of traditional and Western practices. William Ellis, English missionary, recorded the scene of Ke'eaumoku, the late Maui governor and brother of Ka'ahumanu, lying in state. He should not be confused with his father, Ke'eaumoku Pāpa'iahiahi, who died two decades earlier. Ellis wrote: "A day or two after the decease of Keeaumoku [he died March 23, 1824], governor of Maui, and the elder brother of Kuakini, governor of Hawai'i, I was sitting with the surviving relatives, who were weeping around the couch on which the corpse was lying, when a middle-aged woman came in at the other end of the large house, and, having proceeded about half-way towards the spot where the body lay, began to sing in a plaintive tone, accompanying her song with affecting gesticulations, such as wringing her hands, grasping her hair, and beating her breasts."[28] William Ellis recorded the words of the song, commenting on the lyrics: "She described in a feeling manner the benevolence of the deceased, and her own consequent loss."[29]

The song he recorded uses spellings used before the standardization Hawaiian orthography.

> Ue, ue, ua mate tuu Arii
> Ua mate tuu hatu e tuu hoa,
> Tuu hoa i paa ta aina,
> Tuu hoa i tuu ilihune,
> Tuu hoa i ta ua e ta matani,
> Tuu hoa i ta anu o ta mouna,
> Tuu hoa i ta ino,
> Tuu hoa i ta marie,
> Tuu hoa i mau tai awaru,
> Ue, ue, ua hala tuu hoa,
> Aohe e hoi hou mai.
>
> Alas, alas, dead is my chief
> Dead is my lord and my friend,
> My friend in the season of famine,
> My friend in the time of drought,
> My friend in my poverty,
> My friend in rain and wind,
> My friend in the heat and the sun,
> My friend in the cold from the mountain,
> My friend in the storm,
> My friend in the calm,
> My friend in the eight seas;
> Alas, alas, gone is my friend,
> And no more will return.[30]

The chanting of the *kanikau* or funeral dirge was yet another example of funerary customs that continued after the introduction of the Western ways.

FUNERAL

Hawaiian historian Samuel Manaiakalani Kamakau (1814–1876) gave account of the funeral of Keʻeaumoku: "They were called home in February, 1824, by the illness of Ka-ʻahu-manu's brother, Ka-hekili Keʻe-au-moku. He was treated by foreign physicians but died March 23 at Pakaka in Honolulu. On the night that he died Kua-kini arrived from Hawaii, lay off shore with his ship, and secretly took away the body to Hawaii leaving Mr. Bingham to conduct the funeral services over an empty coffin. The chiefs did not at this time take the missionaries seriously and some of them said, 'Let us see whether the foreign god has power to tell them that the coffin is empty.' How ignorant are the ungodly who say there is no God!"[31]

The missionary account differs, especially concerning the disposition of the body and the cooperation of Kuakini (Governor Adams):

> The chiefs, having concluded to remove the remains of Cox to Kairuah [Kailua, Kona], have had a strong coffin closely made, pitched within, and lined with cloth, and neatly covered without with black velvet, tacked on with brass nails. A glass was set in the lid, and by the request of Gov. Adams, the English name of the deceased, Cox, was put upon the coffin in large capitals. At eight o'clock in the morning we repaired to the house of Kaahumanu, his sister, just at the head of the harbor, where he died and where the chiefs had requested to have a funeral service, previous to the embarkation. The corpse being placed on a bier in the front of the house, the chiefs and mourners arranged themselves around it, and the common people just without the court; part of funeral hymn was sung. Mr. Bingham offered a prayer, and the remainder of the hymn followed. Mr. Ellis then preached a funeral discourse from the words of James, "Go to now, ye that say, Today, or tomorrow, we will go into such a city, and continue there a year, and buy and sell, and get gain, whereas ye know not what shall be on the morrow. For what is your life—it is even as a vapor, that appeareth for a little time, and then vanisheth away. For that ye ought to say, If the Lord will, we shall live, we shall live, and do this or that."[32]

Contrary to the Kamakau version, published some forty years after the event, the glass in the lid certainly would have alerted Bingham, who penned the contemporaneous account, to an empty casket.

Procession

"As soon as the services were closed, the procession moved with the corpse to the King's wharf, a distance of 30 rods, accompanied by a crowd of the common people on each side, 'weeping as they went.' The corpse being placed in the boat, Krimoku [Kalanimoku], dressed in mourning, with great propriety of deportment, stepped into it alone; and while the multitude raised their voices in loud acclamation, it moved off by means of a rope, extending from the boat to the vessel, that was waiting to carry it away, where it was immediately taken on board."[33]

The *Missionary Herald* recorded: "No interment which we have witnessed at this place has appeared to us more affecting, nor have the people at any burial manifested more feeling than on the present occasion."[34]

The canoes accompanying the body of Keʻeaumoku sailed past Maui, where Charles Stewart remarked on Friday, March 26, 1824: "This morning a squadron of native vessels passed, with the body of Governor Cox, who died this week at Oahu, bound to Kairua (Kailua, Kona] where the corpse is to be deposited. All the principal chiefs [...] have now gone to Kairua to the funeral."[35] Of the Kailua funeral, Stewart, who viewed the flotilla from Maui, was silent. A letter from Artemas Bishop and Asa Thurston to the missionary board, however, continued the account: "About noon today [March 27, 1824] Gov. Adams [Kuakini] returned from Oahu, bringing with them the remains of his deceased bother Cox (Keaumoku) who died on Mon. the 20th inst. After a heavy discharge of artillery from the battery, for nearly an hour, the Gov. & suite, accompanied by several of the principal chiefs from the Leeward, his relatives, landed and with great lamentations, deposited the deceased in the cellar of his new framed house [Huliheʻe Palace]. Messrs. T. [Thurston] & B. [Bingham] visited them in the afternoon. At evening they visited them again and attended prayers in the cellar, where during the days of mourning they are to make it their abode."[36]

The "great lamentations" most likely refer to the usual wailing that accompanied the death of a chief. The location for the coffin, too, reflected the traditional practice of burying relatives in or near the house of a relative of the deceased. Other than the prayers in the cellar the missionaries make no reference to Christian services.

Kaumualiʻi (1824)

The death of Kaumualiʻi on May 26, 1824, also occasioned his lying in state in the house in which he died, replete with Western and traditional Hawaiian furnishings and accouterments. Kaumualiʻi, the last king of Kauaʻi, had ceded his kingdom to Kamehameha I, completing the latter's unification of the island chain. Married to Chiefess Deborah Kapule, Kaumualiʻi was forced to move to Oʻahu, where he married Kaʻahumanu, widow of Kamehameha I. Charles Stewart once again recorded the scene surrounding the death of an *aliʻi*:

> The moment it was evident that he was in the very last agony, Kaahumanu ordered the door fastened and the window curtains dropt, and began preparing the corpse for exhibition to the people who had assembled in multitudes about the house. A Chinese lounge, or settee, was spread with a rich mantle of green silk velvet, lined with pink satin; on this the corpse was laid, the lower extremities being wrapped in loose and heavy folds of yellow satin; while the chest and head were without covering, except a wreath of feathers placed round the head, so as to pass over and conceal the eyes. The splendid war-cloak of the king composed of red, yellow, and black feathers, was spread over the arm of the settee at his head, and a large cape of the same material and colours, occupied a corresponding place at his feet. The crowd without had in the mean time received some intimation of the event; and redoubling their lamentations were rushing from all directions towards the windows and the doors, so that it was difficult to keep them closed; as soon therefore as the body was thus laid out, the curtains of the windows in the room were again drawn up, and an indescribable scene of wailing ensued.[37]

Stewart explained the feather wreath covering the eyes in a note: "This was an important matter, connected not only with the adjustment of the body immediately after death, but a necessary act in order to the departed spirit's entering Meru, or joining the society of happy spirits in the other world."[38] Stewart's note confirms the admixture of traditional and Christian funerary practices at the death of Kaumuali'i. The lying in state of Kaumuali'i also exhibited the first recorded use of *ahu'ula*, feather cloaks, in lying in state. The bodies of both Kaumuali'i and Ke'eaumoku lay on couches during the visitations that occurred in their places of death.

Funeral

The funeral of Kaumuali'i took place in Honolulu at 9 a.m. on Friday, May 28, 1824, with Ellis presiding: "After a hymn and a prayer, Mr. Ellis preached from the words, 'Be ye also ready.'" The services were closed by singing a native version of Pope's "Dying Christian."[39] Stewart's account does not record the opening hymn or the content of the prayer that followed, but he does indicate the text for the sermon. The words "Be ye also ready" come from Matthew 24:44, a traditional verse for funerals: "Therefore be ye also ready: for in such an hour as ye think not the Son of man cometh."[40]

Stewart refers the closing hymn as the "native version of Pope's "Dying Christian," a shortened title for Alexander Pope's ode, "The Dying Christian to His Soul." The final song for the funeral was available in *Na Himeni Hawaii*, printed a year before death of Kaumuali'i. William Ellis and Hiram Bingham had collaborated to publish *Na Himeni Hawaii*, and a printing of 2,000 copies had been completed by March 1823.[41] The closing music of the funeral, Hymn XXX, opens in *Na Himeni Hawaii* with a quote from the Old Testament: "*I make au ke make ana o ka poe maitai. Numbers XXIII. 13*," although the citation more likely should refer to Numbers 23:10: "Let me die the death of the righteous."[42]

The lyrics of Hymn XXX, a rough Hawaiian translation Pope's poem, read:

> 1. Kuu uhane ora mau,
> Tuu e tuu kuu kino nei,
> Nani mai ke oli ana
> 'Ko ke kino make ana.
> Ua oki pela—tuu ia'u
> 'Rere au 'ke ora mau.
>
> 2. Ka!—ka reo runa ae,
> E Kaikaina—hele mai—
> Ka! Ua paupau aho wau
> Ua poere kuu naau
> He pouri e hui mai;
> Keia anei ka make nei?

> 3. Ke naro e nei keia ao;
> Ua wehe mai ka lani mau,
>   He mele 'kani mai,
> Kii mai iau—kii mai, kii mai
> Ua pau no nae kuu enemi,
>   Ua pau ia Iesu Kraist.

Hymn XXX ends with the English word and abbreviation: "-Dying Ch.," indicating the tune for the lyrics. The original ode in English, as penned by Pope, reads:

> 1. Vital spark of heav'nly flame!
> Quit, Oh quit this mortal frame:
> Trembling, hoping, ling'ring, flying,
> Oh the pain, the bliss of dying!
> Cease, fond Nature, cease thy strife,
> And let me languish into life.
>
> 2. Hark! they whisper; angels say,
> Sister Spirit, come away.
> What is this absorbs me quite?
> Steals my senses, shuts my sight,
> Drowns my spirits, draws my breath?
> Tell me, my soul, can this be death?
>
> 3. The world recedes; it disappears!
> Heav'n opens on my eyes! my ears
> With sounds seraphic ring:
> Lend, lend your wings! I mount, I fly!
> O Grave! where is thy victory?
> O Death! where is thy sting?[43]

The account in *Missionary Records, Sandwich Islands*, published in London by the Religious Tract Society, makes no reference to the name of the closing hymn, only noting that the "solemn services were afterwards closed by singing a suitable hymn in the Hawaiian language."[44]

Procession

William Ellis wrote: "and on the 30th, which was the Sabbath, his interment took place at Lahaina, in a style somewhat similar, though less imposing, than that in which Keopuolani's remains had been conveyed to the tomb."[45]

Burial

The burial of Kaumuali'i took place not on the island of Kaua'i, where he had once reigned as king, nor on O'ahu, where he had lived as a captive consort of Ka'ahumanu, but on Maui, next to fellow Christian, Keōpūolani.

Ellis explained: "Kaumualii and Keopuolani agreed, prior to her decease, that directions should be given to have their bodies deposited side by side together in the grave, that they might rise together in the morning of the resurrection. This was complied with, and the body of Kaumualii was placed by the side of his late departed friend."[46]

Today, the bodies Kaumuali'i and Keōpūolani remain together after the transfer from the grounds of Halekamani, to Moku'ula, and eventually to the graveyard of Waine'e Church.

Kamehameha II and Kamāmalu (1824)

Other individuals who had a profound impact on funerary practice were King Kamehameha II and Queen Kamāmalu. Kamehameha II, 'Iolani Liholiho, was born in 1796, the son of Kamehameha I and Keōpūolani. His act of eating with Ka'ahumanu and Keōpūolani effectively ended the *kapu* system. His half-sister and favorite queen, Kamāmalu, was the daughter of Kamehameha I and Kalakua. The couple traveled to London, England, where they contracted the measles and died. Unlike the explicit commands of his mother, Keōpūolani, restricting forms of mourning, the influence of the royal couple came from the practice associated with British royal funerals. The place of the deaths of Hawaiian king and queen, therefore, influenced the funerary practices that took place following their deaths, for themselves, and those who succeeded them. A letter from George Burder, secretary of the London Missionary Society, to Jeremiah Evarts, of its American counterpart, describes the initial treatment of the deceased:

> I called at the house of their residence (Osborne Hotel in the Adelphi) several times before and during their illness, but could not see them. Their bodies have been deposited (pro tempore) in St. Martin's Church and will be taken home by order of our Government next month (August) in a ship commanded by Lord Byron, brother of the deceased poet.[47]

Sixty-five years later, Theo H. Davies, gave a more detailed account of the funerary preparations in England, in a letter to Princess Lili'uokalani dated July 26, 1889:

> On Saturday, July 7, the remains lay in state in a large apartment on the ground floor of the hotel, the central part of the room was divided from the rest by a frame-work 14 feet square, open on three sides, the floor being covered with small feather cloaks, and a number of capes and helmets. The large royal cloak was at the head of the coffin.
> On Sunday, July 18th, a 5 o'clock, a hearse and six horses conveyed the coffin to St. Martin's Church, and it was deposited beside the coffin of the Queen. [...]
> On Tuesday night, [September] 7th, at 10 o'clock, two hearses, mourning coaches..., conveyed the remains from St. Martin's Church to the London Dock, where they embarked onboard the Frigate "Blonde" for conveyance to Honolulu.
> ... On Wednesday, Sept. 30th, the "Blonde" sailed for Honolulu.[48]

The dates of the account by Wyllie differ from other accounts. The inscription on the coffin of Kamāmalu dates her death to July 8, a day after Wyllie's date. The account in the *Voyage of HMS Blonde* has the ship receiving the coffins on September 8 and sailing for Hawai'i on September 29, 1824, a day before and a day after respectively the Wyllie dates.[49] Byron also has them "in a vault under the church of St. Martin's in the Fields."[50] Today the crypt there, once a place of royal repose, has a café.

The return of the bodies of Kamehameha II and Kamāmalu from England, on May 11, 1825, on board the *Blonde* established an entirely new level of extravagance for the funeral practices for Hawaiian royalty.

The *Blonde* returned with a wax bust of King Kamehameha II. The funerary practices of English royalty formerly included a wax effigy on the bier. The use of the effigy ended after the funeral of James I on May 7, 1625. Elizabeth Keka'aniau Pratt donated the bust to the Bishop Museum in 1897 (courtesy Hawaii State Archives [PP-97-6-003]).

LYING IN STATE

The lying in state of Kamehameha II and Kamāmalu would mark the royal standard for future arrangements. The elaborate coffins prepared for the royal Hawaiian pair in England displayed an elegance provided by the English monarch, George IV, whom they had come half way around the world to visit. A wax bust of Kamehameha II, which accompanied the coffins, reflected a past practice of producing wax effigies of English royalty for placement on their biers.

Ephraim Eveleth provides a description of the sumptuous caskets: "The ponderous and elegant triple coffins, of lead, mahogany, and oak, covered with crimson velvet, and richly studded with gilt nails and ornaments, and weighing together about 2200 pounds."[51] Byron reported that the bodies of the king and queen "were properly cased, and external coffins were covered with crimson velvet with gilt ornaments, a kind of decoration of death which so pleased the Eriis [Aliʻi], that on the arrival of the bodies at Oahu, more than one said it would be a pleasure to die in England to have their bodies so honoured."[52] Kamakau provides a description that juxtaposed the past practices with the new ones. The people "looked with admiration at the handsome caskets the like of which had never been seen before in this country, where the chiefs had been put away in basketwork woven of braided cord (kaʻai)."[53]

Though the cost of the caskets for Kamehameha II and his queen had been borne by the British crown, future expenses would be the sole burden of the Kingdom of Hawaiʻi. As lying in state became more formalized, the costs associated with the royal Hawaiian way of death also increased. Unlike the sennit *kāʻai* used to enclose the bones of the chiefs in ancient times, the new royal way of death required the purchase of foreign goods, though native *koa* and *kou* would later replace the oak and mahogany.

Funeral

The funeral service for Liholiho and Kamāmalu took place outdoors. The nascent chapel could not hold the numbers of mourners, nor could the massive coffins easily enter, so the ministers conducted the service outdoors: "The procession stopped at the door of the chapel, where a few appropriate passages, selected from the church service, were read by Mr. Bloxam, chaplain of the Blonde." Charles Stewart, in his description of the funeral, noted that "Mr. Bloxam read part of the burial service of the Episcopal Church." Since the Church of England still used the 1662 *Book of Common Prayer*, the passages that opened the service would have been from the following verses:

> I am the resurrection and the life, saith the Lord: he that believeth in me, though he were dead, yet shall he live: and whosoever liveth and believeth in me shall never die. St. John xi. 25, 26.
> I know that my Redeemer liveth, and that he shalt stand at the latter day upon the earth. And though after my skin worms destroy this body, yet in my flesh shall I see God: whom I shall see for myself, and mine eyes shall behold, and not another. Job xix. 25, 26, 27.
> We brought nothing into this world, and it is certain we can carry nothing out. The Lord gave, and the Lord hath taken away; blessed be the Name of the Lord. 1 Tim. vi. 7. Job I. 21.

Eveleth gave the following description of the service: "A hymn was read, a short discourse in the native language, delivered by one of the missionaries, from the words of Paul,—"Since by man came death, by man came also the resurrection from the dead." The Authorized (King James) Version of the Bible uses the phrase "resurrection of the dead." Eveleth does not specify whether the hymn was read in English or Hawaiian. The hymnal, *Na Himeni Hawaii*, used during the funeral of Kaumualiʻi certainly would have been available. For this funeral the American missionaries provided the message in the Hawaiian language. William Ellis, who had delivered the message at the funeral of Keōpūolani, had already left for England in August 1824, a month after the royal couple had died in London. The coffins of Liholiho and Kamāmalu ended in the *hale pili* of Kalanimoku where the service was ended with the hymn sung to Pleyels, most likely the tune of "Pleyels Hymn," written by Joseph Pleyel in 1791.

Hymn XXIV in *Na Himeni Hawaii* has Pleyels listed as the tune at the end of the hymn. Hymn XXIV, with its opening Bible verse, reads:

Ua hana heva makou.......Ke pule nei makou ia Oe, e hoora mai ia makou nei.—Na Kilo X. 15 (Judges 10:15).

1. IEHOVA e aroha mai,
Ia makou nei ke heva no ;
He pono mau ko kanawai,
He rohe ore ko makou.

2. Ke uhi nei ka naau po,
Ia makou nei ke hara pau;
Hoora mai nei ia makou,
Kokoke i ka make mau.

3. IEHOVA e ahonui mai,
O make mau makou a pau;
Homai i naau ao maitai,
Ke mihi nei 'ka hara mau.

4. Horoi i ko makou naau
'Ko Iesu koko mana nae,
I pau ka hara o makou,
Ia Oe makou e ora'i.

Pleyels, Windham.

PROCESSION

Because their deaths took place abroad, the procession for Kamehameha II and Kamāmalu started at Honolulu harbor on the *Blonde*. From the ship the coffins "were placed upon two wagons, covered with black *tapa*, in the form of a hearse, and drawn by forty chiefs of the middle and lower ranks."[54] The order of procession was set by someone very familiar with the protocols of the British monarchy. Charles Stewart noted that the British diplomat provided counsel regarding the funeral march: "Mr. Charlton improved the period in forming them in the order in which they were to walk."[55]

As a result of the great numbers of persons who had gathered to mourn the deaths of their *aliʻi*, the path was guarded by "two lines of native soldiers, extending from the beach to the chapel, a distance of half a mile."⁵⁶ Eveleth recorded the order of the procession:

> First the lofty and superb national kahiles [*sic*], eight or ten in number, black, green, and red, from twenty to twenty-five feet in length. Next the marines of the Blonde in their uniform; then the band of music; then the gentlemen of the mission, and the chaplain and surgeon of the Blonde; then the corpses, followed by Kauikeouli [*sic*] and Nahienaena [brother and sister of Kamehameha II], the former supported by Mr. Charlton, the consul, and the latter by Lord Byron; then came Kaahumanu, Kaniu [Kalakua Kaheiheimālie] mother of Tamehamaru [Kamāmalu, also know as Kamehamalu], the deceased queen; then Boki, Adams [John Adams Kuakini], Opira [Piʻia, also known as Nāmāhāna], Hoapiri [Hoapili], the step-father of Riho Riho.
>
> The procession moved in a slow and decent order, between the two lines of the guard. The gazing multitude from the chiefs, prohibited from approaching within fifty yards. Minute guns were fired from the fort and ships, and the bell tolled.⁵⁷

BURIAL

The Western-style Royal Tomb at Pohukaina was built to house the remains of King Kamehameha II and Queen Kamāmalu. The initial resting place, though, for the royal couple was the *hale pili* of Kalanimoku that had served as an audience hall. The thatched house, "lined with black *kapa* [...] was prepared as a temporary repository. [...] The government soon erected a more permanent but very simple mausoleum of stone, about twenty-four feet square, in which they were deposited with funeral solemnity."

The inscription on the coffin was in Hawaiian and English: "KAMEHAMEHA 2D | Elii no nahina o Awhai | Make I Pelekani 28 Makaiki Kaiku | I ke mahoe mua o Kamakaiki 1824 | Aloha ino no komako Elii Iolani. | KAMEHAMEHA 2ND KING | of the Sandwich Islands | Died July 14th 1824 | in London | in the 28th year of his age | May we remember our beloved King Iolani."⁵⁸ The inscription on the coffin of Kamāmalu, according to *Ke Au Okoa*, reads: "Kamehamalu Elii | no na aina o awahi | Make i Pelekani | 22 ma Raiki Taitu | London 8 Re mahoe o Re ma Raiki 1824. | Tamehamalu | Queen | of the Sandwich Islands | Departed this life in London | on the 8 July 1824 | Aged 22 years." The spelling of the Hawaiian language inscription reflected the orthography prior to its standardization.

The missionary letters to the American Board of Commissioners for Foreign Missions reported the extent of the change of practices surrounding the death of aliʻi: "Great decency and sobriety were observed on this occasion—What a contrast to the funerals of their former kings—Then the heavens were insulted & the earth polluted by the grossest abominations."[59]

With each new funeral, the old ways slowly passed. With the death of Kamehameha's last child on Oʻahu, and the death of Keōpūolani on Maui, chiefs on those islands had been introduced to the new forms of respect following the death of royalty. From the mission station on Kauaʻi, Mr. Bishop, reported: "This morning [December 8, 1825], I was requested to perform the funeral service after the Christian manner. I prepared, therefore, a short address, and a prayer suited to the occasion. [...] After service a procession was formed, preceded by chiefs, when we walked with stillness and regularity to the grave. The scene was novel, and excited much attention among the people. Some of the chiefs observed that this was the right way to conduct a funeral, instead of their old custom of carrying out their dead in the night."[60] For Western missionaries and visitors the new form of mourning indicated a different level of civilization in Hawaiʻi.

Kalanimoku (1827)

Kalanimoku, who adopted the Western name William Pitt, in honor of the British Prime Minister, served as Kalaimoku, or Prime Minister, to Kamehameha I and Kamehameha II. Kalanimoku died in Kailua, Kona, on February 8, 1827.[61] Kamakau related the events surrounding his death, especially the return to some of the former practices. "Some expressed their grief in extravagant ways," Kamakau wrote, "to the terror of Dr. [John] Pellham [who had accompanied Kalanimoku to Kailua]. One man named Kiaʻi-moku hung himself head down from the ridge of the house where Ka-lani-moku's body was laid, and wailed bitterly."[62] Kamakau gave no account of the burial of Kalanimoku.

Nāmāhana (1829)

Queen Nāmāhana was the mother of Kaʻahumanu, who served as Kuhina Nui during the reign of Kamehameha II and as regent of the young king, Kamehameha III. The practices following her death illustrate the continuation of tradition expressions of grief following the death of chiefs. The death of aliʻi still prompted the composing of the *hē kanikau* or funeral dirge. As she had done for her father, Keʻeaumoku Pāpaʻiahiahi, Kaʻahumanu composed one following the death of her mother, Nāmāhana, also known as Piʻia, on September 12, 1829:

> Kuʻu makua, i ke hale uluoʻa kanaka,
> Hale malumalu komo poʻo o maua,
> E hoʻomaha ai i ka wela ke hele—

Hele kuʻu makuahine me ke aloha,
ʻAuwana wale iho ko au i Kuahea,
O ʻoe o ka wahine ʻai makani,
ʻAi makani malanaʻi-e—
E ʻai e ʻai ana i ke aloha,
E ʻai e ana i ke aloha o na makua,
Kenakena i ke aloha o na keiki,
O kou kaikaina muli pokiʻi
O Pokiʻi-kauna, o kuʻu kaikaina.

My mother in the house well-peopled,
House into whose shelter we entered
To rest from the heat of the way,
Love to my mother who has gone,
Leaving me wandering on the mountainside.
You are the woman consumed by the wind
Consumed by the trade wind,
Consumed, consumed, consumed with love,
Consumed, consumed with love for parents.
Bitter with grief for the children,
For your beloved little sister,
For the four younger sisters, for my younger sister.[63]

Missionary Levi Chamberlain recorded in his journal that Nāmāhana lay in state "in a richly ornamented coffin covered with crimson velvet, her name marked upon it and age Viz L. Piia AE 37."[64]

Funeral

The funeral service for Nāmāhana took place on the afternoon of Sunday, September 13, 1829, at the recently completed Kawaiahaʻo Church, a *hale pili* with dimensions of 196 by 63 feet. "The theme of the funeral discourse was the language of Simeon, 'Lord, now lettest thou thy servant depart in peace according to thy word, for mine eyes have seen thy salvation,' and was supposed capable of being appropriately applied to her case."[65] As at the funeral of Kaumualiʻi, the ode "Dying Christian" was sung in Hawaiian.[66]

Procession

The procession for Nāmāhana, who had participated in the procession of Kamehameha II and Kamāmalu just four years earlier, also drew numerous mourners, this time in Honolulu. Hiram Bingham recorded: "On the Sabbath, her funeral was attended by great numbers who respected her. The procession moved from the house to the church. The remains were followed by the husband [Laʻanui] and two sisters [Kaʻahumanu and Kaheiheimālie], the king [Kamehameha III], Auhea [Kekāuluohi] and Kinau [both nieces], Kekūanāoʻa [husband of Kīnaʻu] and Kanaina [husband of Auhea], Boki [Governor of Oʻahu] and Liliha [wife of Boki], all in deep mourning. There followed, two by two, the native members of the church to which she belonged; then the members of the mission family, twelve in numbers; then nearly five times the number of foreign residents; after them, a great company of natives."[67]

BURIAL

Levi Chamberlain wrote of the burial of Nāmāhana on September 13, 1829, that the coffin was interred: "in the Selpuchre built for the remains of the King & Queen who died in England. [...] The chiefs built a stone enclosure within the house for the remains of Opiia i.e. The grave in which the coffin is to be put is to be laid up around the side with stone & lime."[68]

Kamanele (1831)

Kamakau mentions little regarding the death and burial of Kamanele, daughter of the governor of the island of Hawaiʻi, Kuakini. He does note, however: "During this troubled year of 1834, some of the young chiefs died, among them Ke-ola-loa, the son of Pauli Ka-ʻo-lei-o-ku and the brother of Konia, who was to have been the husband of Princess Harriet Nahi-ʻenaʻena, and Ka-ʻuaʻa-moku-o-Kamanele, the daughter of J.A. [John Adams] Kuakini, governor of Hawaii, who was affianced to Kamehamea III. Both of these young chiefs were about twenty years of age."[69]

According to *Au Okoa*, the inscription on the coffin of Kamanele reads: "Kamanele | Make Mei 7, 1831 | 19 | Kona mau Makahiki."[70]

Keaweaweʻulaokalani I (1832)

Keaweʻulaokalani I was the son of Kamehameha III and Kalama Hakalelleponi. Little is written of the child, but Kamakau recorded that just after the child's birth, Keoni Ana was caught with Kalama and sentenced to death, a sentence that was not carried out.[71] P. Christiaan Klieger claimed in *Mokuʻula: Mauiʻs Sacred Isle* that Keaweaweʻulaokalani I was a "probable burial at the tomb at Mokuʻula."[72] The body was likely moved by Bernice Pauahi Bishop in 1884.[73]

Queen Kaʻahumanu, Kuhina Nui (1832)

Perhaps the most powerful woman in the Kingdom of Hawaiʻi, Queen Kaʻahumanu was the widow of Kamehameha the Great. With Keōpūolani, Kaʻahumanu overthrew the *ai kapu*, the prohibition of women eating with men, by dining with Kamehameha II. Kaʻahumanu served as Kuhina Nui,

Queen Kaʻahumanu broke the prohibition against men and women eating together, effectively ending the entire *kapu* system (courtesy Hawaii State Archives [PP-99-6-004]).

a position that exercised authority equal to that of the king. Just three years after she had written a *kanikau* for her mother, Nāmāhana, Kaʻahumanu herself would be subject of funeral dirges. Kaʻahumanu had died at her house in Mānoa called Pukaʻōmaʻomaʻo on June 5, 1832. "I well remember seeing her on her deathbed in Manoa Valley. It was night. She lay in a dying state on a high pile of mats, in a thatched house, with many people around her. She passed away that evening."[74] Her obsequies took place during the course of the day.

LYING IN STATE

The lying in state for Kaʻahumanu took place at her Mānoa house. The scene was chronicled in the account in *Wreck of the Glide*: "By twelve o clock nine or ten thousand people had collected to pay the rites of burial."[75]

PROCESSION

In a scene reminiscent of the procession of Liholiho and Kamāmalu, an open path required the presence of a military escort. Dix reported: "The funeral procession moved with measured steps and with muffled drums from the late residence of Kaahumanu to the chapel. Several hundred native soldiers, dressed in becoming uniform, were present, and divided to the right and left, while, through the midst the coffin was borne by six pall-bearers, and was followed by near relatives, the missionaries, English and American consuls, and a large portion of the natives and resident foreigners."[76]

FUNERAL

One of the authors of *Wreck of the Glide* described the simplicity of her bier: "Though I had never seen Kaahumanu, I was deeply affected by observing in the chapel the coffin covered with crimson velvet and the pall, the badges of mourning, many of which were of the simplest sort, but showed as deep sorrow as the most costly trappings of woe."[77]

At the funeral of Ka'ahumanu, "Mr. Bingham preached from the triumphant words of Paul—'I have fought a good fight, I have finished my course, I have kept the faith. Henceforth there is laid up for me a crown of righteousness, which the Lord, the righteous Judge, shall give me at that day; and not to me only, but to all them also that love is appearing.'" Another observer described the emotion of the event: "The discourse was preached by the Rev. Mr. Bingham, who having been the religious counsellor of the late queen, was peculiarly qualified faithfully and feelingly to portray her character. Tears coursed down his face as he described Kaahumanu's renunciation of idolatry, her interest in the progress of knowledge and piety, her last illness and death."[78]

BURIAL

The final procession went from Kawaiaha'o to the royal tomb at Pohukaina. "The services being concluded the procession moved from the chapel to the place where lie buried the deceased sovereigns and where also were laid the remains of this island queen to await the bright dawn of an endless day."[79]

The inscription on the coffin, in Hawaiian only, reads: "Elisabeta | Kaahumanu | Kona, 1793, | Hanau ana | Kona, 1842, | Make Ana."[80]

David Kamehameha (1835)

David Kamehameha, the son of Kīna'u and Matiao Kekūanāo'a was the *hānai* son of Ka'ahumanu. At the time of his death, his mother, Kīna'u, had assumed the position of Kuhina Nui, styling herself Ka'ahumanu II. Kīna'u was the daughter of Kamehameha I and Kaheiheimalie, making David Kamehameha the grandson of the great chief. Two of his younger brothers occupied the throne as Kamehameha IV and Kamehameha V. His sister, Victoria Kamāmalu, served as Kuhina Nui under the name of Ka'ahumanu. In a column titled "Make," *Kumu Hawaii* listed the death of David Kamehameha: "Dek. 15. Ua make o Davida Tamehameha ma Honolulu. Ehiku kona mau makahiki."[81] He was first buried at the royal tomb at Pohukaina and later transferred to Mauna 'Ala.

His coffin features the following inscription: "Davida Tamehameha | I hanau i Mei 20 la, 1828 | I make i Detemapa 15 la 1835 | O kona mau makahiki e 7 | 6 malama 16 la."[82]

John Young (1835)

War companion of Kamehameha the Great, father of Kuhina Nui Keoni Ana and grandfather of Queen Emma, John Young died on December 18, 1835, in the residence of the latter. He was born in Lancastershire, England, in 1742. Abandoned in 1790 by his American ship, the schooner *Eleanora*, when he went missing, Young's skills concerning Western armaments gave Kamehameha I an edge in the conquest of the island chain. Given chiefly status, Young served as governor of the island of Hawai'i. His death was announced in the same issue of *Kumu Hawaii*[83] as that of David Kamehameha, their deaths falling just three days apart.

According to Levi Chamberlain, the funeral of John Young took place "at the meeting house where prayers were offered and an address both in native & Eng. Delivered by Mr. Bingham—the theme of the address was from the Ninetieth Ps. "The days of our years are three score and ten and if by reason of strength they be four score years yet is their strength labor & sorrow—So teach us to number our days that we may apply our hearts to wisdom."[84]

PROCESSION

Levi Chamberlain recorded in his journal: "The funeral was attended this afternoon [December 18, 1835] from the house of Dr. Rooke. [...] The procession formed and proceeded to the meeting house."[85]

BURIAL

John Young was interred at the Pohukaina tomb. He was among the individuals later transferred to Mauna 'Ala.

Nāhi'ena'ena (1837)

Princess Nāhi'ena'ena died on December 30, 1836, at Hale Ali'i, the residence of her brother, King Kamehemeha III. Her obsequies took place in Lāhainā, Maui. The vessel carrying the body of Nāhiʻenaʻena, the Man of War *Kae*, displayed the Royal Standard for the first time.[86]

PROCESSION

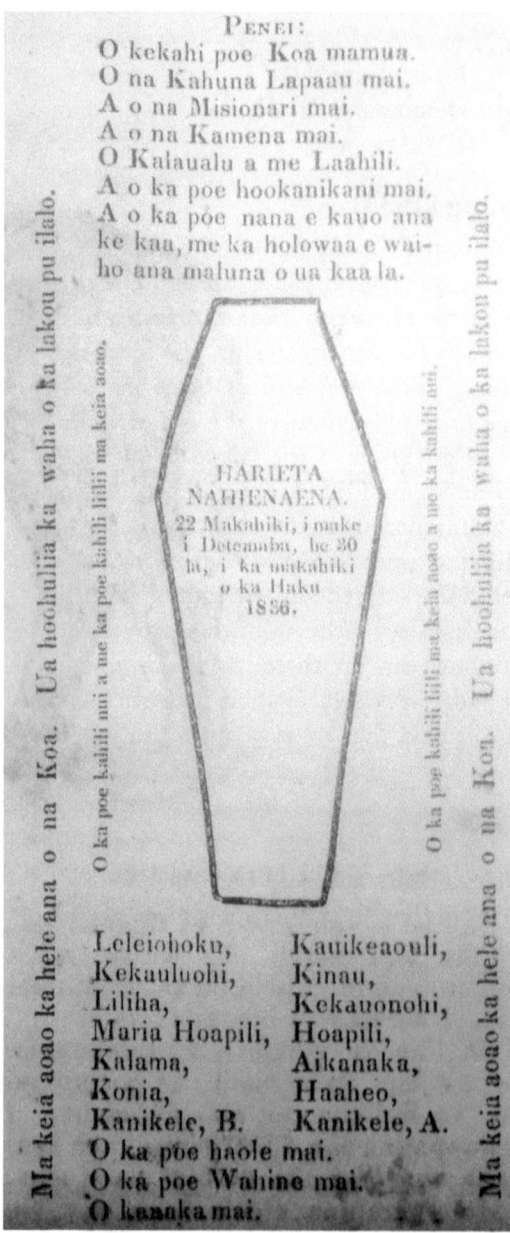

The order of procession for Nāhiʻenaʻena, daughter of Keōpūolani, displayed a more complex form than that of her mother. The introduction of the written Hawaiian language and printing allowed the organizers of the procession to communicate precise locations of the participants. The order for Nāhiʻenaʻena appeared in the Hawaiian language in *Kumu Hawaii*, on February 15, 1837.[87] *Kumu Hawaii*, the first newspaper in Hawaiʻi, had published its inaugural issue just four years earlier. The order of procession gave the positions of the other aliʻi by name. The outline of a coffin was inscribed inside the outline of a coffin were her name, age and the date of her death, December 30, 1836.

The order of procession was:

O kekahi poe Koa mamua. | O na Kahuna Lapaau mai. A o na Misionari mai. | O Kalaualu a me Laahili. |A o ka poe hookanikani mai. | A o ka poe nana e kauo ana | ke kaa, me ka holowaa e

The announcement of the procession of Nāhiʻenaʻena in *Kumu Hawaii* in 1837 showed the specific positions of the participants.

wai- | ho ana maluna o ua kaa la. | Ma keia aoao ka hele ana o na Koa. Ua hoohuliia ka waha o ka lakou pu ilalo. O ka poe kahili nui a me ka poe kahili liilii an keia aoao. [*outline of a casket containing the words*: HARIETA NAHIENAENA. 22 Makahiki, i make i Detemaba, he 30 la, i ka makahiki o ka Haku 1836.] O ka poe kahili liili (*sic*) ma keia aoao a me ka kahili nui. Ma keia aoao ka hele ana o na Koa. Ua hoohuliia ka waha o ka lakou pu ilalo. | Leleiohoku, Kauikeaouli,| Kekauluohi, Kinau | Liliha, Kekauonohi, | Maria Hoapili, Hoapili, Kalama, Aikanaka, | Konia, Haaheo, | Kanikele, B., Kanikele, A. | O ka poe haole mai. | O ka poe Wahine mai. | O kanaka mai.

The following is an English translation:

Soldiers | Doctors | Missionaries | Carpenters | Kalaualu and Laahili | Musicians | Those who pulled the cart | Coffin placed on the cart. | Leleiohoku, Kauikeaouli, | Kekauluohi, Kinau | Liliha, Kekauonohi, | Mary Hoapili, Hoapili, | Kalama, Aikanaka, | Konia, Haaheo. | Consul B. Consul A. | Foreigners. | Hawaiian Women. | Hawaiian Men. |

The identities of Kalaualu and Laahila are open to speculation. A Kalaualu is mentioned in the Native Testimony.[88] Sworn testimony about Kapena Molakeke (Harriet Blanchard) also mentions Kalauala: "Lanai, sworn by the Word of God and stated, I have often heard Kapena Molakeke say that he [she] had paid $100.00 to Kalaualu for that place on which he [she] had lived and he [she] had believed that Kalaualu had no right there. This was close to the time Kaahumanu had died."[89] Kalaualu is also mentioned in a letter from Queen Emma to Peter Kaeo regarding a "*kalaipahoa* [poison wood image]."[90] Land records also mention Laahila.[91] Laahili was the subject of a complaint in March 1846 regarding "a native, Laahili, at Lahaina" for "not paying up his share of the expenses of a vessel built by [John] Dawson."[92] An account in the *Friend* refers to "the home of Laahila a chief" in Lāhainā.[93]

The importance of carpenters in the early Kingdom of Hawai'i was reflected by their presence in the royal procession. Kamehameha I had relied on carpenters to construct the fleet for his planned invasion of Kaua'i. Other foreigners in the procession included Kanikele B. and Kanikele A., most likely the British Consul and American Consul in front of the *haole* people. Unlike the funeral procession of Keōpūolani, where the foreigners had led the procession, the foreigners formed further back in the train of mourners.

The route of the funeral procession to the church and cemetery became known as Luakini Street, Hawaiian for temple or church.

Burial

Andelucia Lee Conde, member of the Eighth Company of missionaries, eight months after her arrival in Hawai'i, visited the chamber where Nahienaena was entombed. She wrote in her journal on December 11, 1837:

We were also escorted by himself alone to the chamber where were deposited the remains of his deceased mother and sister the young Princess and his sister's child. The room was a large chamber elegantly furnished with chairs tables with large mirrors set under them, beautiful Chinese matting and a small organ upon which he played for our entertainment. Nearly in the centre of the room was placed a beadstead, nearly the magnitude of 3 common bedsteads, upon which was a bed very neatly spread, and upon this were placed the three coffins, side by side, most splendidly ornamented. Each of these corpses were enclosed in 3 coffins—the first zinc—the second lead and the third or outside one, of wood. These were covered with scarlet silk velvet, put on with a multitude of brass nails—gilded plaits, with their names upon them, and various other gilded ornaments that gave us almost any impression but that of a tomb. [...] Without this, around the bed were stationed several Kahilis like so many tall sentinels to keep unceasing vigil over the dead.[94]

Kīna'u (1839)

Queen Kīna'u, the mother of two future kings, Kamehameha IV and Kamehameha V, and Kuhina Nui Victoria Kamāmalu, died April 4, 1839. She had served as Kuhina Nui from July 1832 until her death.

LYING IN STATE

The cost of the casket, called *pahu* in the Hawaiian language document, was sent soon after the account of the death of Kīna'u, called by the

Kīna'u (center) served as the second Kuhina Nui (courtesy Hawaii State Archives [PP-98-2-007]).

name she used as Kuhina Nui, Ka'ahumanu II. It detailed the expenses associated with the creation of the coffin for Kīna'u. From the foreign stores came the materials required for the Western style ceremony. From Brewer, 114 yards of black cloth at one dollar per yard, 11 yards of red plush at four dollars a yard, three yards of lace at a dollar a yard, and three yards of black ribbon at twenty-five cents a yard; Mr. Ladd supplied thirty yards of black silk at two dollars a yard and four spools of silk thread for 50 cents. Thomas provided 3,500 nails at five dollars for a thousand.[95] The inscription for the coffin of Kīna'u used the name she used as Kuhina Nui. It read: "Kaahumanu II | i make | Ape 4 1839 | I Kona | Makahiki | 33."[96]

Captain Edward Belcher of the HMS *Sulphur*, who stopped in Hawai'i on his voyage around the world, gave a detailed account of the funeral of Kīna'u:

> Royal Funeral in the Sandwich Islands.—The funeral of Kinau was appointed for the Wednesday following, and, accompanied by the consul and my officers, we proceeded to the house where the remains of the princess (now designated as Kahamanu II. by the missionaries) reposed in state. The coffin, which was six feet and a half long, by three wide, and the same in depth, covered with crimson cloth and gilt ornaments (*similar to that of Rihoriho made in England*) [*italics* mine], was placed on a bedstead ; the curtains of which were black silk, trimmed with white lace. The body of a carriage having been removed from the wheels, the bedstead was adapted to it, thus forming a very handsome car.
>
> We were received with great attention by the king and chiefs, and his majesty, in further proof of his good will, sent the order of the procession the day previous to ascertain if I wished to make any alteration. The troops and militia, amounting to four hundred, were all well clothed in white uniforms. Their evolutions were admirable. The king's body-guard, amounting to twenty officers in scarlet jackets, some few with epaulets, tinsel, crape &c., marched, with their swords reversed [end of curve of scabbard in front], on each side of the car; the troops with arms reversed, preceded. The king as chief mourner, with the deceased's husband, and the other chiefs, followed the car, the residents, consuls, and officers, bringing up the rear. The concourse of well-dressed females (from all the islands I imagine) in black silk mourning, astonished me. I am quite satisfied they equaled the number of troops.
>
> The moment the procession advanced, the natives not included in the procession, but who lined the roads (which had been previously strewed with rushes, over which mats were laid) commenced the *wail*,—a low noise which can only be compared to the shrill noise of the bull frogs of America ; and the buzz of so many voices in such melancholy notes certainly did not diminish the solemnity of the scene. Many I noticed shed tears, and some I thought really wailed *in earnest*. Kinau, whatever her failings might have been, was much esteemed by her subjects. The kahali, or feathered plume, and the badge of royalty was carried on this occasion. It is constructed of the dark tail-feathers of the cock, very similar to the Chinese fly-dusters or resembling the feathers worn by our regimental bands. It is, however, of great size, measuring as follows:— length of pole and plume, eighteen feet six inches ; length of plume, four feet and twenty-eight inches in diameter. On the car reaching the church, a thatched house about two

hundred feet in length by sixty wide, the canopy was lowered, the troops marched through, and the car was placed abreast of the pulpit. The consul and myself were assigned seats with his majesty.[97]

Her procession was the first that mentioned soldiers with reversed arms.

Kuini Liliha (1839)

Kuini Liliha died at Leleo in Honolulu on August 25, 1839. She had served as governor of Oʻahu following the purported death of her husband in December 1829 until her dispute with Kaʻahumanu, ending her term on April 1, 1831. Liliha, along with her husband, Boki, was a member of the party that accompanied Kamehameha II on his ill-fated trip to London.

Native historian S.M. Kamakau gives one his longest accounts regarding the mourning for a chief in his account regarding Liliha: "Before the mourning had ended for Kinaʻu and Ka-iki-o-ʻewa, another sorrow came to the chiefs in the death of Kuini Liliha. She was the daughter of Ka-lili-kauoha the daughter of Ka-hekili ʻAhumanu, king of Maui and Oahu, and of Ulu-maheihei Hoapili. Her death is said to have been caused by poison mixed in her liquor by her own relative. She had already taken a drink and went back for another. After finishing what was left in the bottle she fell down moaning and foaming at the mouth and died."[98]

While the burial place of Liliha is known, her husband, Boki, was lost on an expedition to find sandalwood (courtesy Hawaii State Archives [PP-96-2-00]).

Her popularity among the common people swelled the ranks of her mourners. "It is said that never before had there been heard such lamentation for the death of a chief as on the night she died at Leleo, and her body was brought back to Honolulu. The river of Kiki-hale was stamped dry by the feet of people of all ranks crossing over to the city."[99] Kīkīhale was "old section of Honolulu bordered by Maunakea and King streets to Nuʻuanu Stream."

Besides wailing, the people reverted back to prior mourning practices. Kamakau reported: "Common people loved the name of Liliha, and when she died they tattooed their skins with the words 'Liliha Leleo' as an everlasting memorial to their affection."[100]

BURIAL

By the time Liliha died the mausoleum at Halekamani had been replaced with one at Mokuʻula. Kamakau wrote: "Her [Liliha's] body was sent back to Mokuʻula at Lahaina on Maui and placed with that of Nahiʻenaʻena, and chiefs and commoners bewailed her life with a sorrow that abides in the in the hearts of many."[101] Kamakau makes no mention of the procession to the burial site.

Her body was transferred to Waineʻe Cemetery (now call Waiola Cemetery), where the marker reads: "Liliha | Wife of Gov'r Boki | Daughter of Ulumaheihei | Died In | Honolulu. Aug. 25, 1839."

Hoapili (1840)

Ulumaheihei Hoapili, who served as governor of Maui, was entrusted by Kamehameha I with concealing his bones, one of the most important tasks in the traditional funerary practices. He was married to Ka-lilikauoha, and later to Kaheiheimālie, one of the widows of Kamehameha I and sister of Kaʻahumanu. Unlike his daughter, Liliha, Kamakau only briefly mentioned the death of Ulumaheihei Hoapili, limiting his remarks to his religious status: "A chief of true piety was Ulu-maheihei and he died in the faith of life through the sinless blood of Jesus Christ the beloved son of God."[102] At some point his remains were transferred to the Waineʻe cemetery.

Chiefess Kapiʻolani (1841)

Chiefess Kapiʻolani, not to be confused with her namesake who married King Kalākaua, was famous because of her act of defying the Hawaiian goddess of the volcano, Pele. English poet, Alfred Lord Tennyson, wrote of the courage of the early Christian convert in his poem, "Kapiolani":

> Great and greater, and greatest of women, island heroine, Kapiolani
> Clomb the mountain, and flung the berries, and dared the Goddess,
>   and freed the people.

Of the death of the chiefess Kamakau mentions only "but going about so much in the heat of the sun to see her friends she was overcome by a fever, and she died in Honolulu on May 5, 1841, the same day of the year as her birth."[103]

The *Polynesian*, an English language newspaper that had started a year earlier, reported a more detailed account of the death of Kapiolani:

> Died in this village [Honolulu] on Wednesday last, Kapiolani, a chief woman of some distinction, from Kealakekua, Hawaii.
>
> She came to Honolulu about six weeks since, for the purpose of being operated on for a cancer, from the effects of which she had just recovered; but owing probably to going out too soon, she was seized with an erysipelatous inflammation, which eventually fell on the brain, producing palsy and death.[104]

The record is silent regarding her obsequies. She is reputed to have been buried at Mauna 'Ala, though no marker bears her name.

Keaweawe'ulaokalani II (1842)

Amos Starr Cooke recorded the date of the birth of the son of Kamehameha III and Kalama, the second son bearing the name, Keaweawe'ulaokalani. "The Queen gave birth to a son," Cooke wrote, "on the 14th inst. [January 14, 1842]." According to Juliette Montague Cooke, the "King commanded a general hula and the people turned out in great numbers to dance in honor of the new baby. There were strange goings on, carousing, etc. The King wrote a letter to us and our family announcing its birth and calling it one of our scholars. Said when it could walk he should send it here [Chiefs' Children's School]. When he died he wrote and said *ua make ka hanai a oukou* [your child is dead]. Oh, that the King might learn wisdom from his troubles!"[105]

Like his brother, Keaweawe'ulaokalani I, P. Christiaan Klieger claimed in *Moku'ula: Maui's Sacred Isle* that Keaweawe'ulaokalani II was a "probable burial at the tomb at Moku'ula."[106]

Hoapili Wahine (1842)

Hoapili Wahine, also known as Kalakua or Kaheiheimālie, was one of the widows of Kamehameha the Great, and later the wife of Hoapili. With Kamehameha I she bore two daughters: Kamāmalu and Kīna'u. The former was the wife of Kamehameha II; the latter served as Kuhina Nui and was mother of Kamehameha IV and Kamehameha V. Hoapili Wahine died January 16, 1842. Little is recorded concerning her death or obsequies. According to Kamakau: "Ka-heihei-maile Hoa-pili-wahine died of croup at Lua-ehu, Lahaina, and was taken to the mausoleum at Waine'e."[107]

Ha'alilio (1845)

Ha'alilio, also known Timoteo Ha'alilio, was born on O'ahu in 1808. He died in the service to the King on December 3, 1844, aboard the *Mon-*

treal on route back from the United States. Along with William Richards, Ha'alilio had been meeting there as an early envoy of the Kingdom of Hawai'i. His death occasioned the preservation of bodies at sea. The *Polynesian* reported: "The corpse of Haalilio was brought here, preserved in alcohol in a lead coffin. It was taken on shore on Monday evening [March 24, 1845], and an examination took place in the presence of His Majesty and a few of his officers. It was found to be in a perfect state, the features unchanged since death. The left lung was entirely gone, and hypertrophy of the right ventricle of the heart had taken place. The other viscera were healthy."[108]

Ha'alilio served the kingdom as an envoy (courtesy Hawaii State Archives [PP-96-5-004]).

FUNERAL

The funeral services for Ha'alilio took place inside Kawaiaha'o Church on Thursday, March 27, 1845, "with the coffin placed immediately in front of the pulpit."[109] With the dedication of the coral edifice of Kawaiaha'o Church on July 21, 1842, Honolulu had a covered venue of sufficient size to hold royal funerals indoors.

While the *Polynesian* records neither the Bible verses nor the names of the hymns at the service, it does note the bilingual nature of service and eulogy: "The services were conducted partly in Hawaiian and partly in English by Mr. Armstrong and the Rev. Mr. Dole.—A brief notice of the character and career of the deceased was given in both languages and the crowded audience manifested a deep sympathy for the loss the chiefs and country have sustained."[110]

PROCESSION

The *Polynesian*, dated March 29, 1845, contains the Order of Procession for Ha'alilio:

Native Officers. Native Officers. | Troops with Reversed Arms. Troops with Reversed Arms. | Band. | Colors with Guard. | British Marines with arms reversed. | Seamen from H.B.M. Talbot and Basilisk. | Merchant Seamen. | Masters and Officers of Merchant Ships. | Foreigners. | Missionaries. | Halai. Waolani | Honokaupu { The Body } Halai | Kuhia. Piikoi. | Halilea. The Widow. Kaleokokoi. | H.M Kamehameha III | G.P. Judd, esq. Gov. Kekuanaoa. | T.C.B. Rooke. Mast. Cer. | John Ricord, Esq. Kalama | John Ii. John Young. | J. Dudoit, Esq. | G. Brown., Esq. W. Miller, Esq. | Cons. For France. |U.S. Com. Br. Cons. Gen. | Capt. Sir Thos. R.T. Thompson, Bart. | William Hooper, Esq. U.S. Vice Com. Agent. | H. Sea. Lieut. Com. Hunt. | Br. Vice Consul. H.B.M.K. Basilisk. | Paki. Konia | Leleiohoku. Alapai. Keliiahonui. | British Officers. | The Young Chiefs. | Other Chiefs. | Government Officers. | Natives.

On either side of Kamehameha III were Guard with Arms Reversed and on the outside of the procession were Police.[111]

The voyage of the H.B.M. Ketch *Basilisk* to Hawai'i would be its last as a British warship. It was condemned, and sold in 1847 and rebuilt by James Robinson.[112] It sailed with the H.B.M *Talbot*, which had also done duty in Tahiti.

BURIAL

The burial of Ha'alilio featured military honors. The *Polynesian* reported: "On the body being deposited [in the Royal Tomb], three vollies were fired by the marines of the H.B.M. Ship *Talbot*, which were followed by salutes of 15 guns from the fort and the Talbot."[113] Ha'alilio was the first individual who was buried in the royal tomb based on his service to the crown rather than his chiefly status.

Kekāuluohi (1845)

Kekāuluohi, also known as Miriam Kekāuluohi and Auhea, died on June 7, 1845. She followed Kīna'u as Kuhina Nui upon her appointment on June 8, 1839. The daughter of Kaheiheimālie and Kaleimamahū, she was the wife of Kamehameha I, Kamehameha II and Charles Kana'ina. Her son by Kana'ina, William Charles Lunalilo, would later reign as the last king of the Kamehameha dynasty. She may also have been the mother of Kauwai, the last daughter of Kamehameha I.

FUNERAL

The *Polynesian* reported: "Her funeral took place yesterday [Friday, June 20]. Her remains were conveyed to the stone church [Kawaiaha'o], where an obituary discourse was preached by the Rev. R. Armstrong; thence they were removed to the Royal Cemetery, where they were deposited with military honors, beside those of the late king and other members of the royal family. The occasion being similar to those attendant upon the recent interment of Ha'alilio, it is needless at this date for us to recapitulate them."[114]

PROCESSION AND BURIAL

Wyllie sent notice of the procession to Lieutenant Hunt of the Royal Navy indicating that the procession would be from the house of Kekāuluohi, in the Palace yard, to Kawaiahaʻo and then back to the Royal Cemetery, also in the Palace yard.[115]

Unlike the others who were later transferred to Mauna ʻAla, Kekāuluohi was eventually buried at sea by her son King Lunalilo and others. Edwin North McClennan witnessed the interment at sea.[116]

William Pitt Leleiohoku, Kaʻiminaʻauao and Moses Kekuaiwa (1848)

The deaths of three royal individuals in just over a month

Kekāuluohi was the third Kuhina Nui (courtesy Hawaii State Archives [PP-98-1-001]).

from measles resulted in shared funerals: William Pitt Leleiohoku, died October 21, 1848; Kaʻiminaʻauao, twenty days later on November 10; and Moses Kekūāiwa, fourteen days after that on November 24. William Pitt Leleiohoku, the son of Kalanimoku, prime minister under Kamehameha I and II, was the husband of the late Princess Nāhiʻenaʻena, sister of the Kamehameha III; Kaʻiminaʻauao was the ward of Queen Kalama; and Moses Kekūāiwa was brother of the king. Although Kaʻiminaʻauao was also the sister of future King David Kalākaua and future Queen Liliʻuokalani, the funeral took place during the Kamehameha dynasty, so the honor accorded her related to her status as ward of Queen Kalama.

Dying around the same time as Moses Kekūāiwa was his *hānai* mother, Keaweamahi, but she was not included in the state funeral. She had served as governor of the island of Kauaʻi from 1839 until her death.

The delay in the funeral of Leleiohoku resulted in the cancellation of the Hawaiian independence day holiday that recognized the reestablishment of Hawaiian sovereignty five years earlier. The Chamberlain's Office announced on November 23, 1848: "On account of the funeral of the late Chief Leleiohoku not having yet taken place, and their Majesties the King and Queen being indisposed, the celebration of the 28th November, 1848, will not be performed this year."[117]

The funeral would not take place for another month. The Chamberlain's Office announced on December 14, 1848:

> The funeral obsequies of the late Chief Wm. Pitt Leleiohoku (brother-in-law to the King), of the late young Chief Moses Kekuaiwa, Son of His Excellency the Governor of Oahu by the late Kinau (Kaahumanu II.) and of Kaiminaau; ward of the Queen, will take place on Sunday the 30th instant, at 12 o'clock, M.
> A general invitation is hereby extended to foreigners and natives to be present on the occasion. A programme of the order of procession will be issued, and sent to all Foreign Representatives and Consuls at an early period, previous to the funerals.[118]

In 1882, the *Saturday Press* looked back at the funeral for the three, including a description of the coffins: "Large sums were expended on the coffins, which were made of the beautiful island woods, the *Koa* and *Kou*, inlaid with satin and profusely ornamented with silver trappings. The bodies were preserved with alcohol in metal coffins, enclosed in the costly outside caskets."[119] The preparation of the bodies was the same as had previously occurred for Haʻalilio in 1845.

PROCESSION

The Order of Procession published by the Chamberlain's Office on December 22, 1848,[120] and signed by A. Paki, explicitly stated the royal relationships and orders the names accordingly. William Pitt Leleiohoku was husband of the late Princess Nāhiʻenaʻena, sister of Kamehameha III, making him "brother-in-law to the king." Moses Kekuaiwa was "son of His Excellency Governor Kekuanaoa by the Late Kinau Kaahumanu II," linking him both to the governor of Oahu and the former Kuhina Nui. Kaʻiminaʻauao, who died at age 3, is listed as "Ward of the Queen." The shared order:

> Order of Procession | For the Funerals of the late | William Pitt Leleiohoku, Brother-in-law to the King, | Of the late Young Chief | Moses Kekuaiwa, Son of His Excellency Governor Kekuanaoa by the late Kinau Kaahumanu II., | and of | Kaiminaauao, Ward of the Queen.| [*Rule*] | Undertakers | Two Kahili Bearers | Officer | Twenty-Four Soldiers, Four Deep. | Band Playing Dead March. | Hawaiian Flag, | Borne by an Officer. | Medical Attendants. | Officiating Clergyman. | Guard of Soldiers and Police. Friends of the Deceased. } Young Chiefs. [*outline of coffin*] Young Chiefs { Friends of the Deceased. Guard of Soldiers and Policemen. | Three Kahili Bearers | His Majesty the King. | Officer Bearing the Royal Standard. | The King's Ministers. | Governors of Islands, Members of the Privy Council and Their Ladies, Four Deep. | The Foreign Representatives. | and | Foreign Consuls | Judges, Officers of Customs, And Other Officers in the Service of the King, Four Deep. | The Clergy, Protestant and Catholic, Indiscriminately, Four Deep. | Native Judges and Tax Gatherers, 4 Deep. | Foreign Res-

idents and Foreigners Belonging to Ships, Six Deep. | Military Officer, Bearing Hawaiian Flag. | Twenty-Four Soldiers, Four Deep. | Natives Indiscriminately, Six Deep. | Four Policemen.| [*pointing hand*] The Procession to start at 12 o'clock from the House of M. Kekaounohi, on Saturday the 30th instant.| [*pointing hand*] The Place of Interment the Royal Cemetery. | A. Paki. | Chamberlain's Office, December 22, 1848.[121]

The Order of Procession omitted the route of the procession. It was, however, the first order of procession to explicitly mention the Hawaiian flag. The announcement also refers to another flag, the Royal Standard, since the list uses the words "Kahili Bearers" elsewhere. The prominent presence of the national banner may have been influenced cession of sovereignty to the British in 1843.

The *Polynesian* reported briefly concerning the funerals: "On Saturday last, the 30th ultimo, the funeral ceremonies of the late Chiefs Leleiohoku, Moses Kekuaiwa, and Kaiminaauao, were performed, their remains deposited in the vault which contains the ashes of so many of their relatives. The King assisted on the melancholy occasion; and a large body of persons, consisting of the chiefs, foreign and native officers of Government, Foreign Agents, merchants, and others, and thousands of natives took part in the procession."[122]

The coffin of Leleiohoku bore the simple inscription: "LELEIOHOKU | Hanau | Malaki 21 1821 | make | Okatoba 21 | 1848. [Leleiohoku | Born | March 21, 1821| Died | October 21| 1848]."[123] The inscription for Moses Kekūāiwa included the same information: "MOSE KEKUAIWA | Hanau Iulai 20 | 1829 | Make Novemaba 28 | 1848."[124]

Keali'iahonui (1849)

Although he had never ruled as sovereign over Kaua'i, as had his father Kaumuali'i, Keali'iahonui was accorded the honor of a state funeral. He had at one time been married to Ka'ahumanu until her conversion to Christianity had forced her to choose just one husband, and to Kekau'ōnohi, granddaughter of Kamehameha the Great. He served on the House of Nobles from April 1, 1841, to June 12, 1848.[125] Keali'iahonui was appointed as the first Chamberlain from September 6, 1846 to May 26, 1847. He died June 23, 1849.

PROCESSION

Abner Paki, who succeeded Keali'iahonui as Chamberlain, and the Chamberlain's Office issued a broadside containing the Order of Procession on June 26, 1849:

54 **1. Royal Deaths**

> Order of Procession | for the Funeral of the late | Chief, Kealiiahonui, | Son of Kaumualii, the late King Of Kauai | [*Rule*] | Undertakers. | Kahili Bearers | Officers. | Soldiers Four Deep | Hawaiian Flag, Borne by an Officer. | Medical Attendants. | Officiating Clergyman. | Guard of Soldiers and Policemen. Friends of the Deceased } Young Chiefs [*Cut Of Coffin*] Young Chiefs { Friends of the Deceased. Guard of Soldiers and Policemen. | Kahili Bearers. | Chief Mourners. | Hawaiian Flag, Borne by an Officer. | His Highness the Premier. | The King's Ministers | Governors of the Islands, Members of the Privy Council and Their Ladies, Four Deep. | Consular Corps. | Judges, Officers of Custom, and Other Officers in the Service of the King, Four | Deep. | The Clergy, Protestant and Catholic, Indiscriminately, Four Deep. | Native Judges and Tax Gatherers, Four Deep. | Foreign Residents and Foreigners Belonging to Ships, 6 Deep | Military Officer Bearing the Hawaiian Flag. | Soldiers, 4 Deep. | Natives Indiscriminately, Six Deep. | Four Policemen.[126]

Like other orders of procession, the one for Keali'ihonui gives the status of the deceased calling him "the late chief" and "Son of Kaumualii, the late King of Kauai." Unlike previous orders, though, the one for Keali'iahonui lacked a band and prominently placed a "Chief Mourner," presumably the late chief's wife, Kekau'ōnohi, immediately behind the *kāhili* following the casket. Significantly, the King was represented by Keoni Ana, Kuhina Nui, listed in the order as "His Highness the Premier." The procession left from Hōlani, house of Kekau'ōnohi, wife of the deceased, and started at 11 a.m., on Saturday, June 30, 1849.[127] The earlier hour may have been scheduled to avoid the heat of the day during the summer. It ended at the Royal Cemetery at Pohukaina on the opposite side of Hale Ali'i. Although no route for the procession is indicated, it most likely traveled down Richards Street to King Street and then to the Royal Cemetery.

Burial

Although the funerary ceremonies for Keali'iohonui initially reflected Western practices, the traditional Hawaiian form subsequently took place. According to W.D. Alexander:

> It seems that by Kakauonohi's orders the coffin containing her late husband's remains were removed to Puuloa, Ewa, with the view of having it afterwards taken out to sea, and there sunk. It was temporarily deposited in a cavern in the coral limestone back of Puuloa, and has lately been closed up.
>
> [Deborah] Kapule [widow of Kaumuali'i] strongly objected to the plan of sinking the coffin in the sea, and delayed its execution for a considerable time. At last certain chiefs from Honolulu paid her a visit and succeeded in overcoming her opposition. During the following night she and her husband [Simon Kiau], with one or two assistants, removed the outer coffin, which they afterwards buried somewhere near Puuloa.
>
> [...] There is a particular superstition among the native Hawaiians in regard to the disposal of the outer coffin in such cases, of which we have had illustrations in recent times. In their opinion, if such a coffin is left unburied it bodes death to some near relative of the deceased. During the same night they took out the sacred bones, the "uni-

hipili," which they "hunakele'd" or concealed, according to ancient custom. I am informed that they were sunk in the sea.[128]

Ka'ōana'eha (1850)

High Chiefess Ka'ōana'eha, wife of John Young, was mother of Fanny Kekelaokalani, Grace Kama'iku'i, Keoni Ana, and Jane Lahilahi. She died on January 22, 1850. After the death of her husband, she took on the name, Kuamo'o, which reflected a critical battle between the supporters of the Hawaiian *kapu* system and the Western customs that supplanted the old religion.

Today, she is supposedly buried with her husband, John Young, at Mauna 'Ala, in the style of the Western customs.

Kekau'ōnohi (1851)

Kekau'ōnohi, the wife of the late Keali'iahonui, died on June 2, 1851, eleven months after her husband's death. A granddaughter of Kamehameha I, Kekau'ōnohi had previously been one of the wives of Liholiho, Kamehameha II. Five months after the death of Keli'iahonui, Kekau'ōnohi married Levi Haalelea, in November 1849. Haalelea was the brother of Ha'alilio.

The House of Representatives and House of Noble adjourned on account of her death, from June 4 to June 8, 1851.[129] She had served as the governor of Kaua'i from 1842 to 1844.

FUNERAL

Her funeral took place on Monday, June 30, 1851, in her house on Richards Street. The Chamberlain Notice announced in the *Polynesian* on June 28, 1851: "The procession will move from her residence in Richard Street, to the large native church, and from thence to the Royal Cemetery."[130]

PROCESSION

The Chamberlain's Office issued the Order of Procession for Kekau'ōnohi on June 21, 1851. The broadside read:

> Order of Procession | for the Funeral of the late | Lady Chief Kekauonohi, | Grand Daughter of Kamehameha I., and Niece of His Majesty the King. | [*Rule*] | Undertakers. | Kahili Bearers. | Officers | Soldiers Four Deep. | Hawaiian Flag, | Borne by an Officer. | Medical Attendants. | Officiating Clergyman. | Guard of Soldiers and Police Men. Friends of the Deceased. } Young Chiefs. [*outline of a coffin.*] Young Chiefs } Friends of the Deceased. Guard of Soldiers and Policemen. | Kahili Bearers. | Chief

Mourners. | Hawaiian Flag, Borne by an Officer. | His Highness The Premier [Keoni Ana]. | The King's Ministers. | Diplomatic and Consular Corps.| Governors of Islands, Members of the Privy Council and Their Ladies, Four Deep. | Judges, Officers of Customs, and Other Officers in the Service of the King, Four Deep. | The Clergy, Protestant And Catholic, Indiscriminately, Four Deep. | Native Judges and Tax Gatherers, 4 Deep. | Foreign Residents and Foreigners Belonging to Ships, Six Deep. | Military Officer, Bearing Hawaiian Flag. | Soldiers, Four Deep. | Natives Indiscriminately, Six Deep. | Four Policemen.| [*Rule*] | The Procession to Start at 10 o'clock from the House of the Deceased, on Monday the 30th Instant.| [*pointing hand*] The Place of Interment The Royal Cemetery. | A. Paki. | Chamberlain's Office, June 21, 1851.[131]

The procession had no *kāhili* at the corners of the catafalque and prominently positioned three Hawaiian flags. The diplomatic and consular corps moved up in the procession of Kekauʻōnohi from behind the island governors to in front of them.

BURIAL

She was buried at the royal cemetery at Pohukaina. A some point her remains were transferred to Maui. A marker at Waiola Cemetery in Lāhainā has the inscription: "Kekauonohinui | Granddaughter of K. I, | Died In | Honolulu. June 2, 1847."

James Young Kanehoa (1851)

James Young Kanehoa, son of John Young (Olohana) and Young's first wife, Namokuelua, died in the morning of October 1, 1851,[132] at the residence of his brother-in-law, Thomas Charles Byde Rooke.[133] His half-brother, Keoni Ana, was appointed as administrator of his estate. He was born in Kawaihae on August 7, 1797. He married Sarah Davis, a daughter of Isaac Davis, the other *haole* war companion of Kamehameha I. His widow when he died was named Hikoni. Kanehoa was one of eight chiefs advanced in rank by the 1845 legislature and served from then in the House of Nobles until June 21, 1851. He was a member of the Privy Council from October 18, 1846. Kamehameha III named him on October 21, 1846, as governor of Maui.

His funeral took place on Saturday, October 4, 1851. R.C. Wyllie communicated to the foreign ministers: "The procession will start at 10 a.m. precisely, on that day, from the House of Dr. Rooke, whence it will proceed to the Royal Cemetery, in the same order, as that which was observed in the case of the late Governor of Hawaii [William Pitt Leleiohoku who died in 1848]."[134]

The Chamberlain gave notice in the "Published by Authority" column of the *Polynesian* that "the Court will go into mourning for His Excellency

James Young Kanehoa, the late Governor of the Island of Maui, for 15 days from this date [October 4, 1851]."[135]

Kanehoa may be buried with his father, John Young, at Mauna 'Ala, though he has no marker to confirm his burial there.

James Kaliokalani (1852) and Polly Pa'a'āina (1853)

Two students of the Chiefs' Children's School, eligible for the throne, died in 1852 and 1853, but have no recorded state funerals. Both were not direct descendants of Kamehameha. Kaliokalani descended from a cousin of Kamehameha; Polly Pa'a'āina born in 1833, descended from Keli'imaikai, the brother of Kamehameha. Born of the union of Fanny Kekelaokalani Young and Henry Lewis, she was the *hānai* daughter of John Papa 'Ī'ī and his wife, Sarah. She had entered the school for young chiefs a decade before her death. Had Kaliokalani died during the reign of his brother, David Kalākaua, much more substantial obsequies would probably have occurred, as took place for his sister, Likelike, when she died in 1887.

The *Polynesian* reported little information about his death: "At Lahaina, Maui, April 21, James Kaliiokalani [*sic*] son of Kapakea [*sic*] and Keohokalole, aged 16 years. His remains were brought to Honolulu for interment, on the 4th inst. [May 4, 1852]."[136] In comparison, the *Polynesian* report of the funeral of G.W. Hunter, just below that of Kaliokalani, was three times longer than that of the young chief.

The *Friend* recorded the death of Polly Pa'a'āina in greater detail: "At the residence of the Princess Victoria Kamamalu, Saturday morning, May 28, 1853, Mrs. Mary P., wife of J.A. Griswold—aged 28. The subject of the above notice was the adopted daughter of Hon. John Ii, and was a pupil in the Royal School, for seven years, where she endeared herself to her teachers and fellow pupils. She was married Dec. 30, 1851 ; and left an infant daughter, aged two months. Her suffering during her last sickness were extreme. She felt conscious of danger, and, as far as human eye could see, prepared herself for her departure. She took a calm and effecting leave of her friends that were present, and sent her last message to absent ones. She expressed the wish that others whom she loved would prepare while in health for the trying hour of death."[137] Her place of death indicates the social circles that endured even after leaving school.

The notice ended in a poem, which called her Mary:

> "Dearest Mary thou hast left us,
> *Here* thy loss we deeply feel,
> But 'tis god who hast bereft us.
> He can all our sorrow heal."[138]

The timing of a royal death had an impact on whether the individual was accorded a state funeral. If she had died a year later, she probably would have been honored with an elaborate state funeral as the half-sister of Queen Emma, in the same way that Ka'imina'auao had been honored as *hānai* daughter of Queen Kalama. For other royalty timing had no bearing on the grandeur of the obsequies.

Kamehameha III (1854)

Kamehameha III, the longest reigning monarch of the Kingdom of Hawai'i, presided over some of the greatest changes the island nation faced. He was born in Keauhou, Kona, on the Big Island of Hawai'i, the son of Kamehameha I and Keōpūolani. The death of his brother, Kamehameha II in London had resulted in the early start of his reign under the regency of Queen Ka'ahumanu. The introduction of Christianity prevented his marriage to his sister, Nāhi'ena'ena. He married, instead, Kalama, with whom he had two children who died as infants. He adopted Alexander Liholiho, son of Kīna'u and Kekūanāo'a, who succeeded him to the throne. Under the king, the constitutional monarchy was established and the division of lands resulted in ownership by the king, *ali'i*, commoners and foreigners. His death, on December 15, 1854, resulted in widespread mourning and a state funeral of unprecedented spectacle.

Kamehameha III had the longest reign (courtesy Hawaii State Archives [PP-97-7-003]).

The shift in the royal Hawaiian way of death was noted in the *Sailor's Magazine and Naval Journal* following the death of Kamehameha III: "He [Kamehameha IV] commenced by issuing one good order, viz., that the old practice of Hawaiians when their kings died should be strictly *tabu*. The meaning of this is, that no person should show respect for the dead by getting drunk, knocking out their front teeth, or rioting in licentiousness."[139] The order certainly achieved its end. The writer, Samuel Chenery Damon, was able to relay following the funeral of Kamehameha III: "I am most happy to report that the utmost order and quiet reigned throughout the whole day. The becoming and appropriate style in which everything passed off, called forth the admiration of the numerous foreigners and strangers within the city. It was truly a memorable day in Hawaiian history."[140] Damon had arrived in Honolulu in 1841 to serve as chaplain to American seamen. He pastored the Bethel Church in Honolulu for forty-two years.

The *Polynesian*, however, did report a couple of instances of the continuance of of a traditional Hawaiian funerary practice. The wailing that took place was mild compared to the total breakdown in social behavior that previously occurred. When the funeral procession of Kamehameha III hit the intersection of Nuuanu and Beretania streets in Honolulu, the newspaper reported: "At this point there had assembled a dense throng of people [...] could no longer contain themselves, but burst forth in a low suppressed wail." When the procession reached the Sepulcher: "Again did the natives yield to ancient custom, and a long low wail arose from the thousands congregated here. Except these, nor indeed in these traces of former customs, was there anything during the day, inconsistent with the most perfect order and decorum."[141] Thus the newly adopted funerary practices served as evidence for civilization to outsiders.

CANOPY OF KAMEHAMEHA III

Other aspects of the funeral of Kamehameha demonstrated the melding of ancient and Western practices. The canopy, absent from previous Hawaiian royal funerals, but present in English royal funereal practices, appears in the drawing titled "Kamehameha III Laying [sic] in State" by Paul Emmert. The Hawai'i canopy, like ones in England, was suspended on poles, but the poles for the Hawai'i ceremonies were *kāhili*, topped with feathers. Instead of a Holland sheet and purple velvet pall that covered the coffin of King George III, the feather *pā'ū*, or skirt, of his late sister Nāhi'ena'ena served as the pall on the casket of Kamehameha III. The *pā'ū*, twenty feet in length, had been cut in half with the two pieces sewn together.[142]

Once again, the example set by the funeral of Kamehameha II and Kamāmalu influenced the trappings for the obsequies of Kamehameha III. The local replacements for the Western coffins were created using rare Hawaiian wood. Lafrenz & Fischer were paid $1,121.50 for the caskets for Kamehameha III. The expenses included:

1 Polished Koa Coffin	50
1 Stand (Koa) for the same	30

1. Royal Deaths

"Kamehameha III Lying in State" by Paul Emmert (courtesy Hawaii State Archives [Kahn 37/12]).

1 large Royal Parade Coffin	250
1 Mourning Canopy	200
2 long & 10 small beams	28
20 Galns Alcohol @ $4	80
1 Lead Coffin	45
6 Coffin Handles	20
Coffin Screws	30
Engraving, Gilding and Painting Crown	125
10 Iron Hooks	10
33½ yds. Crimson Velvet @$4	134
Gold Lace & thread	15.50
Covering & Polishing Throne Chair	15
Engraving Silver Plate for Coffin	60
Silver Screws for Silver Plate for Coffin	5[143]

The expenses also indicate the means of preserving the body of Kamehameha III was the same as had been used for Haʻalilio, Leleiohoku, Moses Kekūāiwa and Kaʻiminaʻauao—alcohol in a lead coffin. On January 16, 1855, Prince Lot Kamehameha presented a report to the meeting of the Privy Council, "giving a list of expenses in connection with the funeral of His late Majesty." The expenses totaled $26,025.42.[144] At the same meeting the minister of finance reported the "amount of cash the Treasury to be $47,807."[145] Thus, the expenses represented 54 percent of that amount. The monies, however, were not taken directly from the treasury. Alisha Allen, minister of finance, noted in his report to the legislature: "On the 9th of April I had the honor to make a communication on the subject of the funeral expenses of his late Majesty. You will have learned from that communication that a loan was made, to meet those expenses on the undoubted security of his Majesty Kamehameha IV. and seventeen members of his Privy Council, so the Treasury is entirely secure. A proper respect for the memory of his late majesty, as well as a due regard for the opinions of his people, required public obsequies; and it is in conformity to the usage of all civilized nations, that expenses of this kind should be paid from the National Treasury."[146]

The committee also recommended the source of funding for the funeral: "The undersigned taking into consideration the great and many benefits which the Hawaiian people owe to His late Majesty support the view adopted in the Resolution moved in this Council by Mr. Wyllie that the expenses of His Majesty's funeral to be paid out of the National Revenues."[147]

Funeral

The description of the funeral services for Kamehameha III appeared in the *Sailor's Magazine and Naval Journal*, simply put: "Religious exercises were held at the Palace."[148] The location for the funeral service of Kamehameha III, originally proposed for Kawaiahaʻo Church, was changed by a Privy Council resolution. Resolution 1 read: Resolved that the resolution directing that the religious services to be performed at the burial of His late Majesty at the stone church, be rescinded, and that the same shall be performed in front of the Palace."[149]

Procession

In contrast to the simple procession of his mother, Keōpūolani, the procession of Kauikeaouli, who reigned as Kamehameha III, featured dozens of *kāhili*, tall and hand-held. The *Friend* published the Order of Procession in January 1855:

1. Royal Deaths

Order of Procession | for the | Funeral of His late Majesty, | Kamehameha III. | [*rule*] | Grand Marshal. [King David Kalākaua] | Marshal. | Hawaiian Cavalry. [Lieutenant F. Manini, Lt. P. Manini, Lt. M.R. Harvey, Surgeon Smythe, Capt. Vincent] | Clergymen of All Denominations. | Free Masons. | Odd Fellows. | Royal School | Faculty and Students of Oahu College | Other Schools and Their Masters, 6 Deep. | Artillery | The King's Band. | Household Troops. | The King's Purveyor [Called H. St. John in P. Emmert lithography of funeral procession, named Steward in Privy Council] and Servants. | The Physician and Assistant Physician of the Late King. | Two Kahilis. | The Late King's Standard. | Soldiers. High Chiefs. Small Kahilis. Hearse. Small Kahilis. High Chiefs. Soldiers. | Two Kahilis. | Her Majesty, The Queen | Her Royal Highness, The Princess | Victoria ; His Majesty, the King ; | His Royal Highness, Prince Kamehameha. | The King's Chancellor, The Chamber- | lain, The Kuhina Nui. | The Ministers. | The Representatives of Foreign Nations. | The Governors of Islands. | The Members of the Privy Council. | And Ladies of the Court. | The Foreign Consuls, and the Post | Captains, Commanders and Of- | ficers of Ship's of War | The Judges, Officers of Customs and Other | Government Officers,—Four Deep. | Drummers | Hawaiian Infantry. | First Hawaiian Guard. | Foreign Marines, Taking Place Ac- | cording to the Rank and Sen- | iority of Their Respective | Commanders. | Fire Companies—Four Deep. | Hook and Ladder Company—Four deep. | The King's Yeomanry. | The Foreign Residents and Foreigners belong- | ing to foreign merchant vessels. | The Native Population generally.[150]

Led by Mataio Kekūanāoʻa, the grand marshal of the Kingdom, the procession stretched for half a mile. The drawing of the procession by Paul Emmert is approximately 10 inches by 349 inches.[151]

The inclusion in Hawaiʻi of a riderless horse in the procession, called

Funeral procession of Kamehameha III (courtesy Hawaii State Archives [Kahn 37/13]).

a caparisoned horse because of the covering on the saddle, started with the obsequies for Kamehameha III. A decade later, Abraham Lincoln was the first U.S. president to have a caparisoned horse in his procession.

The king's horse made quite an impression of young Mary Waterhouse. Waterhouse, then seven or eight, recalled the "stirrups of the saddle reversed."[152] The procession grouped members of the clergy together regardless of denomination. The procession featured the earliest appearance of Masonic organizations, the Free Masons and Odd Fellows. Hawaiian Lodge No. 21, Free and Accepted Masons had been established in 1852. The Odd Fellows were from the Excelsior Lodge No. 1, I.O.O.F., founded in 1846.[153]

Although the sepulcher sat within a stone's throw of Hale Aliʻi, the procession took a circular route to accommodate the great numbers of official mourners: "The procession moved from the Palace, down King's St., then up Nuuanu St. to Beretania St.—[...] The procession proceeded with no other incident up Beretania to Punch Bowl St., thence to King Street and the Sepulcher."[154]

Abner Pākī (1855)

Abner Pākī, who had served in the House of Nobles and on the Privy Council, died on June 13, 1855. While the Chamberlain for Kamehameha III, from May 26, 1847, to around March 31, 1848, Pākī had issued the Orders of Procession for Leleiohoku, Moses Kekūāiwa and Kaʻiminaʻauao, also for the Chamberlain who had preceded him, Prince Kealiʻiahonui, and for Kekauʻōnohi. He had served in the House of Nobles from April 1, 1841 through August 12, 1855. Pākī was father of Princess Bernice Pauahi and *hānai* father of Queen Liliʻuokalani.

The *Friend* praised Pākī: "For reasons which it would be extremely difficult to explain to foreign readers, the family from which he was descended, has been for many years, or generations, under a cloud. 'Rebel' blood ran in their veins, but it was still acknowledged as

Pākī was the father of Bernice Pauahi (courtesy Hawaii State Archives [PP-98-17-002]).

'Royal.' It might be said, that there was not power enough in the kingdom to suppress its influence. (…) As Chamberlain of His late Majesty, he sustained an honorable and noble character."[155]

Though no final action is indicated, the Privy Council minutes record a proposal by Kekūanāo'a for "some appropriation" for the funeral of Pākī.[156] At the following meeting, on June 25, 1855, Lot Kamehameha read from the funeral program,[157] though no program survives in the collection of the Hawaii State Archives.

The inscription on his coffin reads: "A. PAKI | Hanau Aug. 1808 | Make Iune 13th 1855."[158]

Kōnia (1857)

Konia, also known as Laura, was the wife of Abner Pākī and mother of Princess Bernice Pauahi Bishop. Born about 1807, Konia was the daughter of Pauli Kaoleioku, the son of Kamehameha I and Kanekapolei. She married Pākī on June 7, 1826.[159] She served in the House of Nobles from April 1, 1841 through June 21, 1851.[160] She died in Honolulu on July 2, 1857.

Sixteen days later, Keoni Ana, died. Once again, the quick succession of deaths of two notable chiefs caused a joint announcement to be circulated.[161] Unlike the earlier deaths of William Pitt Leleiohoku, Moses Kekūāiwa and Ka'imina'auao, the funerals of the two were not held together.

FUNERAL

The funeral of Konia took place at her home called Haleakala on Tuesday, August 4, 1857. "The religious services were performed by the Rev. Mr. Clark, and the ceremony was conducted throughout with a decorum and feeling which was remarked by all present."[162]

Kōnia, mother of Bernice Pauahi, was a granddaughter of Kamehameha I (courtesy Hawaii State Archives [PP-98-17-002]).

Her coffin bears the inscription: "L. KONIA | Wahine a A. Paki | Hanau M. H. 1808 | Make Iulai 2d 1857."[163]

Keoni Ana (1857)

Keoni Ana, son of John Young (Olohana), died on July 18, 1857. He was born in Kawaihae in 1810, son of Kaʻōanaʻeha, the second wife of his father. He married chiefess Juliana Alapaʻi Kauwā, who died August 2, 1849. He served as Kuhina Nui from June 10, 1845, to January 16, 1855, when an act of the Legislature separated the Kuhina Nui from the Minister of the Interior, and he resigned from the former office. In his role as Kuhina Nui, he had participated in the processions of Kekauʻōnohi and Kealiʻiahonui. He continued as Minister of the Interior until June 6, 1857, when Lot Kamehameha, later Kamehameha V, took over the post. He then assumed the role of Chamberlain from June 10, 1857, until his death.

"The funeral of His Excellency the late John Young took place on Sunday afternoon last [August 30, 1857], as advertised. The services were conducted at the late residence of the deceased, by the Rev. A. Bishop."[164]

Keoni Ana, son of John Young, war companion of Kamehameha I (courtesy Hawaii State Archives [PP-82-5-016]).

Procession

In contrast to the procession of Kamehameha III, the funeral line of the first male Kuhina Nui, Keoni Ana, displayed a much simpler form. Interestingly, the circular notifying the public of his death makes no reference to his time as Kuhina Nui, or as Minister of the Interior, referring instead to his most recent title of Chamberlain of His Majesty's Household.[165]

The *Polynesian* announced the order of procession:

Order of Procession | for the Funeral of | His Excellency, the late John Young, | Chamberlain of His Majesty's Household. | [*rule*] | Clergymen | Hawaiian Flag |

Company of the Household Guards | Medical Attendants. | Pall Bearers [*cut of coffin*] Pall Bearers. | Chief Mourners. | His Majesty the King. | High State Officers. | Foreign Representatives. | Members of the Privy Council. | Consular Corps. | All Officers of the King's Government, taking place according to rank. | Foreign Residents. | The King's Yeomanry. | The Public Generally.[166]

The order of procession is notable for its brevity, just 15 lines. Another interesting aspect of the order of procession for Keoni Ana is the lack of *kāhili*.

BURIAL

The *Pacific Commercial Advertiser* reported: "The remains were escorted with military parade to the Royal tomb, where they were deposited."[167] Inscribed on his coffin, according to *Ke Au Okoa*, is the following information: "Keoni Ana, | Hanau i ka la 12 o Maraki, 1810, | Make Iulai 18, 1857."[168]

Joshua Kaeo (1858)

Joshua Kaeo was one of eight chiefs advanced in rank to high chief by the Privy Council. T.C.B. Rooke said, "I think he died on the 20th June, last [1858]."[169] His son, Peter Young Kekuokalani, stated: "I think he died on the 27 or 29 June."[170] "Prince L. Kamehameha communicated to the Nobles the intelligence of the decease of Hon. J. Kaeo, a member of this House. The Prince also moved a series of resolutions condoling with the family of the deceased, and voting that the House go into mourning for one month. Adopted."[171] The *Friend* published his death notice: "In this city, June 27, 1858, Hon. J. Kaeo, of disease of the heart, aged 49. Mr. Kaeo was for many years an intimate friend and associate of the late king [Kamehameha III], and was the husband of Jenny [Gini] Lahilahi, a daughter of the late Mr. John Young, the Foreign Adviser of Kamehameha I. The deceased was one the first Representatives chosen under the Constitution of 1840, and for a number of the latter years of his life, held the office of Privy Councillor and a member of the House of Nobles. His remains were yesterday deposited in the Royal Cemetery."[172]

BURIAL

Kaeo was buried in the Royal Cemetery at Pohukaina on July 25, 1858.

Thomas Charles Byde Rooke (1858)

The procession for Thomas Charles Byde Rooke reflected his role as *hānai* father of Queen Emma, the wife of the reigning monarch.

Thomas Charles Byde Rooke, Emma Rooke and Grace Kamaʻikuʻi Rooke (courtesy Hawaii State Archives [PP-9-3-018]).

PROCESSION

The Chamberlain's Office published the Order of Procession on a broadside on December 15, 1858:

Order of Procession | for the | Funeral | of the | Honorable Thos. Chas. Byde Rooke, F.R.C.S. [Fellow of the Royal College of Surgeons], | Member of His Majesty's Privy Council of State and Physician to the King and Royal Family. | [*Oxford rule*] | Clergymen. | Hawaiian Flag (Draped), | with Color Guard. | Detachment of Troops of the Line. | The Masonic Bodies. | Excelsior Lodge I.O. of O.F. | Polynesian Encampment I.O. of O.F. | The Honolulu Mechanics' Benevolent Union. | The Medical Faculty. | Privy Councillors and Their Ladies. | The Tenants, Retainers, and Servants of the Deceased. | The Queen's Household Servants. | Detachment of Rifles. Kahilis. Pall Bearers. [*cut of coffin*] Pall Bearers. Kahilis. Detachment of Rifles. | Chief Mourners. | Their Majesties the King and Queen. | Her Royal Highness the Kuhina Nui [Victoria Kamāmalu], His Royal | Highness the Alihikaua [Commander-in-Chief], and the | Queen Dowager. | The Chancellor of the Kingdom. | Ministers of State and Foreign Representatives, | Other High Officers of the Crown, and Officers | of Foreign Ships of War. | Governors of Islands. | Consular Corps. | Friends of the Deceased. The King's Yeomanry. | The Public Generally. | Officers of Police. | [*Oxford rule*] | [*pointing hand*] The Procession Will Leave the late Residence of The Deceased | at Four o'clock, p.m. on Tuesday [Handwritten] the 28th [Handwritten] Instant. | M. Kekuanaoa, | Chamberlain. | Chamberlain's Office. | December 15th, 1858.[173]

The Mechanic's Benefit Union, a Hawaii labor organization started in September 1853,[174] made their first appearance in the procession for Rooke.

BURIAL

According to *Ke Au Okoa*, the inscription on his coffin reads: "T.C. Byde Rooke | F.R.C.S. [Fellow of the Royal College of Surgeons] | Born May 18, 1806, | Died May 28, 1858. It is unclear whether the mistake in the date of death, which should be November 28, 1858, is on the inscription or a typographical error in the newspaper."[175]

John William Pitt Kīna'u (1859)

John William Pitt Kīna'u, the son of the late William Pitt Leleiohoku and Ruth Ke'elikōlani, the nephew of King Kamehameha IV, died at Kapa'au, Kohala, on Hawai'i island, on September 9, 1859, at age 17.

The *Pacific Commercial Advertiser* reported the death of Kīna'u: "He was one of the highest and wealthiest chiefs upon the islands. In his veins flowed the blood of a long line of Hawaiian Princes. Ruth, the present Governess of Hawaii, was his mother, and consequently he was grandson of Governor Kekuanaoa of this island. His grandfather on the paternal side was 'Billy Pitt,' a chief of high repute in years gone by."[176] It is not surprising that the son of the woman who was reputed to have stopped Pele's advance into Hilo would be reputed to have been visited by his own signs. The *Pacific Commercial Advertiser* recounted an earlier event: "It will be remembered that William landed on the island of Hawaii, in January last, on the *very day* when the present lava eruption burst forth from Mauna Loa; and it was believed by a large proportion of the native population of the island, that Pele had thrown forth the lava stream in special honor of his arrival."[177]

FUNERAL

The eight-day visit of magician John Henry Anderson, the self-proclaimed "Wizard of the North," coincided with the funeral of John William Pitt Kīna'u and resulted in an extended account of the event. He wrote of the service at Kawaiaha'o, held on Sunday, November 6, 1859:

> In the native church, at the end of the service, there was to be buried a chief of high standing. The funeral was attended by some thousands, many of whom had walked as far as twenty miles from the interior, to be present at the last rites of the beloved chief. His name in English was John William Pitt, or "Kinau" in the native tongue. He was young. That your readers may have an idea of the respect the people have for their chiefs, a recital (after the burial service of the church was read), given by thousands of the natives, was commenced at his tomb by a single voice, and rising until one full, passionate burst of grief filled the air—resounding amongst the neighbouring rocks and hills, whose echoes gave back the sorrowful cry. The effect—as thus borne from voice to voice, and from one valley to another, now rising almost into a shriek of bitterness,

then subsiding in a low, sad murmuring wail—was (to my unaccustomed ear) most startling and impressive.[178]

Unfortunately, Anderson recorded little detail of the funeral itself, other than its timing, nor the procession, being most impressed by the wailing that occurred at the Pohukaina tomb. Anderson does acknowledge his "high standing"; like Kamehameha IV, Kīna'u had been designated by Kamehameha III as eligible for the throne and had attended the Chiefs' Children's School.

The *Pacific Commercial Advertiser* dates the state funeral to Tuesday, December 27, 1859. "The funeral of J.W. Pitt Kinau, one of the last of the pure descendants of the ancient Kings of Hawaii, the dynasty conquered by Kamehameha the Great, took place Tuesday last. Keoua, the great grandmother of Kinau, is reputed to have possessed the highest chief blood, according to Hawaiian genealogy. The funeral drew out a large concourse of spectators. The remains were escorted from the residence of Kekūanāo'a [grandfather of John William Pitt Kīna'u] through Fort and King streets and deposited in the palace premises. It is sad to see the young as well as the older chiefs passing away without any prospect of their places being filled. The stock of *Aliis* is dwindling down to a mere handful, and some are now living who may follow to his resting-place the last of the ancient Royal line."[179]

According to *Au Okoa*, the coffin includes the inscription: "John William Pitt Kinau, | Born Dec 27, 1842, | Died on the 9th of Sept. 1857 [*sic*, should be 1859]."

The *Pacific Commercial Advertiser* also recorded the costs associated with the Western funeral. "The preparations for the funeral of the Young Prince John Pitt Kinau, created some liveliness, but that being over, will be followed by a reaction. Those who are not acquainted with the facts, will be surprised at the prodigality of the natives in preparing for state funerals. One firm alone in Honolulu has sold for this purpose nearly four thousand dollars worth of mourning goods, and in one day its sales amounted to nearly $600. The estate of the Prince, which [is] said to be very large, is understood to pay for the expenses of the funeral, which must amount to at least $10,000."[180]

Bennet Nāmākēhā (1860)

Bennet Y. Nāmākēhā, the uncle of Queen Emma, died during the reign of Kamehameha IV. The *Polynesian* reported: "It is our painful duty to announce the death of the Honorable Bennett Namakeha, who expired at his residence in Pauoa Valley on the morning of the 27th inst., of dropsy. The deceased was the son of Kamauna, descended from the ancient Kings of the northern districts of Hawaii, and of Kukaeleiki, a Chieftainess of high rank from the island of Kauai, and he was a brother of the late Honorable George Naea, and therefore an uncle of Her Majesty the Queen. At the time of his death he was about sixty-two years of age. For a long number of years he had been a member of the House of Nobles and of the Privy Council of State, and for a considerable time he acted as Governor of Maui."[181]

FUNERAL AND BURIAL

Inclement weather twice postponed the funeral of Nāmākēhā. The *Polynesian* noted: "The funeral was to have taken place yesterday afternoon [Friday, December 28, 1860] and the coffin deposited in the Royal Cemetery, but on account of the weather being very unpropitious the ceremony was deferred to today [Saturday, December 29, 1860]." The *Pacific Commercial Advertiser*, however, reported yet another delay, dating the funeral and burial to Monday, December 31, 1860: "The funeral of this Hawaiian Nobleman took place on Monday afternoon, and his returns were deposited in the Royal Tomb, under a military escort. Like most of the Nobles, he was possessed of a large amount of real and personal property, which under good management would produce a revenue of perhaps $10,000 a year."[182]

The inscription on the coffin, according to *Ke Au Okoa*, reads: "B. Namakeha, | Make i ka la 27 Dek. 1860, | He 62 kona mau makahiki."[183]

Abigail Maheha (1861)

Another student at the Chiefs' Children's School, Abigail Maheha, did not have as impressive a ceremony at her death as William Pitt Kīnaʻu. The lifestyle of members of royalty often had an impact on whether a state funeral was accorded the individual. Such was the case of Maheha. Born July 10, 1832, the daughter of High Chief Namaile and High Chiefess Kuini Liliha, Maheha was a *hānai* daughter of Kekauʻōnohi, a wife of Kamehameha I and later Kamehameha II. At age 12, Maheha was listed in the *Polynesian* on July 20, 1844, as one of the "Princes and Chiefs Eligible to be Rulers." With the other royal children, Maheha attended Chiefs' Children's School. Her tuition at the school was paid by A. Kealiiahonui, the last prince of Kauaʻi and husband of Kekauʻōnohi. Her destiny, however, abruptly changed course when she was forced to leave the school, reputed to have become pregnant by another student at the missionary-run school. Though the father remained unnamed, speculation has focused on Lot

Kapuāiwa, later Kamehameha V, or his brother Moses Kekūāiwa, the expected future governor of Kaua'i. Lot is suggested because he later aided the husband who Maheha had been forced to marry and Moses because he left the school two days before Maheha for unspoken reasons. The journal that Lot kept at the school ends with an entry dated September 1, 1845, with an unknown number of pages removed from it after that date.[184]

Fourteen-year-old Maheha married Keaupuni a servant of Kekau'ōnohi, on February 4, 1847. Because Maheha was under the age of eighteen, the consent of her parents would have been required.[185] Amos Starr Cooke does not record the reason for her leaving what by then was called the Royal School. On February 4, 1847, he recorded, "Abigail left us & bade all goodbye. In the evening I [...] accompanied Brother Armstrong to Abigail's marriage to Keaupuni. Only he & Konia & Kekauonohi & I were witnesses to it."[186] She promptly moved to Kaua'i, where she gave birth to a baby girl. A couple of years after her marriage Maheha returned to Honolulu, where she lived first with her *hānai* mother, Kekau'ōnohi, and later with Frederick James Porter. Porter and Frederick Ogden arrived in Honolulu on July 12, 1850, where they started an importing business called Porter & Ogden. Maheha bore two children with Porter, both of whom died shortly after their births. Porter shot himself on August 11, 1854, after shooting a native woman, who survived. Ogden continued the firm solely under his name. Maheha later gave birth to a child by Ogden. In the case of *Keaupuni* vs *Fred Ogden*, before the Supreme Court, during its March 1855 Special Term, "the plaintiff in this action sought to recover damages for criminal conversation with the plaintiff's wife, Abigail Maheha. The Jury was unable to agree, after an absence of four hours were discharged by the Court." In February 1855 Maheha filed to divorce Keaupuni. In addressing the court, Maheha gave her credentials as "formerly a pupil at the Honolulu Royal school." She cited the grounds as her husband's inability to "support her in the necessaries of *civilized* life to which from her education considered herself to be justly entitled." Regarding the circumstances of the marriage, a witness named Mele testified: "I was present when they were married by Mr. Armstrong. [...] She was about 13 years old at the time and the reason for her being married was that she was pregnant at the time. She was a Scholar at the Royal School at the time. Five months afterwards a child was born, child of Keano, not her present husband's child. They lived together about 2 years since which time they have been separated. They then returned to Honolulu. I don't know the reason of their separation." The court granted a decree of separation on April 25, 1855, and provided that the decree could be "modified or discharged; and that neither of the said parties shall be at liberty to marry again during the lifetime of the other party." The legislature in 1856 passed an act, approved by Kamehameha and Kaahumanu IV (Victoria Kamāmalu), that authorized the supreme court to "grant permission to persons [...] to marry again."[187] Permission must have been secured, because on July 17, 1857, in Waimea, Kauaʻi, Apigaila Maheha married Kiaaina Wahineaea of Hanapepe, Kauaʻi. Maheha died on February 3, 1861, at Hale Aliʻi. Only the Hawaiian language *Ka Hae Hawaii* reported her death, with only her name, date of death and place of death.[188]

Jane Lahilahi Young (1862)

Born around 1812, Jane Lahilahi Young was sister Keoni Ana, Grace Kamaʻikuʻi and Fanny Kekelaokalani. By Joshua Kaeo, she was the mother of Peter Young Kaeo; by Kamehameha III, she bore Albert Kūnuiākea. Young died at her residence called Kuaihelani on Sunday, January 12, 1862. The *Polynesian* reported: "Mrs. Kaeo was the youngest daughter of His Excellency John Young, Sen., the Minister, Adviser and friend of Kamehameha I., and of Kaowanaeha, descended from one of the most ancient Chief families in Hawaii, consequently she was own Aunt to her Majesty Queen Emma. Mrs. Kaeo suffered from a stroke of paralysis, yet bore her lot with exemplary fortitude and a contented, cheerful temper. Her remains were deposited in the Royal Cemetery on King Street."[189] The inscription on her coffin, interestingly only in English, reads: "Jane Lahilahi Kaeo, Died Jan 12 1862, Aged 50 years."[190]

Prince of Hawaiʻi (1862)

The "pride and hope of Hawaii,"[191] Prince Albert Edward Kauikeaouli Leiopapa a Kamehameha, the son of Kamehameha IV and Queen Emma, died at 8 a.m. on Wednesday, August 27, 1862.[192] Born on May 2, 1858, the Prince of Hawaii was four years and three months old.

FUNERAL

Unlike the very public funerals of the past, the obsequies of the Prince of Hawaii were a private affair. The *Polynesian* announced:

> The Ceremony of the Funeral of His late Royal Highness Albert the Prince of Hawaii, will be performed at the Palace, at 11 o'clock, a.m. on Sunday the 7th of September, proximo.

The Funeral will be strictly a private one. By order of the Chamberlain of the King's Household.
PALACE, 29th August, 1862.[193]

Besides being ostensibly private, the funeral service would diverge markedly from the services of the past in its ritual. Even in the absence of clergy of the Church of England, the service was conducted using its rites. The *Pacific Commercial Advertiser* reported briefly concerning the ceremony: "The funeral of the late Prince of Hawaii, was held on Sabbath last at 11 o'clock a.m., at the Palace. The ritual of the church of England was read, the Rev. E.W. Clark and S.C. Damon officiating. Despite the notice that the service was to be strictly private, the attendance was large, comprising the chiefs, ministers, representatives of foreign governments, military and other organizations, government officers, &c., &c."[194]

Prince Albert Edward Kauikeaouli Leiopapa a Kamehameha, son of Queen Emma and Kamehameha IV, was called Prince of the Hawaii (courtesy Hawaii State Archives [PP-95-10-004]).

Although the procession did not take place, the residents of the city would experience the funeral in a very memorable way: "From sunrise till the conclusion of the services—about 11½ o'clock—guns were fired every five minutes."[195] From 6:16 that morning, Honolulu reverberated with more than five dozen volleys.

The young prince's death was visibly displayed, too. The court determined specific marks of mourning, with the Privy Council setting how his death would be observed; it "resolved that members of the Privy Council not in uniform shall at the Funeral of the Prince of Hawaii, wear crape with streamers on the hat, [and] a crape scarf from the left shoulder."[196]

BURIAL

Because the Pohukaina tomb had run out of space for the burial of the Prince of Hawaii, a temporary structure was built to shelter his coffin.

He remained there until February 4, 1864, when his body was brought to the partially completed Royal Mausoleum.[197] The poignant inscription on his coffin, partly in Hawaiian and partly in English, reads: "Ka Mea Kiekie | Albert Edward Kauikeaouli, | Leiopapa a Kamehameha, | Haku o Hawaii | Hanau i ka la 27 o Mei, 1858, make i ka la 27 o Augate, 1862. | Suffer little children to come unto me, and forbid them not, for of such is the Kingdom of God."[198] The English portion is a quotation from Matthew 19:14 in the Authorized (King James) Version of the Bible that reads: "But Jesus said, Suffer little children, and forbid them not, to come unto me: for of such is the kingdom of heaven." It constitutes the only known inscription to include a Bible verse.

Cost

The limited scope of the funeral and lack of a procession resulted in one of the least expensive obsequies for royalty. The cost of the funeral for the Prince of Hawai'i amounted to $4,569.62.[199]

Another royal child would die a year later, but not an heir to the throne.

Keolaokalani Pākī Bishop (1863)

Keolaokalani Pākī Bishop, *hānai* son of Bernice Pauahi and Charles Reed Bishop, was the son of Ruth Ke'elikōlani and Isaac Young Davis. He was the grandson of Isaac Davis, the *haole* war companion of Kamehameha I. Born at the house of Major W.L. Moehonua, he lived just seven months and twenty-nine days.

Not in the immediate family of the king, the death of Bishop would not be mourned in the same way. The only element of his obsequies preserved is the inscription on his coffin, only in English, which reads: "Keolaokalani Paki Bishop | Born Dec 30, 1862, | Died Aug 28, 1863."[200] It is one of four known inscriptions written solely in English.

King Kamehameha IV (1863)

Kamehameha IV, the grandson of Kamehameha I, was born February 9, 1834, the son of Kīna'u and Mataio Kekūanāo'a. He was the *hānai* son of Kamehameha III and preceded his older brother, Lot, to the throne. He married Emma Rooke, granddaughter of John Young, and the kingdom rejoiced when their union resulted in an heir to the throne, Prince Albert Edward Kauikeaouli Leiopapa a Kamehameha. The couple established the Queen's Hospital. Saddened by the death of his only son, Kamehameha IV would join him in death less than fifteen months after the funeral, on

November 30, 1863. The lack of a suitable burial location for the king extended the time between his death and funeral to two months and four days, one of the longest periods for any royal obsequies, exceeded only by the observances for Liholiho and Kamāmalu who died half a world away.

LYING IN STATE

The lying in state of Kamehameha IV took place at Hale Aliʻi, in the throne room of the palace. The *Pacific Commercial Advertiser* described the scene on the palace grounds:

Kamehameha IV (courtesy Hawaii State Archives [PP-97-8-011]).

For several days and evenings previous to the funeral, the palace yards were filled with natives [...] engaged with singing *meles* or lamentations composed for the deceased King. [...] Some of these songs, though accompanied by ancient forms, are sung with such pathos, and embody such touching incidents, as to frequently plunge the whole assembly of hearers into tears.

On Tuesday night, (that preceding the funeral,) there was a crowd of five or six thousand natives and foreigners collected around the palace, and the scene is represented as quite exciting. At 12 o'clock, midnight, Bishop Staley read the Litany over the corpse in the throne room. There were only a few present, perhaps twelve or fifteen foreigners.[201]

Though strictly in Western form, the coffin was made locally of local materials by Mr. Fischer, and was called by the newspaper "a most elaborate piece of workmanship, of *koa* and *kou* woods." Fischer's business was located on the property of the *hānai* mother of Queen Emma, Grace Kamaikui, at Union and Hotel streets.[202] The inscription on the coffin, written in English, according to *Au Okoa*, was: "ALEXANDER KALANIKUA LIHOLIHO | IOLANI MAKA O IOULI KUNUIAKEA, KUKAILIMOKU, | KAMEHAMEHA IV. | King | of the | Hawaiian Islands. | Born, February 9, 1834, Succeeded to the Throne, | December 15, 1854. Died November 30, 1863."[203] The *Pacific Commercial Advertiser* described the "heavy silver plate surrounded with scroll work and surmounted with a crown" and added: "The engraving of this plate was executed by Dr. J. Mott Smith, and could hardly be excelled for beauty and finish in any Eastern city. The plate itself was cast here, by Mr. J. Hopper, and the whole shows that our artisans can, when required, perform work not surpassed anywhere else."[204]

Funeral

As with his son's funeral, during the funeral of Kamehameha IV, guns sounded every five minutes, from 6 a.m. until his remains were entombed in the Royal Mausoleum.

The funeral, viewed by a non–Anglican resident of Honolulu, featured elements not present at past funerals. The account was contained in *Missionary Herald*, a publication of the American Board of Commissioners for Foreign Missions, that had sent the first missionaries to Hawai'i. The writer, who possessed a card of admittance, described the service: "Nothing could well be more popish. From 150 to 200 candles were burning in that little church, at noon-day. The Bishop's back was towards the audience most of the time, with his altar and pictures and candles before him. A chapter was read by a native—a former pupil of ours—from our translation of the Bible, which was the most sensible part of the services. The display of the Bishop's crook, or crozier, and all the other flummery, was not a little disgusting."[205]

Cost

The Privy Council passed a "Resolution approving the action of His Majesty's Cabinet Council in authorizing the Minister of Finance [C. de Varigny], under the painful and extraordinary emergency caused by the death of His Majesty Kamehameha IV to be expended for the Funeral obsequies [...] a sum not exceeding Ten thousand dollars to be expended by the Minister of Finance and the Chamberlain of the Royal Household [Charles Gordon Hopkins] conjointly."[206] Charles Gordon Hopkins made a motion at the January 26, 1864 Privy Council meeting to authorize the expenditure of "the further sum of $10,000 to defray the remaining expenses attending upon the funeral of His late Majesty Kamehameha IV."[207]

The cost was not lost to critics of aspects of the funeral. The *Missionary Herald* informant wrote: "The funeral of the late king, after a good deal of delay and parade and expense, has passed off."[208] In the end, the cost of the funeral for Kamehameha IV amounted to $17,897.11.[209]

Procession

The King's Chamberlain issued the Order of Procession two days after the Privy Council had approved the expenses. The broadside read:

Order of Procession for the Funeral | of His | late Majesty Kamehameha IV. | [rule] | Artillery. | Undertaker to the late King. | Faculty and Students of Oahu College. Royal School, Kahehuna School, G.B.C. Inagraham's School, Miss Fayerweather's School, Palolo | School, Manoa School, Pauoa School, Waiahao School, Loma School, Palama School, Wai- | lupe School, Moanalua School, Select Hawaiian School, Kaumakapili School, Ka- | lihi School, Maemae School, Makiki School, Kamoiliili School. | Honolulu Fire Department, Mechanic's Benefit Union. | Odd Fellows, Free Masons. | Members of the Medical Faculty, Apothecary and Attend- | ing Physicians of the late King. | The Konohikis of the Crown Lands. | The Konohikis of the Late King's Private Lands, Com- | Missioner of the Crown Lands. | General Commanding and Staff. | Honolulu Rifles, Household Troops. | Honolulu Yeomanry, The Queen's Servants, | The late King's Purveyor. | The late King's Servants. | Ministers of Religion of the Several | Denominations. | The Clergy of the Roman Catholic Church. | His Lordship Louis, the Right Rev. Bishop of Arathea and | Vicar Apostolic of the Hawaiian Islands. | The Choir of the Hawaiian Cathedral. | Officiating Clergy. | His Lordship The Right Reverend Bishop of Honolulu. | The late King's Horse. | The late King's Aids. | H.R.H. Prince William | Bearing the Sword and hat of the late Majesty. | The Honorable Colonel Peter Y. Kaeo, Bearing the Crown of the late King. | Large Kahilis. | Escort of Honolulu Cavalry. Large Kahilis. Small Kahilis. Pall Bearers. [cut of coffin] Pall Bearers. Small Kahilis. Large Kahilis. Escort Of Honolulu Cavalry. | Large Kahilis. | Carriage Bearing | Her Majesty Queen Emma. | Carriage Bearing | Her Royal Highness the Princess. | Carriage Bearing | Queen Dowager, Hakaleleponi. | His Majesty the King | Supported by H.R.H. the Kuhina Nui, and attended by the Hon. Col. C. Kapaakea. | The King's Chancellor. | The Cabinet Ministers: | His Ex. R.C. Wyllie, Minister of Foreign Relations and Secretary of War and of the Navy; His Ex. | G.M. Robertson, Minister of the Interior; His Ex. C. de Varigny, Minister of Finance; | His Ex. C.G. Hopkins, Acting Minister of Finance; the Hon. C.C. Harris, | Attorney General.| [rule] | His Ex. The Minister Resident of the United States, Jas. McBride; H.B.M.'s Commissioner, W.W. | Follett Synge; H.I.M.'s Commissioner, Mons. Desnoyers. | [rule] | Ladies of the Court. | Members of the Privy Council of State; | Members of the House of Nobles. | Judges of the Supreme Court. | [rule] | Consular Corps | [rule] | Circuit Judges. | Clerks of Government Departments ; House of Representatives ; Collector | General, Custom House Officers, and Officers of the Customs ; the Marshal and Sheriffs of the | different Islands ; the King's Household Servants ; the King's Yeomanry; Foreign | Residents ; Ahahui Aloha o Lahaina. | Hawaiian Population Generally. | Police Force.| [rule] |

The King's remains will lie in state at Iolani Palace on Tuesday night of the 2d February.

Any persons wishing to recite "Kanikaus" for the memory of the late King, will be allowed to do so on that occasion.

At 12 o'clock, midnight, there will be Church Service at the Palace.

Those who attend the Funeral are to assemble in front of the Palace at 10 a.m., on Wednesday, the 2d of February, and the procession to start at 10½.

The line of procession *preceding* the remains of His late Majesty, will be formed on King street, the right line resting on Alakea street. Those who *follow* the remains, will be formed on King street, their right resting on the Waikiki side of the Palace gate.

The procession will proceed to the Hawaiian Cathedral, and the Body will be received there by his Lordship the Bishop of Honolulu and his clergy, and conveyed into the Cathedral, when the Funeral Service will be performed.

The public generally are invited to attend.
Issued from the Chamberlain's Office, Honolulu, January 28, 1864.[210]

The procession added a new organization to the usual participants in the funeral parade, one that would have a significant impact on the kingdom in the future. The Honolulu Rifles made its first appearance in a funeral procession during the obsequies for Kamehameha IV. The Privy Council had first approved their Charter on January 11, 1858. In 1860, the Honolulu Rifles had elected Kamehameha IV as Colonel.[211] His wife, Queen Emma, and other Honolulu women had presented colors to the Honolulu Rifles shortly after their organization in August 1857. Unmentioned by name in the published Order of Procession, a group of one hundred native Hawaiians volunteers, called the Zouave Guard, marched after the Household troops. The *Pacific Commercial Advertiser* provided a detailed description of the Zouave uniforms: "The dress, consisting of white leggings, rich scarlet trowsers, tucked up at the knees, after the Zouave style, blue shirts and scarlet caps made one of the most striking and attractive uniforms that could be devised."[212] Named for a regiment of French soldiers in Algeria, drawn from a Berber tribe, the uniforms reflected clothes suitable for an arid North African desert climate.

The highly crafted order, too, was scrutinized in detail. The wording of the Order of Procession elicited comment in the *Missionary Herald*: "You will notice the peculiar manner in which Protestant clergy are put down in the programme, arranged doubtless, to suit the Bishop" noted the Honolulu resident who wrote the letter. "They are not mentioned as clergymen, but only *ministers of religion*, while a great flourish is made of the Roman Catholic and Episcopal Bishop and clergy."[213] The result was that "of the American clergy (the most numerous here) we observed but one representative, and understood that the reason for their non-appearance was the sneering way in which they were thought to be referred to in the programme. We cannot believe that there was any intention to offend them. An occasion like a royal funeral is not the place to create or foster religious jealousies, by sectarian rivalry."[214] The Order of Procession was the first to mention the bishops by name.

The order also included "The Late King's Horse." Other examples of caparisoned horses position the horse after the catafalque.

The instructions for the funeral of Kamehameha IV were the first to set aside a specific time for individuals to recite *kanikau* or funeral dirges.

Robert Crichton Wyllie (1865)

The first unrelated foreigner to be buried at the Royal Mausoleum, Robert Crichton Wyllie, advisor to three kings, died on October 19, 1865. He was born in Scotland on October 13, 1798, arriving in Honolulu in 1844 as secretary to British Consul General William Miller, and later served as the acting British Consul in Miller's absence. He served as Minister of Foreign Affairs for the Kingdom of Hawai'i from March 26, 1845, through October 19, 1865. C. De Verigny distributed the circular to foreign consuls that announced his death: "It is my painful duty to announce to you the death at 5 minutes to 11 AM., in Honolulu, of His Excellency, Robert Crichton Wyllie, His Majesty's Minister of Foreign Affairs and Secretary of War."[215]

FUNERAL

The funeral took place on October 30, 1865, at 2 p.m., at the Hawaiian Temporary Cathedral. The Anglican Church, called then the Reformed Catholic Church, had been established in Hawai'i in 1862 at the invitation of King Kamehameha IV and Queen Emma, with its first Bishop, Thomas Nettleship Staley, arriving in October of that year. The cornerstone for the permanent cathedral would not be laid until March 5, 1867.

PROCESSION

The Order of Procession appeared in the *Pacific Commercial Advertiser* on October 28, 1865:

> Order of Procession | For the Funeral of His Late Excellency | Robert Crichton Wyllie, | His Majesty's Minister of Foreign Affairs, Secretary at | War, and Grand Cross of the Order of | Kamehameha I., &c., &c. | [rule] | Undertaker. | Band. | Artillery. | Governor of Oahu. | Honolulu Rifles. | Hulumanu Company. | Household Troops. | Master and Crew of the Schooner "Prince." | Household Servants. | Overseers of Princeville Plantation. | Manager of Princeville Plantation. | Medical Attendents. | Free Masons. | Protestant Clergy. | The Clergy of the Roman Catholic Church. | Choir of the Reformed Catholic Church. | Officiating Clergy. | Escort of Honolulu Cavalry. Pall Bearers. The Corpse. Pall Bearers. Escort of Honolulu Cavalry. | Chief Mourner. | His Majesty's Carriage. | His Highness M. Kekuanaoa. | Majesty's Staff. | The King's Chancellor. | Cabinet Ministers. | Judges of Supreme Court. | Members of the Privy Council of State. | Members of the Legislative Assembly. | Consular Corps. | Circuit Judges. | District Judges. | Clerks of Government Departments. | Members of the Bar and Officers of the Supreme Court. | The Collector General. Custom House Officers, and Officers of | Customs. | The Marshal and Sheriffs of the different Islands, | Fire Department. | The Public. | Police Force.[216]

Unlike in other processions to the Royal Mausoleum, no kāhili were present. It included for the first and last time the manager of Princeville

Plantation, named for the Prince of Hawai'i, the son of Kamehameha IV and Queen Emma.

Princess Victoria Kamāmalu (1866)

Princess Victoria Kamāmalu, the daughter of Kīna'u and Mataio Kekūanāo'a, was sister of two kings: Kamehameha IV and Kamehameha V. Appointed as Kuhina Nui by the former, she used the name Ka'ahumanu. In that position, she named her other brother, Lot Kamehameha Kapuāiwa as heir to the throne following the unexpected death of Kamehameha IV. She died at her father's residence, called Papakanene, on May 29, 1866. Her funeral took place more than a month later, on June 30, 1866.

In his letter of July 1, 1866, Twain wrote of the religious jockeying surrounding the funeral.[217]

> The sermon was preached by the Rev. Mr. Parker, pastor of the great stone church—of which the Princess was a member, I believe, and whose choir she used to lead in the days of her early womanhood. To the day of her death she was a staunch, unwavering friend and ally of the missionaries, and it is a matter of no surprise that Parker, always eloquent, spoke upon this occasion with a feeling and pathos which visibly moved the hearts of men accustomed to conceal their emotions.
>
> The Bishop of Honolulu, ever zealous, had sought permission to officiate in Parker's stead, but after duly considering the fact that the Princess had always regarded the Bishop with an unfriendly eye and had persistently refused to have anything to do with his church, his request was denied.

Victoria Kamāmalu was named Kuhina Nui at age 17 (courtesy Hawaii State Archives [PP-97-11-002]).

A contemporaneous account in the *Pacific Commercial Advertiser* expressed a similar sentiment:

> Saturday last [June 30, 1866], in accordance with the programme issued. The funeral services were performed at the Palace, at 9½ o'clock, by the Rev. Henry H. Parker pastor of the Kawaiahao Church, of which the deceased was a member. It is reported to have been the wish of her venerable father and others that the body

should be taken to that Church and the exercises held there, but in this their wishes are said to have been over-ruled by Bishop Staley, who appears to have had more to say in the matter than prudence dictated or the public interests called for. The officiating clergyman was not even allowed to take the place in the procession which custom assigns to him, next to the hearse, but that was appropriated by the above officious functionary. Neither was the officiating clergyman allowed to close the exercises at the tomb, on account of a new dogma set up by this same functionary that it is "consecrated ground," where no one but he can officiate. The Hawaiian Government may tolerate such bigotry, but we hesitate not to say it is more worthy of the middle ages than of the nineteenth century. There is an intense feeling of disgust provoked, not among his own people merely, but among all thinking minds, against the bigoted conduct of Bishop Staley at the late funeral.

The procession was not so large nor so imposing as previous ones that we have witnessed, but the display of kahilis was really magnificent, surpassing in number, variety and beauty anything of the kind that has ever been known here on State occasions. The remains of the Princess were deposited in the Royal Tomb, where repose those of nearly all the Aliis of the Kamehameha dynasty. May it be long before we are called upon to witness another such pageant.[218]

PROCESSION

The *Pacific Commercial Advertiser* printed the official Order of Procession:

Programme of the Funeral | of | Her Late Royal Highness the Princess | Victoria Kamamalu Kaahumanu. | Undertaker. | Royal School, Kawaiahao School, Roman Catholic School, | Maemae School. | Honolulu Fire Department. | Mechanic's Benefit Union. | Attending Physicians. | Konohikis of Crown Lands, Konohikis of Private Lands of | His Majesty, Konohikis of Private Lands of | Her late Royal Highness. | Governor of Oahu and Staff | Hulumanu | Prince of Hawaii's Own. | Household Troops. | The King's Household Servants. | Servants of Her late Royal Highness. | Protestant Clergy. The Clergy of the Roman Catholic | Church. | His Lordship Louis Maigret, the Rt. Rev. Bishop of Arathea, | Vicar Apostolic of the Hawaiian Islands. | The Clergy of the Hawaiian Reformed Catholic Church. | His Lordship the Right Reverend Bishop Staley of Honolulu. | Escort Haw. Cavalry, Large Kahilis, Small Kahilis, PALL Bearers. [black coffin] Pall Bearers. Small Kahilis, Large Kahilis, Escort Haw. Cavalry |Her Majesty Queen Emma's Carriage. | His Majesty's Staff. | Carriage of Her late Royal Highness. | Carriage of Her Majesty the Queen Dowager. | The King's Chancellor. | Cabinet Ministers. | His Excellency the Minister Resident of the United States, | James McBride. | H. I. M.'s Commissioner, Mons. Desnoyers. | H. B. M. — Acting Commissioner, W. L. Green. | Judges of Supreme Court. | Privy Councillors. | Members of the Legislative Assembly. | Consular Corps. | Circuit Judges. | Clerks of Government Departments. | Members of the Bar. | Collector General, Custom House Officers and Officers of the | Customs. | Marshal and Sheriffs of the different Islands. | King's Yeomanry. | Foreign Residents. | Ahahui Kaahumanu. | Hawaiian Population Generally. | Hawaiian Cavalry, | Police Force. |

The Procession will form at 10 o'clock a.m. on Saturday, June 30th, on King street, in front of Iolani Palace. Those who are to precede the Catafalque will form between Richard street and Fort street, and those who are to follow, on the Waikiki side of the Palace gate.

> The Procession will start at 11 o'clock a. m., precisely, and will proceed through King street to Nuuanu street, thence by Nuuanu street to the Royal Mausoleum.
> The Procession will be under the direction of the Governor of Oahu.
> Iolani Palace. June 27, 1866.[219]

The government changed the wording that had offended the writer to the *Missionary Herald* two years earlier regarding the Order of Procession for Kamehameha IV. In the Order of Procession for Victoria Kamāmalu, "Protestant Clergy" replaced the offending phrase, "ministers of religion."

They were immediately followed by military units, the Prince of Hawaii's Own and the Household Troops. The former unit was named for the Prince of Hawai'i, Albert Edward Kauikeaouli Leiopapa a Kamehameha, who had died four years earlier. The procession included the Mechanics Benefits Union, an organization chartered in 1857. The Roman Catholic bishop was listed by his name and title "Bishop of Arathea." He was the titular bishop of a see no longer in existence.

Author Mark Twain also wrote extensively about the procession and burial of Victoria Kamāmalu in *Roughing It*. His description of the procession follows the list in the *Pacific Commercial Advertiser*, but has minor variations. He leaves out the name of the Anglican Bishop, Thomas Nettleship Staley, as well as the three named diplomats: James McBride, Mons. Desnoyers, and W. L. Green.

Cost

The expenses of the funeral for Victoria Kamāmalu amounted to $12,766.65.[220]

The death of Victoria Kamāmalu had a profound impact on her father Mataio Kekūanāo'a, so much so that the *Pacific Commercial Advertiser* reported: "The venerable Ex-Governor has not been enjoying his customary good health, since the death of his daughter, the Princess, which has weighed heavily upon him. He has been able to be about, however, and rides out daily, and we trust will soon recover his usual vigor and health."[221] Despite the positive report, Mataio Kekūanāo'a would die just under two and a half years later.

Grace Kama'iku'i (1866)

The death of the *hānai* mother of Queen Emma, Grace Kama'iku'i Rooke, on July 26, 1866, occasioned simpler obsequies. Grace Kama'iku'i, the daughter of John Young and Ka'ōana'eha, was born in Kawaihae on September 8, 1808. The *Pacific Commercial Advertiser* reported: "The funeral of the late Mrs. Dr. Rooke, foster mother of Queen Emma, will take place at 10 o'clock to-day [August 18, 1866], from her late residence, corner of Nuuanu and Beretania streets."[222] C. De Varigny sent a copy of the funeral program and circular to D.C. Waterman, consul for Chile.[223] Unfortunately the program is no longer attached to the circular.

As with many of the royal obsequies, the funeral of Rooke disrupted another scheduled event. The afternoon performance of "Birch's Holiday Trip!" was postponed. The death also disrupted the travels of Queen Emma, who was still abroad when her *hānai* mother died. She had arrived in New York City from Liverpool, England, aboard the Cunard steamer *Java*[224] on Wednesday, August 8, 1866.[225] On August 10, 1866, she visited Greenwood Cemetery, New York. Following the visit to the cemetery, "she remarked, 'our people live so fast I wonder they find the time to bury their dead so superbly.'"[226] She later went toured Washington, D.C. (where she met with President Andrew Johnson), Niagara Falls and had just arrived in Montreal, Canada, when she received the news of the death of her *hānai* mother. She immediately hurried back to New York to catch the California steamer that was scheduled to leave on September 1, 1866.[227] She arrived in San Francisco on Monday, September 24, 1866,[228] where she accepted the offer of U.S. Secretary of State William H. Seward to travel on the United States steamer *Vanderbilt* to Hawai'i. She arrived on October 22, 1866, "after a passage of nine days."[229] Thus a combination of a delay in notification (the message had to be transported to San Francisco and telegraphed to Montreal) and the length of time it took to travel from the East Coast of the United States to Hawai'i meant Queen Emma arrived back in the islands more than nine weeks after the obsequies for her *hānai* mother, Grace Kama'iku'i Rooke, took place. She wrote to Kamehameha V when she returned: "I loved my mother above everything on this side of the grave and perhaps it was my erring in making too much of my earthly thing that she has been taken from me, it is only through the severest of trials that we can ever lift our eyes and see our Saviour's beaming face and outstretched arm."[230]

Kaisara (Caesar) Kapaʻakea (1866)

Kaisara (Caesar) Kapaʻakea Kaluaikau Kamakaehukai Kahana Keola was father of David Kalākaua, who would later reign as king, and Lili'uokalani, who would reign after her brother. He was born in Kuiaha, Hamakualoa, Maui, about 1816 or 1817. He married Ana Keohokālole in 1835. Kapaʻakea served as a member of the House of Nobles from 1845 and a member of the Privy Council from 1846.

1. Royal Deaths

Kapaʻakea (right) and his wife, Keohokālole, were parents of David Kalākaua, the founder of a new dynasty (courtesy Hawaii State Archives [PP-97-13-003]).

The Order of Procession for Caesar Kapaʻakea appeared in the *Hawaiian Gazette*:

Order of Procession—For the funeral of the late Honorable Colonel Ceasar [*sic*] Kaluaiku Kamakaehukai Kahana Keola Kapaakea. Member of the House of Nobles; Privy Council of State and Knight Companion of the Order of Kamehameha. | Undertaker. | Artillery Company "The Prince of Ha- | waii's Own. || Hulumanu Company. | Household Troops. | Household Servants. | Medical Attendants. | Escort of Cavalry. Large Kahili's. Small Kahili's Pall Bearers. [*cut of coffin*] Pall Bearers. Small Kahili's. large Kahili's. Escort of Cavalry. | Chief Mourners. | The Carriage of H.R.H M. Kekuanaoa. | Staff Officers.| Her Majesty Queen Emma, The Queen Dowager. | Members of the Privy Council and | House of Nobles and their Ladies. | The Public. | Detachment of Cavalry. |

The Funeral Services will take place at 3 p.m. on Sunday, December 9th, at the Kawaiahao Church. The Procession will be formed on King Street, and will be under the direction of Major Moehonua.

Adjutant's Office, Dec. 6, 1866.[231]

Burial

Though a high chief, he was not of the Kamehameha family and was not accorded the honor of being buried at the newly built Royal Mausoleum. Although early accounts speculated that he would be buried in Kealakekua,[232] on the island of Hawaiʻi, or in the Kewalo on Oʻahu, Kapaʻakea was buried in Kawaihaʻo Cemetery. Nine years later, the founding king of the new dynasty, his son, David Kalākaua, reinterred Kapaʻakea in the Royal Mausoleum on November 30, 1875. The transfer was made "under a military escort, with torches."[233]

Mataio Kekūanāoʻa, Kuhina Nui (1868)

Named for the masts of Captain Vancouver's ship, Mataio Kekūanāoʻa was born in Hilo during the British explorer's visit in 1794. His marriage with Pauahi resulted in birth of Ruth Keʻelikōlani; the subsequent union with Kīnaʻu made him the father of King Kamehameha IV, King Kamehameha V and Kuhina Nui Victoria Kamāmalu. He died November 24, 1868, at his Honolulu residence called Papakanene.[234] Kekūanāoʻa served as a member of the House of Nobles starting in 1841 and a member of the Privy Council from 1845. He was governor of Oʻahu from November 17, 1846, through February 18, 1864. He served as the King's Chamberlain starting August 31, 1857. A member of the board of education from September 26, 1860, he served as president from January 21, 1865. Following the death of his daughter, Victoria Kamāmalu, Kekūanāoʻa assumed her role as Kuhina Nui from December 19, 1863, until the position ceased on August 20, 1864.

The Chamberlain, Henry Prendergast, published the notice for mourning the death of Mataio Kekūanāoʻa:

> The Court will go into full mourning for His late Highness Mataio Kekuanaoa, G. C. K., Commander-in-Chief and member of His Majesty's Privy Council of State, from the date of this notice until two weeks after the funeral, and will wear half mourning from that time until the expiration of two mouths from the day of the funeral. Ladies will wear black with white trimmings for full mourning, and white with black trimmings for half mourning. Gentlemen will wear black with crape on the hat and left arm for full mourning, and crape on the hat and left arm with their ordinary dress for half mourning. The members of the Government and gentlemen connected with the Court will wear crape with

Mataio Kekūanāoʻa was father of Ruth Keʻelikōlani, Kamehameha IV, Kamehameha V and Victoria Kamāmalu. He served as Kuhina Nui following the death of his daughter, Victoria Kamāmalu (courtesy Hawaii State Archives [PP-98-2-003]).

their several uniforms. Members of the Legislative Assembly, and all the Representatives of Foreign Countries, Consuls and Commercial Agents are invited to observe the period of mourning herein prescribed, and the public generally are requested to show their respect for the memory of His late Highness, by wearing badges of mourning during the time specified.[235]
  Chamberlain's Office, Nov. 30, 1868
  Adjutant General Office
  Honolulu, Nov. 30, 1868

General Order No. 113 directed members of the military to cover parts of their uniforms as a sign of mourning:

The Adjutant General to the forces has been commanded to direct, on the present melancholy occasion of the death of His late Highness Mataio Kekuanaoa, G. C. K., Commander-in-Chief, etc., etc., that the officers of the forces and the several volunteer companies wear, when in uniform, black crape over the ornamental part of the hat or cap, over the sword knot, and on the left arm, with black gloves, and a black crape scarf on the sash. The drums are to be covered with black, and black crape is to be hung from the color staff of the Infantry and from the standard of the cavalry.

When officers appear at Court in their uniforms, they are to wear black crape over the ornamental part of the hat or cap, over the sword knot, and on the left arm, with white gloves and a black crape scarf over the sash.

The period of mourning specified by the Court will be observed by the forces.
JNO. O. DOMINIS
Adjutant General.[236]

A subsequent order, General Order 116, specified the formation and parade at the funeral of Kekūanāoʻa.

Funeral

The *Pacific Commercial Advertiser* announced: "The funeral of His Highness M. Kekuanaoa will take place on Tuesday next [Dec. 22, 1868]. The procession will form on King street, opposite the palace, at 10 a.m., and will proceed on the line of march at 11 a.m."[237]

Procession

The Order of Procession was issued on December 11, 1868, by the Office of the Governor. John O. Dominis, husband of Liliʻuokalani, had succeeded Kekūanāoʻa as governor of Oʻahu in February 1864. The broadside read:

Order of Procession | for the | Funeral | His late Highness | M. Kekuanaoa, | Grand Cross of the Order of Kamehameha I Alihikaua | Nui, Member of His Majesty's Privy Council of State, | Etc., Etc., Etc. | [*rule*] | Undertaker. | Prince of Hawaii's Own. | Hulumanus. | The Public Schools. | Honolulu Fire Department. | Mecancis' [*sic*] Benefit Union, | Indepnd't Order of Odd Fellows. | Free Masons. Attending Physicians. | Hulumanus. | Konohiki, Tenants, and Retainers | of His Late Highness' Estate. | Governor of Oahu and Staff. | Honolulu Rifles. | Marines of U.S.S. Ossipee. | Household Troops. | Household Servants of His Late | Highness. | The Roman Catholic Clergy. | The Right Rev. His Lordship the | Bishop of Arathea. | The Clergy of the Hawaiian | Reformed Catholic Church. | The Protestant Clergy. | The Pastor of the Kawaiahao | Church | Kahili Bearers | Escort Hawaiian Cavalry. Large Kahilis. Small Kahilis. Pall Bearers. [Rectangle] Pall Bearers. Small Kahilis. Large Kahilis. Pall Bearers. | His Majesty the King. | Mourning Carriages. | The King's Chancellor. | The Cabinet. | Governors of the different Islands. | Foreign Representatives and Cap- | tain of the U.S.S. 'Ossipee.' | Judges of the Supreme Court. | Privy Councilors | Members of the Legislative Assembly. | Consular Corps. | Officers of the U.S.S. 'Ossipee.' | Circuit Judges. Government Officers. | Members of the Bar. | Foreign Resident. | The Public. | Police Force. | Hawaiian Cavalry. | [rule] | The funeral will take place on Tuesday, the 22d inst. The procession will be formed on King Street, in front of the Palace, at 10 o'clock a.m., and will move punctually at 11 a.m. The procession will be under the direction of the Governor of Oahu. | Office of the Governor of Oahu, | Honolulu, Dec. 11, 1868.[238]

The USS *Ossipee*, a screw sloop-of-war, had been commissioned in 1862 for service in the U.S. Civil War, a war during which the Kingdom of Hawai'i had declared its neutrality. Decommissioned after the war, the ship was recommissioned in October 1866. In 1867 the ship had carried U.S. officials to the ceremony that transferred Alaska to the United States.

BURIAL

The father of kings, Kekūanāo'a, was buried with his son, Kamehameha IV, daughter, Victoria Kamāmalu, and grandson, the Prince of Hawai'i, at Mauna 'Ala. As the father of the reigning monarch, Kamehameha V, Kekūanāo'a rested with the remains of Kamehameha Dynasty.

High Chiefess Keohokālole (1869)

High Chiefess Keohokālole was a descendant of Keawe-a-Heulu and Kame'eiamoku, war companions of Kamehameha the Great.[239] Keohohiwa, the daughter of Keawe-a-Heulu, married Kepo'ookalani, son of Kame'eiamoku, and bore his a son named Aikanaka, father of Keohokalole. Had she died during the reign of her son, King David Kalākaua, the obsequies would, no doubt, have taken on a much more elaborate form. During the reign of King Kamehameha V, however, she was simply one of many high chiefs. She did, however, serve as a member of the House of Nobles from 1841 to 1846 and on the Privy Council from 1846 to 1847. Her death was notable, and a report of it appeared in the *Pacific Commercial Advertiser*:

> Death of Hon. Mrs. Keohokalole—The *Kate Lee* arrived this morning from Hilo bringing the corpse of the Hon. Mrs. A Keohokalole, mother of the Hon. Col. D. Kalakaua, Hon. Mrs Dominis, Miss Likelike Kapaakea and a younger son. She died at Hilo on

the 5th inst., of congestion of the lungs. Her funeral will take place during the coming week.[240]

The unnamed younger son was William Pitt Leleiohoku Kalahoolewa, the *hānai* son of Princess Ruth Keʻelikōlani.

PROCESSION

Though not an official state funeral, a procession formed to bring Keohokālole to her final resting place. The most notable feature of the procession was the lighted kukui nut torches present at the obsequies of the descendants of Iwikauikaua. Unlike the state funerals, the order of procession was not noted in the newspaper's report of the procession: "On Sunday last [April 18, 1869], p.m., the remains of this honored lady, more generally known as Keohokalole, were taken from the residence of Maj. Moehonua, where they had been deposited since being received from Hilo [April 10, 1869], and were conveyed to the vault in the Kawaiahao burial ground. A large concourse of natives and foreigners assembled at the house, and followed the hearse to the church at Kawaiahao. Some thirty Kahili bearers, marched on each side of the hearse. A marked feature of the procession was four torch bearers—insignia of the family to which the deceased chiefess belonged—the torches were composed of kukui-nuts wrapped or enfolded in ti-leaves. There were four of them, two alight, and the other two unlighted."[241]

FUNERAL

The funeral services for Keohokālole, that took place on Sunday, April 18, 1869, reflected the funerary practices of the Protestant missionaries who had founded Kawaiahaʻo Church:

> At the church, the services were very solemn and impressive. The choir sang several chants and anthems with admirable skill and precision, the words being original and composed for the occasion. The funeral sermon was preached by the Rev. H.H. Parker, pastor of the church. 22, v. 7: "Behold I come quickly; blessed is he that keepeth the sayings of the prophecy of this book." The remarks of the Reverend gentlemen were very eloquent, and his allusions to the many amiable qualities of the deceased brought tears into many eyes.[242]

Queen Kalama (1870)

Queen Kalama, also known as Hakaleleponi or Hazaleleponi (derived from the Biblical name, Hazelelponi, mentioned in I Chronicles 4:3) was born about 1818, the daughter of Naihekukui and I (also known as Kepooku). She married Kamehameha III on February 4, 1837. She served as a member of the House of Nobles from 1845 to 1848, and on the Privy Council from September 7, 1846. Kalama died on Tuesday, September 20, 1870, at her residence in Honolulu.[243]

LYING IN STATE

The outside coffin was manufactured locally by Wilhelm Fischer. The *Hawaiian Times* described it as "a very highly finished and beautifully manufactured piece of workmanship. As might be expected, it is entirely made of native wood the main body being koa and kou; the ornamental work in the design is Gothic, and extremely chaste in appearance."[244]

FUNERAL

Funeral took place at 11 a.m. on Saturday, October 8, 1870.[245]

Chamberlain Henry Prendergast announced the observance of the funeral of Queen Kalama: "The Court will go into full mourning for Her late Majesty, Dowager Queen Kalama, relict of His late Majesty Kamehameha. III., for three weeks from this date [September 27, 1870]."[246]

Queen Kalama, wife of Kamehameha III, died fifteen years after his death (courtesy Hawaii State Archives [PP-96-17-001]).

PROCESSION

The Order of Procession appeared in the *Hawaiian Times*, a newspaper that was printed, fortunately, from September 13, 1870 to December 13, 1870:

Undertaker | Hawaiian Cavalry. | Attending Physician. | Konohikis, Servants' and Retainers of Her late Majesty. | Governor of Hawaii and Staff. | Prince of Hawaii's Own. | Honolulu Rifles. | Detachments from Foreign War-Vessels now in Port. | Household Troops. | Household Servants of Her late Majesty. | The Roman Catholic Clergy. | The Clergy of the Hawaiian Reformed Catholic Church. | The Protestant

Clergy. The Officiating Clergyman. | Kahilis. | Escort Hawaiian Cavalry. Small Kahilis. Pall Bearers. [*rule*] The Coffin. [*rule*] Pall Bearers. Small Kahilis. Escort Hawaiian Cavalry.| His Majesty's Carriage. | Her Majesty's Carriage. | The Cabinet. | Judges of Supreme Court. | Foreign Representatives. | Governors of the different Islands. | Privy Councillors. | Members of Legislative Assembly. | Consular Corps.| Officers of Foreign Vessels of War. | Circuit Judges. | Members of the Bar. | Foreign Residents. | The Public. | Police Force.[247]

It also, strangely, found its way into the *Daily Southern Cross*, a New Zealand publication: "The order of procession comprises—undertaker, Hawaiian cavalry, attending physician of the Queen, servants and retainers of her late Majesty, Governor of Oahu [John O. Dominis] and his staff, Prince of Hawaii's Own, Honolulu Rifles, detachments from forces of vessels in harbor, household troops, household servants of her late Majesty, Roman Catholic clergy, the Protestant clergy, the officiating clergy, the hearse with pall-bearers, his Majesty's carriage, her Majesty's carriage, the Cabinet Ministers (Kuaha Kuhina), Judges of the Supreme Court, foreign representatives, Governors of the different islands, Privy Councillors (nahoa ahakukamahi), members of the Legislative Assembly, Consular corps, officers of foreign vessels of war, Circuit Judge, members of the Bar, foreigners, the public, and the police force bringing up the rear."[248]

Robert Wilson Andrews, assistant engineer on the *Kilauea*, recorded October 9, 1870, the impact of the funeral on the community along with a participant's assessment of the procession. He wrote in his log: "The funeral of late Queen Kalama has caused a partial suspension of business. The Rifles, Artillery, 2 cavalry companies, and 2 companies of marines from the 'Jamestown' and 'Ringdove' swelled the procession. The march was extremely hot and wearisome."[249]

The USS *Jamestown* and the HMS *Ringdove* were warships anchored in Honolulu Harbor. The USS *Jamestown*, built in 1844, had served during the Mexican-American and U.S. Civil wars. The ship served as supply ship at Sitka, Alaska, during the transfer of the Russian possession to the United States.

Among the officers of the *Jamestown*, Captain Cochrane noted that he "had assisted Prince David Kalakaua [...] in some military instruction for the funeral of Dowager Queen Kalama when he was a clerk in the foreign office and an officer if the volunteers."[250] Another officer of the *Jamestown*, Commodore William T. Truxtun, was involved in a diplomatic incident related to the funeral observances when he ordered his men to lower the U.S. consulate flag to half staff in respect for the late queen, a move refused by the American Consul Adamson.[251]

HMS *Ringdove*, the fourth to bear that name, had been launched three years before its visit to Honolulu as a wooden screw gun vessel. The ship had arrived on September 27, 1870, from Mazatlan.[252]

ROUTE OF PROCESSION

The *Pacific Commercial Advertiser* reported on the specific route of the procession: "According to the programme the procession will form on Richard street between Palace Walk and King street, at 10 o'clock, under the direction of the Governor of Oahu. Her remains will be deposited in the Royal Mausoleum, in Nuuanu Valley."[253]

"The Funeral of Her late Majesty, the Queen Dowager Kalama, took place last Saturday, according to the published programme. During the procession, twenty-one guns were fired from a shore battery, and also from the men-of-war in port. The remains were deposited in the Royal Mausoleum."[254]

The *Hawaiian Times* gave a detailed description of the obsequies conducted at the Royal Mausoleum: "When the corpse was carried into the Mausoleum, it was placed on a bier in front of the Royal coffins, which were arranged in the N or chancel end. It was then covered in a black silk pall, leaving the plate and coronet exposed. Queen Emma placed a handsome wreath at the head of the coffin, another was placed at the foot. The Rev. W. Parker offered a short prayer in native, which concluded the service."[255]

The *Hawaiian Times* also included the final disposition of the remains: "The coffin will be ultimately placed in proper position by the side of the Queen's husband."[256] Queen Kalama eventually was reinterred in the Kamehameha Crypt, where the arrangement of the coffins is unknown.

The *Pacific Commercial Advertiser* used the funeral of Queen Kalama as an opportunity to reflect on the reign of her husband, Kamehameha III: "As we viewed the impressive cortege conveying the remains of this estimable lady to their final resting place, on Saturday last, in memory we were taken back to those times when she appeared as the Consort of His late Majesty Kamehameha III."[257] The funeral also prompted the writer to consider the deaths of the *ali'i* in general.

> Another reflection also came upon us, that the high chiefs of the country are so rapidly passing away, without leaving descendants to fill their places when they too shall have passed off the stage. It may be said that the people of pure native origin are also passing away, and it is a matter of deep sorrow to all friends of the Hawaiian race ; but as the country may be said, by the admission of foreign elements, conjoined with the Hawaiian stock, to be re-peopling itself into a mixed race, we desire the Hawaiian Dynasty to be perpetuated, as we have often heard it remarked by foreigners, that they had not lived under a government more protective of their rights than the present con-

stitutional government, founded by Kamehameha III. We feel that the above sentiments were freely echoed by the Hawaiians who followed the funeral procession, as we heard them exclaim: *Ua hala hou kekahi makua o makou*—another parent and benefactress has departed.[258]

Kamehameha V (1872)

Named king after his younger brother, Lot Kamehameha would reign as Kamehameha V after the deaths of Kamehameha IV and his son, the Prince of Hawai'i. He would not marry, so when Kamehameha V died on December 11, 1872, the throne would be filled by election the day after the funeral.

LYING IN STATE

The particulars for the lying in state of Kamehameha V included the location, time and instructions concerning funeral chants:

> The King's remains will lie in State at Iolani Palace, on Monday night, January 6th, 1873. Gates will open from 7 p.m. until midnight.
>
> Any persons washing to recite "Kanikaus" [dirges] in memory of the late King, will be allowed to do so on that occasion.
>
> Those who attend the Funeral are to assemble in front of the Palace at 10 o'clock a.m. on Tuesday, the 7th day of January, and the Procession to start at 11 o'clock.
>
> The line of procession *preceding* the remains of His late Majesty, will be formed on King street, the right resting on Alakea street. Those who *follow* the remains will form on King Street, the right resting on the Waikiki side of the Palace Gate.
>
> The public generally are invited to attend.
>
> Iolani Palace, December 31st, 1872.
>
> [*Oxford double rule*]

The instructions for participants in the procession included for the second time a formal mention of the "Kanikaus." The chanting of the *kanikau* marked the continued use of traditional

Kamehameha V did not name an heir, resulting in an election for the next ruler. Photograph by C.L. Weed, 1865 (courtesy Hawaii State Archives [PPWD-15-6-016]).

Hawaiian practices at the funerals of Hawaii's royalty. The directions also failed to include the route of the procession.

Besides the formal publications, Harriet Newell Foster Deming, also recorded her memories of the obsequies surrounding the death of Kamehameha V in her typescript titled "Years of Sunshine Days: Memories of a Childhood in Hawaii." She wrote: "meanwhile the body of Kamehameha was honored by all the ceremonial pertaining to a royal funeral. As he lay in state at the Palace clad in full regalia, and surrounded by a guard of honor and the Hawaiian official mourners, the residents of Honolulu filed through the rooms to view the dead monarch and witness traditional ceremonies that marked his passing. In the Palace yard hula dancing and wailing for the dead were intermingled" (168–169).

Deming also recorded a rarely described activity associated with the royal Hawaiian way of death—the making of the *kāhili*. She wrote:

> A most interesting sight was a collection of large camphor chests filled with the feathers of tropical birds that were used in making the *kahilis* borne in the funeral procession. These *kahilis* were shaped like elongated feather dusters fastened on to long polished wooden handles that varied in length from three feet to six or eight feet according to the position they were to occupy. The feathers used for them were of many colors, red and green from tiny indigenous birds, others pure white or glossy black. Such gorgeous *kahilis* as these were made up for royal pageants only. The need for them accomplished, they were taken to pieces, the feathers carefully protected from moths and packed away in great camphor-wood chests to remain until another King should die.
>
> Native women squatted on the back verandah of the Palace, deftly binding the feathers around and around the *kahili* handles, while all around them rose the shrill wailing for the dead and the rhythmic tom-tom of the hula gourd drums [169].

FUNERAL

The funeral service for Kamehameha V took place not at Kawaiahaʻo Church as had the service for Ana Keohokalole, but at ʻIolani Palace on January 7, 1873, at 10 a.m. The smaller size of the venue necessitated a card of admission, which was enclosed with the announcement of the funeral, sent by the Chamberlain, H. Pendergast, the day after Christmas in 1872. Each small card, 3¼ inches wide by 2⅛ inches high, bore the handwritten name of the invited party.[259]

PROCESSION

The *Pacific Commercial Advertiser* printed the Order of Procession in its issue published on January 8, 1873:

> Order of Procession | *For the Funeral of His late Majesty* KAMEHAMEHA V. | [rule] | Cavalry. | Undertaker. | Honolulu Fire Department. | Mechanics' Benefit Union. |

Good Templars. | Knights of Pythias. | Odd Fellows. | Free Masons. | Members of the Medical Faculty. | The Konohikis of Crown Lands. | The Konohikis of the late King's Private lands. | Governor of Oahu and Staff. | Band. | Artillery Company. | Honolulu Rifles. | Clergy of the Roman Catholic Church. | His Lordship, the Right Rev. Bishop of Arathea. | Protestant Clergy | Clergy of the Anglican Church. | His Lordship, the Right Rev. Bishop of Honolulu. | The late King's Horse. | The late King's Aids. | Major, the Honorable Henry A. Kahanu, bearing the Sword | and Hat of the late King. | Colonel, the Honorable David Kalakaua, bearing the Crown of | the late King. | Large Kahilis. | Escort of Hawaiian Cavalry. Large Kahilis. Small Kahilis. Pall Bearers. [*Oxford ruled rectangle*] Pall Bearers. Small Kahilis Large Kahilis. Escort of of Hawaiian Cavalry. | Large Kahilis. Carriage bearing Her Excellency R. Keelikolani, H.R.H. | Prince William C. Lunalilo, and C. Kanaina | Carriage bearing the Queen Dowager Emma, and the Honor- | abale Mrs. Naea [Fanny Kekelaokalani]. | Mourning Carriages. | The King's Chancellor. | The Cabinet Ministers. | Foreign Representatives. | Judges of the Supreme Court. | Members of the Privy Council of State. | The Legislative Assembly. | Governors of the differennt Islands. | Consular Corps. | Circuit Judges. | Clerks of the Government Departments. | Postmaster-General and Clerks of Post Office. | Collector-General and Custom House Officers. | The Marshal, and Sheriffs of the different Islands. | The Hulumanus. | Ahahui Aloha o Lahaina.| Foreign Residents. | Hawaiian Population. Police Force. | Detachment of Cavalry. |

The Knights of Pythias refers to the Oahu Lodge No. 1; Mystic Lodge No. 2 was not organized until January 10, 1884 (M-186).

The informal account by Deming captured the atmosphere of the funeral procession more powerfully than the official lists. Calling it the "most impressive feature of the day," Deming recounted: "When came the dead king's horse, riderless, his master's boots fastened to the empty saddle, pacing slowly with arched neck, as though conscious of his part in the solemn procession" (170). Deming also noted details unrecorded in newspaper accounts, like the name of the tune played by band in the procession: Chopin's *Funeral March* (170).

Cost

The cost of the funeral for Kamehameha V amounted to $11,661.62.[260]

Jane Loeau (1873)

Under the headline, "Death of a Chiefess," the *Pacific Commercial Advertiser* reported, "Jane Loeau, a descendant in the female line of the ancient high chiefs of Kauai, and a reputed granddaughter of Kamehameha I, died suddenly in this city on Wednesday last [July 30, 1873]. She was 45 years of age, and was in childhood an inmate of the Chief's [*sic*] school under the charge of Mr. and Mrs. Cooke, at the same time with Kamehameha IVth and Vth and His present Majesty [Lunalilo]."[261] The death was indeed "sudden" for she had visited Emma on July 28, 1873. The account made no reference to funeral or burial. It also did not mention her husbands: John Robert Jasper, whom she married September 2, 1847 (O-17:21); Martin Seger, whom she married on March 15, 1855 (O-21a:6;O-30:70); or S.L. Kaelemakule, whom she married December 6, 1862.[262] S.L. Kaelemakule in a letter to *Ko Hawaii Ponoi* did note their ten years, seven months and twenty-five days of marriage.[263] The August 2, 1873, issue of *Ka Nupepa Kuokoa*, however, did report that on Thursday, July 31, 1873, Jane Loeau Kaelemakule was buried at Kawaiahaʻo cemetery.[264] The *Nuhou* published what Alfons Korn called a "tasteless obituary." It read: "Jane Loeau, daughter of Liliha, daughter of Kalani and son of Kamehameha Nui, being the sixth from Keawe, and seventy-sixth from Wakea, and the one hundred and fifth from Kane and Kanaloa. And now oh God, let her rest in peace. Amen."[265] Her rapid burial, a day after her death, contrasted with the two most recent state funerals, with the nineteen days between the death and burial of Queen Kalama and twenty days between the death of Kamehameha V and his state funeral.

King William Charles Lunalilo (1874)

The death of King William Charles Lunalilo on February 3, 1874, marked the end of the Kamehameha dynasty. Born in Honolulu on January 31, 1835, Lunalilo was grandnephew of Kamehameha the Great through his mother Kekāuluohi, the daughter of Kalaʻimamahu, the half-brother of the dynasty's progenitor. Lunalilo served in the House of Nobles from December 24, 1863 to 1872, and as a member of the Privy Council from December 24, 1863, to 1865. He reigned as king from January 8, 1873.

William Charles Lunalilo, the last king of the Kamehameha Dynasty, is buried in a separate mausoleum (courtesy Hawaii State Archives [PP-98-15-007]).

LYING IN STATE

The inscription on the coffin was in Hawaiian. The *Hawaiian*

Gazette translated it to read: "William C. Lunalilo | King of the Hawaiian Islands. | Born January 31, 1835, | Died Feb. 3, 1874. | The length of his reign was one year | and twenty-five days."[266]

FUNERAL

The funeral services for Lunalilo were conducted solely in Hawaiian. The *Pacific Commercial Advertiser* reported that the Rev. Mr. Parker of Kawaiahaʻo "made an eloquent and impressive address in Hawaiian. A Hawaiian hymn, composed by the late Rev. Hiram Bingham,—("Aole make e ue;" "Weep not for him,") concluded the services in the Palace."[267] The closing hymn, titled "Aole make e uwe," and numbered 558 in the 1872 *Buke Himeni Hawaii*, has the following lyrics for the opening stanza:

> Ina e make no,
> Ka hanai a Iesu
> Mai *u*we oukou—e ala hou,
> A pii i kela ao.

PROCESSION

The Foreign Office issued a broadside that detailed the Order of Procession:

Order of Procession | for the | Funeral | of | His Late Majesty | Lunalilo. | Undertaker. | Ahahui Opiopio. | Honolulu Fire Department. | Mechanics' Benefit Union. | Good Templars. | Knights of Pythias. | Odd Fellows. | Free Masons. | Members of the Medical Faculty. | The Konohikis of Crown Lands. | The Konohikis of the late King's Private Lands. | Governor of Oahu [John O. Dominis] and Staff. | Band. | Detachments of Marines and Sailors from | U.S.S. Portsmouth | U.S.S. Tuscarora | H.B.M. Corvette Tenedos | The late King's Servants | The Late King's Purveyor. | His Late Majesty's Chamberlain [Horatio Gates Crabbe]. | Clergy of the Roman Catholic Church. | His Lordship, the Right Rev. Bishop of Arathea. | Clergy of the Anglican Church | His Lordship, the Right Rev. Bishop of Honolulu. | Protestant Clergy. | The Rev. Henry H. Parker. | The late King's Aids. | Colonel Allen, bearing the sword and Hat of the late King. | His Ex. J.M. Kapena, bearing the Crown of the late King. | Large Kahilis. | Large Kahilis. Small Kahilis. Pall Bearers. [*cut of coffin*] Pall Bearers. Small Kahilis. Large Kahilis. | Large Kahilis. | The late King's Charger. | Carriage bearing their Majesties the King and Queen, H.R. | H. Prince Leleiohoku, and H.R.H. Chas. Kanaina. | Carriage bearing Her Excellency the Governess of Hawaii [Ruth Keʻelikōlani], | The Honorable Mrs. Dominis [Liliʻuokalani], the Honorable Mrs. | Cleghorn [Likelike], and the Honorable Mrs. Bishop [Bernice Pauahi]. | Carriage bearing the Queen Dowager Emma, and the Hon- | orable Mrs. Naea [Fanny Kekelaokalani]. | Foreign Representatives, Captains and Officers of Foreign | Vessels of War in Port. | The King's Vice Chancellor. | Members of His late Majesty's Cabinet. | His Majesty's Cabinet Ministers. | Judges of the Supreme Court. | Members of the Privy Council of State. | Governors of the different Islands. | Consular Corps. | The Legislative Assembly. | Circuit Judges. | Clerks of Government Departments. | Collector

General, and Custom House Officers. | Postmaster General, Postmasters and Clerks in Post Office. | The Marshal, and Sheriffs of the different Islands. | District Justices. | Members of the Bar. | The Hulumanus. | Foreign Residents. | Hawaiian Population. | Police Force. | Detachment of Cavalry.[268]

Those who attend the funeral are to assemble in front of the Palace at 10 o'clock, a.m. on Saturday the 28th day of February, and the procession to start at 11 o'clock.

The line of procession *preceding* the remains of His late Majesty, will be formed on King Street, the right resting on Alakea Street. Those who follow the remains, will form on King Street, their right resting on the Waikiki side of the Palace gate.

The Public generally are invited to attend.
IOLANI PALACE, February 23, 1874.[269]

While the Order of Procession gives the position of the various parties, it does not indicate the number of participants. Fortunately, the *Hawaiian Gazette* estimated that one thousand and five hundred individuals participated in the procession.[270] As with previous funerals, the foreign ships in port at the time—the USS *Portsmouth*, USS *Tuscarora* and H.B.M. Corvette *Tenedos*—participated in the procession. The USS *Portsmouth* was launched in 1843 and commissioned in 1844. The *Portsmouth* had captured the port Yerba Buena, now called San Francisco, during the Mexican American War. At the time that it docked in Honolulu, the ship was in the midst of conducting surveys of the Eastern Pacific. The USS *Tuscarora* was launched in 1861. Launched in 1870, the H.B.M. Corvette *Tenedos*, was a small warship armed with 12 guns. The sailors and marines from the three ships had restored order after the election of Kalākaua resulted in a riot sixteen days before the funeral.

BURIAL

Although the sermon at Kawaiahaʻo had been delivered in Hawaiian, a copy of an English language address, titled "Funeral sermon preached by the Rev. H.H. Parker at the burial Lunalilo the first—king of the Hawaiian Islands, Feb. 20th 1874," survives in the collection of the Hawaii State Archives. Parker, who called Lunalilo "the noblest-hearted king that Hawaii ever could boast," expressed the great loss felt at the burial of popular monarch:

> That Lunalilo a king beloved by his people so amiable and so kind should be cut off so in the midst of his years that his reign, begun under such favorable auspices should be so short and fraught with so many trials adds to our grief. No man will ever know the soul struggles he endured. God bless the proud noble sensitive soul, that conscious of its own weakness, struggles alone against adversity. Never were the Hawaiian people subject to so many trials as they have passed through, during the past fourteen months. Never were the principles of their government put to a severer test. Never have they seen so much trouble in so short a period of time.[271]

Visitor Isabel Bird recorded the finality of the funeral, especially after the election of Kalākaua: "When the body was raised from the feather robe, he [Kanaʻina] ordered that it should be wrapped in it, and thus be deposited in its resting place. "He is the last of our race," he said; "it belongs to him."[272]

The *Hawaiian Gazette* added, nearly as an afterthought, a comment on the predominance of Western practice in the obsequies: "It may be added that no hulas, or heathen dances, were allowed during the time that the corpse of the late King was at the Palace. In this respect, to the credit of those having charge, it should be said that the well-known wishes of the deceased and also of his father, were faithfully observed."[273]

Cost

The *Hawaiian Gazette* reported: "The coffin and its silver ornaments were very chaste and must have cost a large sum."[274] All told, an 1888 report found that the funeral for King Lunalilo amounted to $11,988.50.[275]

A second funeral for Lunalilo, nine months after the first, took place on Tuesday, November 23, 1874, with the transfer of his remains from the Royal Mausoleum to his tomb on the grounds of Kawaiahao Church. According to observers, after King Kalākaua had refused a repetition of the 21-gun salute for the second set of obsequies, the heavens themselves honored Lunalilo with thunder claps. "On Tuesday [November 23, 1874], while the remains of the late King were en route for the tomb at Kawaiahao, a heavy thunder storm passed over this city [...] all of which, say the more superstitious of the natives, had some mysterious connection with Lunalilo."[276]

The funeral of King Lunalilo marked the final obsequies conducted for a king of the Kamehameha Dynasty, though not the last funeral for royalty associated with it.

Royal Deaths During the Kalākaua Dynasty

Kukui ʻā mau i ka awakea.
Torch that continues to burn in daylight.
A symbol of the family of Iwikauikaua. After his daughter was put to death by one of his wives, this chief made a tour of the island of Hawaiʻi with torches burning day and night. This became a symbol of his descendants, who include Kalākaua and Liliʻuokalani.[277]
—Hawaiian proverb

Unlike the Kamehameha dynasty that marked only the deaths of its own family with state funerals, the Kalākaua dynasty honored both its family's deaths and the prominent members of its predecessor dynasty. Even the three royal women who refused to attend the coronation of King Kalākaua and Queen Kapiʻolani—Ruth Keʻelikōlani, Queen Emma and Princess Bernice Pauahi Bishop—each received funerary honors befitting their rank.

Charles Kanaʻina (1877)

The first royal funeral during the Kalākaua Dynasty honored the father of the last ruler of the preceding dynasty, King William Charles Lunalilo. Charles Kanaʻina died March 13, 1877, three years after the death of his son. As with the obsequies for Kapaʻakea a decade earlier, had his funeral taken place during the reign of his son, the procession would have been much more elaborate. Indeed, King Lunalilo is not even mentioned by name in the Order of Procession, only referred to as "His late Highness." Instead, the procession was notable in its simplicity. The Order of Procession contained less than two dozen lines:

Charles Kanaʻina, father of King Lunalilo, wears the badge of the Order of Kamehameha I (courtesy Hawaii State Archives [PP-98-15-007]).

Order of Procession for the Funeral of His Late Highness Charles Kanaiana. | Grand Cross of the Orders of Kamehameha I. and | Kalakaua, Member of His Majesty's Privy Council of State, Etc., Etc. | [*rule*] | Undertaker. | Konohikis, Tenants and Retainers of His late Highness. | Military Escort. | Household Servants of His Late Highness. | Officiating Clergyman. | Pall Bearers. [*cut of coffin*] Pall Bearers. | His Majesty's Carriage. | Mourning Carriages. | The King's Chancellor. | The Cabinet. | Foreign Representatives. | Judges of the Supreme Court. | Governors of the Different Islands. | Privy Councillors and Members of the House of Nobles. | Members of the Legislative Assembly. | Consular Corps. | Circuit Judges. | Government Officers | Members of the Bar. | Foreign Residents. | The Public. |

[*pointing hand*] The funeral will take place on THURSDAY, March 29. The Procession will be formed on Hotel Street, in front of the Hawaiian Hotel, at 10 o'clock a.m., and will move punctually at 11 o'clock a.m.[278]

1. Royal Deaths

The procession for Charles Kanaʻina, the father of Lunalilo, lacked the *kāhili* that marked other royal funerals.

Less than two weeks after the funeral, another royal death would take place. The next funeral, however, would honor Leleiohoku II, the brother of the progenitor of the new dynasty, King David Kalākaua.

William Pitt Leleiohoku Kalahoolewa (1877)

William Pitt Leleiohoku Kalahoolewa, the youngest son of Kapaʻakea and Keohokālole, was born in Honolulu on January 10, 1855. His own death on April 9, 1877, ended the possibility of melding the Kamehameha and Kalākaua dynasties. While he lived Leleiohoku held the potential of uniting much of the land holdings of the Kamehameha dynasty with the throne of the Kalākaua dynasty; Leleiohoku II was the *hānai* son and heir of Ruth Keʻelikōlani, the namesake of her late husband and the brother and heir apparent of King David Kalākaua. His names remembered the deaths of Kamehameha I and Kamehameha III: Leleiohoku remembered the death date of Kamehameha I on the day of Hoku; Kalahoolewa recalled the date of the funeral of Kamehameha III.[279] His own funeral would take place sixteen days following his death.

William Pitt Leleiohoku Kalahoolewa was the *hānai* son of Ruth Keʻelikōlani of the Kamehameha Dynasty as well as brother and heir apparent of King David Kalākaua of the successor dynasty (courtesy Hawaii State Archives [PP-98-8-010]).

Lying in State

Because ʻIolani Palace had been demolished prior to January 1875,[280] the lying in state took place in "the house at Iolani Palace known as Ihekapukalani [*sic*]."[281] Ihikapukalani, the former residence of Kamehameha IV and Queen Emma, was a structure located just Waikīkī of the site of the old palace.

Liliʻuokalani composed the funeral dirge, "He Kanikau No Leleiohoku," for her brother in 1877. She included it twenty years later in her unpublished manuscript titled *Hawaiian Songs*.

1.
He aloha paumako
 Hoohakui nakolo,
Haehae i k Manawa,
 Ia oe e Kalani.
Hui:-Lihaliha wale e Kalani,
 Ka ikena aku,
I kau hiolani,
 Lolii kau hooilo.

2.
Ke uwe aku nei,
 Kaulilua i kea nu,
Auhea kuʻu poki?
 Ka hooilina Aupuni.
Hui:-Lihaliha wale e Kalani

3.
Ua hui malanai
 Mamua e noho nei,
Ke hopu hewa nei,
 Ko kina wailua.
Hui:-Lihaliha wale e Kalani.

4.
Eia o Kapili e,
 Ke haalipo nei,
Ana lipo walohia,
 Ia oe e kuʻu Lani.
Hui:-Lihaliha wale e Kalani.

5.
Pau kou hea ana mai,
 Auhea oe kuahine,
Pehea e pau ai?
 Keia eha nui.
Hui:-Lihaliha wale e Kalani.[282]

Thus, Liliʻuokalani preserved the ancient mourning tradition that had been continued by Kaʻahumanu and other native Hawaiian composers.

Funeral

The funeral took place in the same location as the lying in state, in the "large audience-room of *Ihikapukalani* House."[283] Unlike other services for royalty that had taken place in the edifice built by the American missionaries, Kawaiahaʻo Church, the rite was conducted by the Anglican

Bishop of Honolulu using the "funeral service of the English Church—of which the deceased Prince [had] long been a member."[284]

Because of the small size of the location, admission to the religious services required a card that the bearer needed to "present at the gate on King Street."[285] The ceremony took place on April 25, 1877, at 10 a.m.[286]

PROCESSION

At the conclusion of the service, promptly at 11 a.m., the procession began on King Street. Under the direction of the funeral marshal, William Moehonua, assisted by W.C. Parke, the marshal of the Kingdom, the funeral procession displayed the full participation of the various elements of the government and military headed by his brother, the king. For Parke, the procession represented the twentieth state funeral conducted during his career,[287] which started on June 1, 1850. The *Pacific Commercial Advertiser* published the full listing of funeral participants:

> Order of Procession | for | The Funeral | of | His Late Royal Highness, Prince William Pitt Leleiohoku Kalahoolewa. | [*rule*] | Cavalry. | Undertaker of His Late Royal Highness. | Honolulu Fire Department. | Hawaiian Mechanics' Benefits Union. | Improved Order of Red Men | Knights of Pythias. | Independent Order of Odd Fellows. | Order of Free and Accepted Masons | Members of Medical Faculty. | Physicians of His late Royal Highness. | The Governor of Maui and Staff. | Military Escort. | Clergy of Protestant Churches. | Clergy of the Roman Catholic Church. Choir of the Hawaiian Cathedral. | Officiating Clergy. | His Lordship the Right Reverend Bishop of Honolulu. | The Horse of His late Royal Highness. | Large Kahilis. | Ahahui Poola Drawing the Hearse. | Large Kahilis. Small Kahilis. Pall Bearers. [*cut of coffin*] Pall Bearers. Small Kahilis. Large Kahilis.| Large Kahilis. Carriage bearing Their Majesties the King and Queen [Kalākaua and Kapiʻolani], and | Her Highness Ruth Keelikolani. | Carriage bearing Their Royal Highnesses the Princess Lydia | Kamakaeha Liliuokalani and the Princess Miriam | Likelike, His E. Gov. Dominis, and | the Hon. A.S. Cleghorn. | Carriage bearing the Queen Dowager. | Carriage bearing the Hon. Mrs. Bernice Pauahi and Honora- | ble Charles R. Bishop. | Carriages bearing the Ladies of the Court. | Chancellor of the Kingdom. | His Majesty's Ministers. | Members of the Diplomatic Corps and Commander of H.B. | M.'s S. Fantome. | Judges of the Supreme Court. | Governors of the different Islands. | Members of the House of Nobles. | Members of the Privy Council of State. | Consular Corps and Officers of H.B.M.'s S. Fantome. | Circuit Judges. | Members of the House of Representatives. | Clerks of Government Departments. | Custom House Officers and Officers of the Customs. | Marshal and Sheriffs of the several Islands., | Ahahui Hoola Lahui. | The Konohikis and Tenants of His Late Royal Highness. | Servants of His Late Royal Highness. | Teachers and Pupils of the several schools. | The Public Generally. | Police Force.
>
> [*pointing hand*] The funeral will take place on WEDNESDAY, the 25th of April. The Procession will be formed on King Street, opposite the Palace, at 10 o'clock a.m. and will move punctually at 11 a.m.
>
> Office of the Governor of Oahu,
> Honolulu, April 18, 1877.[288]

The HMS *Fantome*, a British vessel, had been launched in 1873.

By the time of the funeral of Leleiohoku II, two lodges of the I.O.O.F existed, the Excelsior Lodge No. 1, and the Harmony Lodge No. 3. Whether the lodges marched together is not known. The procession included the first appearance of the Knights of Pythias, founded 1871. As *hānai* mother of Leleiohoku, Keʻelikōlani rode with the ruling monarch, David Kalākaua, brother of Leleiohoku.

The *Hawaiian Gazette* described the marks of royalty displayed during the procession and exclusive to Hawaiian royalty: "On either side of the hearse waved a large number of stately Kahilis, the unique and ancient symbols of Hawaiian royalty, of various sizes and composed of feathers of various hues from jet black, rich purple, and brilliant green and scarlet, to pure white."[289] The vivid description captures an element sadly lost in the black-and-white photographs of the time.

Also present in the procession were kukui nut torches burning in daylight, the symbol of descendants of Iwikauikaua.

BURIAL

The burial took place at the Royal Mausoleum, with Leleiohoku being the first member of the new dynasty to be interred at what had formerly been considered the tomb of the Kamehamehas. As *hānai* son of Princess Ruth Keʻelikōlani he would have qualified for burial in a tomb for members of the Kamehameha dynasty.

COSTS

The first funeral for a member of the new dynasty lacked the extravagance that marked subsequent royal funerals during the reign of Kalakaua. The funeral costs for Leleiohoku totaled $8,414.62.[290]

Fanny Kekelaokalani Young (1880)

Another death of a parent of a monarch of the previous dynasty took place when Fanny Kekelaokalani Young died in 1880 at the age of 74 years. Fanny Kekelaokalani was born on July 21, 1806, in Kawaihae, on the island of Hawaiʻi, the daughter of John Young and Kaʻōanaʻeha. She married George Naea, and bore him a daughter, Emma, who would later marry Alexander Liholiho, who reigned as Kamehameha IV.

PROCESSION

The Order of Procession gave the full name of Queen Emma's mother: Her Grace the Late Fanny Young Kekelaokalani Kekuaipoiwa Kailikulani

Leleoili Kulua. The familiar form was published in the *Pacific Commercial Advertiser*:

> Band. | Undertaker. | The Public Schools. Law Students. | Honolulu Fire Department. | Free Masons. | Independent Order of Odd Fellows. | Knights of Pythias | Order of Red Men | Ancient Order of Foresters. | Knights of Jerusalem. | Mechanics' Benefit Union. | Attending Physicians. | Konohikis, Tenants and Retainers of the Estates of Her | Majesty Queen Dowager. | Household Servants of the Queen. | The Choirs of All Churches. | The Protestant Clergy. | The Roman Catholic Clergy. | The Clergy of the Reformed Catholic Church. | His Lordship the Bishop of Honolulu. | Four Banners. | Large Kahilis. | Small Kahilis.| The Ahahui Poola. | Ahahui Opiopio. | Large Kahilis. Small Kahilis. Pall Bearers. [*cut of casket*] Pall Bearers. Small Kahilis. Large Kahilis. | Small Kahilis. | Large Kahilis. | Her Majesty Queen Dowager Emma Kaleleonalani. | Carriage bearing Hons. P.Y. Kaeo and A.K. Kunuiakea. | His Majesty's Carriage. | Carriage bearing Her Highness Ruth Keelikolani. | Four Banners. | The King's Chancellor. | The Cabinet. | Governors of the Different Islands. | Representatives of Foreign Powers. | Privy Councillors. | Judges of the Supreme Court | Members of the Legislative Assembly. | Consular Corps. | Honolulu Merchants. | Government Officers. | Members of the Bar. | Foreign Residents. | The Public. | The Police. |[291]

Unlike other processions, this one lacked the Marshal of the Kingdom. Honolulu merchants made their first and last appearance in the funeral procession of Kekelaokalani. The Ancient Order of Foresters made its inaugural appearance in a procession. The friendly society had been organized a year earlier, on July 17, 1879, by David Kalākaua and John M. Kapena, among others, as Court Lunalilo, No. 6600, Ancient Order of Foresters.[292] The Knights of Jerusalem, founded the same year as the Foresters, also participated for the first time.

Though the procession included Roman Catholic clergy, the bishop was not included in the list by title. The omission may be related to the health of the bishop. Because of his illness, in August 1881, Hermann Koeckemann had been ordained as Bishop of Olba to help with the duties of bishop as co-adjutor.

The Order of Procession ended with time and place at which the participants begin the funeral march: "The funeral will take place on Sunday, the 3rd of October. The procession is to be formed on Nuuanu Street, in front of Luka Hale [Rooke House] at 1:30 p.m., and will move punctually at 2:30 p.m."[293] Since the Luka Hale and the Royal Mausoleum were both on Nuuanu Street, no further directions regarding the route were necessary.

Peter Young Kaeo (1880)

Another relative of Queen Emma died shortly following Kekelaokalani. Peter Young Kaeo, grandson of John Young (Olohana), died at 10 p.m. on Friday, November 26, 1879, at his residence on Emma Street.[294] Through his mother he was a cousin of Queen Emma. His mother, Jane Lahilahi, was sister of Fanny Kekelaokalani, the mother of Queen Emma. Through his father, Joshua Kaeo, he was "a descendant of the high chiefs of Kauai."[295] He was a member of the House of Nobles from 1863 until his death. For a time he was sent to Moloka'i, but the board of health later determined that he was free of disease and he returned to O'ahu. While on Moloka'i he actively corresponded with his cousin, Queen Emma. His death did not result in the cancellation of the Independence Day holiday, November 27, as had occurred after the death of Leleiohoku in 1848.

FUNERAL

No description of his funeral exists, other than the report in the *Hawaiian Gazette* noting that the funeral was "largely attended by the retainers and friends of the family."[296]

PROCESSION

Although no known published Order of Procession exists, contemporaneous accounts point to the usual accouterments associated with royal processions. The *Hawaiian Gazette* recorded: "The hearse was surrounded by Kahili bearers as becomes the dignity of a chief."[297] The *Saturday Press* contained the same detail, noting: "the hearse was surrounded by *kahilis* as is customary on the burial of a chief."[298] Interestingly, the procession of his uncle, Keoni Ana, fourteen years earlier, had featured no *kāhili* despite his service as Kuhina Nui.

The carriage of Queen Emma escorted the hearse to Mauna 'Ala. The *Saturday Press* noted: "it seemed doubly trying to be again engaged in the sad task of accompanying the remains of a dear friend and relation to the tomb."[299]

BURIAL

Kaeo, also known as Kekuokalani, was buried on the afternoon of Sunday, November 28, 1880. Although no detailed account of the burial exists, the *Pacific Commercial Advertiser* reported he "was buried with appropriate honors."[300]

Timing may have had an impact on the public observance of his death and funeral, since the death took place on the Sunday following the observance of a national holiday. The anniversary of National Independence actually fell on the same day as the funeral, November 28, but was observed on Saturday, November 27.[301] The funeral, too, took place less than two months following the obsequies for Queen Emma's mother, Kekelaokalani. The *Saturday Press* especially noted the impact of the death of Peter Young Kaeo on Queen Emma so soon after the death of her mother: "Queen Emma is greatly distressed at the loss of this, her near relative and well beloved cousin. Her Majesty had so recently been called upon to mourn over her bereavement, on the occasion of the death of her mother."[302]

Ruth Keanolani Kanahoahoa Ke'elikōlani (1883)

Ruth Keanolani Kanahoahoa Ke'elikōlani was born in Honolulu, on February 9, 1826, the daughter of Pauahi and Mataio Kekūanaō'a. Pauahi was the daughter of Kaoleioku, the son of Kamehameha I and Kanekapolei. Ke'elikōlani married William Pitt Leleiohoku, son of Kalanimoku, with whom she had a son named John William Pitt Kīna'u. Her husband died on October 21, 1848 and she married Isaac Young Davis. Her son, Kīna'u, was born on December 22, 1859. With Davis she had another son, Keolaokalani, who became the *hānai* son of Bernice Pauahi Bishop. She served in the House of Nobles from 1845 to 1855, and as governor of the island of Hawai'i from January 15, 1855 to February 23, 1872, then from March 30, 1872 to March 2, 1874.

Ruth Ke'elikōlani, half-sister of Kamehameha IV, Kamehameha V and Victoria Kamāmalu, died at 9 a.m., on Thursday, May 24, 1883,[303] in her *hale pili* in Kailua, on the island of Hawai'i, after being visited by her cousin, Princess Bernice Pauahi Bishop, and sister-in-law, Queen Emma. As *hānai* mother of Leleiohoku II, the brother of King Kalākaua, she had closer ties with the new dynasty. The court displayed the marks of mourning starting on May 31, 1883. C.H. Judd, His Majesty's Chamberlain

Princess Ruth Ke'elikōlani was half-sister of Kamehameha IV, Kamehameha V and Victoria Kamāmalu (courtesy Hawaii State Archives [PP-97-18-012]).

announced in the *Daily Bulletin*: "The Court will go into Full Mourning for Her late Royal Highness the Princess Ruth Keelikolani from the date of this notice, until the day after the funeral; and will wear half mourning from that time until expiration of the two weeks from the day of the funeral."[304]

LYING IN STATE

The lying in state occurred on June 1, 1883, from 1 to 5 p.m. at her home on Emma street.[305] The *Pacific Commercial Advertiser* described the scene in the next day's issue: "The casket containing the remains was placed in the elegant drawing room mauka of the hall leading from the main front entrance of the mansion. Four attendants, each bearing kāhili were disposed on either side of the catafalc which was covered with wreaths of flowers."[306]

As with the death of her first husband, Leleiohoku, the death of Keʻelikōlani resulted in the postponement of a national holiday. The celebration of Kamehameha Day moved from June 11 to June 18, 1883.[307]

The observances for Keʻelikōlani, as with most of the other royal obse-

Keʻelikolani died in her *hale pili* that stood on the grounds of Huliheʻe Palace in Kailua, Kona (courtesy Hawaii State Archives [PP-32-2-022]).

quies, retained ancient elements, including most audibly, the wailing and funeral dirges. The extent of the custom was reported in the *Daily Bulletin*: "On Friday night [June 16, 1883] there was much wailing for Her late Highness Ruth to be heard. The dismal sounds seemed to spread from one quarter of the city to the other. At midnight the Kawaihau Club song [*sic*] several dirges composed by themselves at Kaakopua Hale."[308] The Hui Kawaihau had been organized in 1876 by Leleiohoku, the *hānai* son of Keʻelikōlani.[309]

FUNERAL

The funeral service for Keʻelikōlani took place on Sunday, June 17, 1883, not at the stone church, Kawaiahaʻo, but at her residence, Kaakopua Hale. The service, nevertheless, was conducted by the pastor of Kawaiahaʻo Church, the Rev. H.H. Parker, and featured dirges sung by the church's choir.[310] Although the procession after the service passed directly by the Anglican cathedral, the service did not use the rite of the church that had been established by the half-brother of Ruth, Kamehameha IV, and Queen Emma.

PROCESSION

An Order of Procession appeared the *Pacific Commercial Advertiser* on June 16, 1883:

Order of Procession | for | The Funeral | of | Her late Royal Highness | Ruth Keelikolani. | [rule] | Undertaker, | Marshal of the Kingdom, | Mechanic's Benefit Union. | Honolulu Fire Department, | Attending Physicians, | Konohiki of Lands of Her late Royal | Highness, | His Excellency the Governor of Oahu | and Maui and Staff, | Band, | Marines from U.S.S. Hartford, | Mamalahoa, | King's Own, | Prince's Own, | King's Guard, | Servants of Her late Royal Highness, | The Clergy of the Roman Catholic | Church, | His Lordship the Right Reverend | Bishop of Olba, Vicar Apostolic | of the Hawaiian Islands, | The Clergy of the Anglican Church | in Hawaii, | His Lordship the Right Reverend | Bishop of Honolulu, | Protestant Clergy, | Officiating Clergyman, | Ahahui Opiopio Puuwai Lokahi, | Ahahui Poola, | Escort of Cavalry, Large Kahilis, Small Kahilis. Pall Bearers. [*cut of coffin*] Pall Bearers. Small Kahilis, Large Kahilis, Escort of Cavalry. | Carriage of the Honorable Mrs. B.P. | Bishop, | Carriage of Her Majesty, the Queen | Dowager | Carriage of Her Majesty the Queen, | His Majesty's Staff, | Carriage of Her Royal Highness the | Princess Liliuokalani, | Carriage of Her Royal Highness the | Princess Likelike, | Carriage of Her Royal Highness Prin- | cess Pomaikelani, | Carriage of Her Royal Highness Prin- | cess Kekaulike, | Carriage of Her Royal Highness the | Chancellor, | His Majesty's Ministers, | Diplomatic Corps, | Nobles, | Judges of the Supreme Court, | Privy Councillors, | Consular Corps, Captain and Officers of | U.S.S. Hart-ford, | Circuit Judges, | Clerks of Government Departments, | Collector –General of Customs, Cus- | tom-house Officers and Officers || of the Customs. | Sheriffs of the different Islands, |

Royal Deaths During the Kalākaua Dynasty 109

The funeral of Princess Ruth Keʻelikōlani took place in her residence called Keōua Hale, in a room just *mauka* of the main entrance (courtesy Hawaii State Archives [PP 92-10-004]).

Members of the Bar, | Foreign Residents, | Hawaiian Population Generally, | Hawaiian Cavalry, | Police Force.
[*pointing hand*] The Procession will form at 2 o'clock p.m. SUNDAY the 17th instant on Emma Street. Those who precede the Catafalque, will form between Beretania street and Emma Square, and those who are to follow on Emma street *mauka* of the residence of the late Royal Highness.
The Procession will start at 3 o'clock p.m. precisely, and will proceed through Beretania street to Nuuanu street to the Royal Mausoleum.
The Procession will be under the direction of the Governor of Oahu and Maui.
KAAKOPUA HALE, June 11, 1883.[311]

The actual participants may have changed by the day of the funeral, because the list of participants in the procession in the *Hawaiian Gazette*, published on June 20, 1883, after the funeral, differed slightly from the one that appeared earlier:

Undertaker. | Mounted Police. | Two Platoons Foot-Police. | Marshal of the Kingdom. | Reformatory School Band. | Engineers, Fire Department, | Honolulu Fire Department. | Governor of Oahu. | Aides. | Band of U.S.S. Hartford. | Guard of Marines from U.S.S. Hartford. | Mamalahoa Guard. | "King's Own" Guard. | "Prince's Own" Guard | Household Troops.| Hawaiian Military Band. | Konohikis and Servants of the Princess. | Clergy of the Anglican Church. | Officiating Clergy.| Poola Society, 200 strong, drawing funeral carriage. | Escort of Hawaiian Cavalry Large Kahilis Small Kahilis Pall Bearers [rectangle] Small Kahilis Large Kahilis Escort of Hawaiian Cavalry. | Chief Mourners (Hon. Mrs. & Mr. C.R. Bishop.) | H.M.Q. Dowager Emma. | Col. Boyd and Col. G.W. Macfarlane. | H.R.H. Princess Lydia | H.R.H. Princess Likelike. | Carriages of the Princesses Poomaikelani & Kekaulike. | Chancellor of the Kingdom. | His Majesty's Ministers. | His Ex. The American Minister Resident | Captain & Officers of the U.S.S. Hartford. | Judges of the Supreme Court. | Members of the House of Nobles. | Government Officials. | Miscellaneous Carriages. | Cavalry.[312]

Reappearance of Military Units

The military units made their reappearance by name in funeral processions in the obsequies for Princess Ruth. Her cousin, King Lunalilo, had disbanded the Household Troops after the mutiny in September 1873. King Kalākaua issued General Order Number One in February 1874 that reestablished one regular company (Royal Guard), and three volunteer companies (Hawaiian Guards, infantry; Leleiohoku Guard, cavalry; and Prince's Own, artillery). The Mamalahoa Guard made its first appearance in the procession of Princess Ruth. Its name is derived from name of a company of warriors of Kamehameha I, and also the Law of the Splintered Paddle, Māmala hoe or hoa. "By order of Kalakaua on June 30, 1874, the Mamalahoas were authorized as a volunteer militia unit."[313]

The Reform School was located across King Street from the Kapālama house of Keʻelikōlani. She had previously invited the school's band to play at her residence.

The published Order of Procession fails to capture the grandeur or scope of the event. While the list indicated the position of the "Large Kahilis, Small Kahilis," the *Daily Bulletin* reported: "No less than 84 kahilis, large and small, were carried beside the hearse." The length, too, cannot be gauged by the printed order. The length of Nuuanu from Beretania to the Royal Mausoleum is a mile and a quarter. The *Daily Bulletin* reported that the "procession was about a mile and a quarter long and took 30 minutes to pass a given point."[314]

Burial

"The services at the Mausoleum were simple and short consisting of a prayer by the Rev. Mr. Parker and a dirge by the Kawaiahao Choir. On the coffin was placed a beautiful crown of flowers made by Mrs. J.A. Carter and some handsome wreaths. Two hundred of the Poola association drew the hearse. The path of the procession was strewn with rushes."[315]

Princess Victoria Kūhiō Kinoiki Kekaulike (1884)

Princess Victoria Kūhiō Kinoiki Kekaulike, born May 12, 1843, the daughter of Kalaniana'ole Kūhiō and Kinoiki. She was a descendant of Kaumualii, the last king of Kaua'i. Kekaulike married High Chief David Kahalepouli Pi'ikoi in 1861. She served as governor of the island of Hawai'i from September 2, 1880. The sister of Queen Kapi'olani, she was given her title at the coronation of King Kalākaua on February 12, 1883. She would die less than a year later, at age 40, on January 8, 1884, at her Makiki residence called Ululani.

As the sister-in-law of the reigning monarch, Princess Kekaulike would receive a state funeral befitting her rank and relation. Her three children, David Kawānanakoa, 16; Edward Keliihonua, 15; and Jonah Kūhiō Kalaniana'ole, 13; would be left without parents; her husband David Kahalepouli Piikoi had died four years earlier. The three princes would be sent to military school in California the year after the funeral.

Princess Kekaulike was sister of Queen Kapi'olani (courtesy Hawaii State Archives [PP-97-19-001]).

The mourning period for court lasted four weeks, with another two weeks of "half mourning."[316]

The Chamberlain's Office issued the Order of Procession on January 10, 1884:

Order of Procession | for | Her late Royal Highness | Mary K. Kekaulike, | Governess of the Island Of Hawaii | [rule] | Undertaker | Marshal of the Kingdom. | Mechanics' Benefit Union. | Honolulu Fire Department. | Attending Physicians. | Konohikis of Lands of Her late Royal Highness. Major Kinimaka and Aids. | Band. | Mamalahoa | King's Own. | Prince's Own. | King's Guard. | Servants of Her late Royal Highness. | Protestant Clergy | The Clergy of the Roman Catholic Church. | His Lordship, the Right Rev. Bishop of Olba | Vicar Apostolic of the Hawaiian Islands. | His Lordship, the Right Rev. Bishop of Honolulu. | Officiating Clergy. | Ahahui Opiopio Puuwai

Lokahi. | Ahahui Poola | Escort of Cavalry. Large Kahilis. Small Kahilis. Pall Bearers. [*cut of coffin*] Pall Bearers. Small Kahilis. Large Kahilis. Escort of Cavalry. | Chief Mourners. | Carriage of Her Majesty the Queen. | Carriage of Her Majesty the Queen Dowager | Carriage of Her Royal Highness the Princess Liliuokalani. | Carriage of Her Royal Highness the Princess Likelike. | The Chancellor | His Majesty's Ministers. | Diplomatic Corps. | Nobles. | Judges of the Supreme Court. | Privy Councillors. | Consular Corps. | Circuit Judges. | Clerks of Government Departments. | [Inspector General of Customs, Custom House | Officers and Officers of Customs. | Sheriffs of the different Islands. | Members of the Bar. | Foreign Residents. | Hawaiian Population Generally. | Hawaiian Cavalry. | Police Force. |

The Procession will form at 1.30 o'clock p.m. Sunday the 13th instant, on Beretania Street. Those who are to precede the catafalque will form on the west side entrance to the residence of Her late Royal Highness.

The Procession will start at 2 o'clock p.m. precisely, and will proceed through Beretania Street to Nuuanu Street to the Royal Mausoleum. The Procession will be under the direction of Major D.L. Kinimaka.

CHAMBERLAIN'S OFFICE, January 10, 1884 [Broadside Scrap Book, HHS, 47].

Queen Kapiʻolani would represent the crown in the procession for her sister, Princess Kekaulike.

The Roman Catholic bishop, the Rev. Hermann Koeckemann, made his first appearance in a royal funeral procession. He was known by the title Bishop of Olba, an extinct see in what is today southern Turkey. Today Olba is called Oura.

COST

The cost of the funeral for Kekaulike amounted to $1,931.36.[317]

Bernice Pauahi Bishop (1884)

Bernice Pauahi Bishop died on October 16, 1884, at Keōua Hale, the house she had inherited from her cousin Ruth Keʻelikōlani. She was born in Honolulu on December 19, 1831, the daughter of Abner Pākī and Kōnia. She was the *hānai* daughter of Kīnaʻu, who would become Kuhina Nui seven months after her birth. Eligible for the throne, Princess Bernice Pauahi attended the Chiefs' Children's School. She married Charles Reed Bishop on June 5, 1851. Though she did not attend the coronation of King David Kalākaua, Bishop nevertheless received a state funeral.

An announcement of her death, printed on a card, read: "In Loving Remembrance of | The Hon. Bernice Pauahi Bishop, | Wife of Hon. Charles Reed Bishop, | Died at her Residence (Keoua Hale) Honolulu, October 16th, A.D. 1884. | [*rule*] | "Into thine hand I commit my spirit: thou hast redeemed me, O Lord God of truth."[318] The inclusion of a Bible verse with the announcement of death was rare. The verse from Psalm 31:5 came from the Authorized (King James) Version.

Lili'uokalani wrote a chant for the funeral of her *hānai* sister, Bernice Pauahi Bishop, the text taken from the book of Job. Unlike the *kanikau* she had written for her brother, Leleiohoku, the chant[319] for Bishop was a Hawaiian translation of Hymn 1134,[320] from Henry Ward Beecher's *Plymouth Collection*, set to a chant tune composed by Charles Beecher.[321] Lili'uokalani prefaces the English translation with the verse reference to Job 14:14, which reads in the Authorized (King James) Version: "If a man die, shall he live again? All the days of my appointed time will I wait, till my change come." The hymn text comes directly from the Bible text, though some stanzas leave out portions of the Bible verses. The stanza numbers and Bible sources are: 1, Job 14:14; 2, Job 14:7; 3, 14:8a and 14:9; 4, 14:10; 5, 14:11a and 12a; 6, 14:13; and 7, 19:25, 26.

Princess Bernice Pauahi Bishop died shortly after her cousin, Princess Ruth Ke'elikōlani (courtesy Hawaii State Archives [PP-96-1-001]).

PROCESSION

The Order of Procession appeared in the *Hawaiian Gazette* on October 29, 1884, in the "New Advertisements" column rather than the "By Authority" column:

> Order of Procession | for | the Funeral | of | the late Honorable | Mrs. Bernice Pauahi Bishop | [*rule*] | Undertaker. | Marshal of the Kingdom. | Mechanic's [Mechanics' in *Daily Bulletin*] Benefit Union. | Independent Order of Odd Fellows. | Ahahui Opiopio Puuwai Lokahi. | Ahahui Poola. | Ahahui Opiopio Imi Pono Kristiano o Kaumakapili. | Attending Physicians. | Konohikis of Lands of the Late Mrs. Bishop. | Governor of Oahu and Staff. | Band. | Namalahoa. | King's Own. | Prince's Own. | King's Guard. | Servants of the Deceased. | The Clergy of the Roman Catholic Church. | Monseigneur The Right Reverend Bishop of Olba | Vicar-Apostolic of the Hawaiian Islands. | The Clergy of the Anglican Church. | The Right Reverend the Bishop of Honolulu. | Protestant Clergy. | Escort of Cavalry, Large Kahilis, Small Kahilis, Pall

Bearers [*cut of coffin*] Pall Bearers, Small Kahilis, Large Kahilis, Escort of Cavalry. | Carriage of the Chief Mourner. | Carriages of Mourners. | Carriage of Her Majesty the Queen. | His Majesty's Staff. | Carriage of Her Royal Highness the Princess Likelike. | Carriage of Her Royal Highness Princess Pomaikelani.[*sic*] [Poomaikelani in *Daily Bulletin*]| The Chancellor. | His Majesty's Ministers. | Diplomatic Corps. | Nobles. | Judges of the Supreme Court. | Privy Councillors. | Consular Corps. | Circuit Judges. | Clerks of Government Departments. | Collector General of Customs. Custom House Officers and Officers of the Customs. | Sheriffs of the different Islands. | Members of the Bar. | Foreign Residents. | Hawaiian Population Generally. | Hawaiian Cavalry.

The Procession will form at 1 o'clock p.m., Sunday, the 2nd prox., on Emma Street.

Those who are to precede the Catafalque, will form between Beretania Street and Emma Square, and those who are to follow, on Emma Street *mauka* of the Residence of Mr. Bishop.

The procession will start at 2 o'clock p.m. precisely, and will proceed through Beretania Street, thence to the Royal Mausoleum.

The Procession will be under the direction of the Governor of Oahu and Maui. Keoua Hale, October 24th, 1884.[322]

The crown was represented by Queen Kapiʻolani alone.

"Last Sunday's [November 2, 1884] state funeral procession was the seventeenth that has taken place under the direction of Governor John Dominis. It is more than coincident—it is almost phenomenal—that each of these should have fair—or at least not stormy weather, and that during the progress of each there should have been a foreign vessel in port."[323] Dominis served as Governor of Oʻahu from February 18, 1864, to October 4, 1886.

The *Saturday Press* recorded the route of the procession: "The line of march was along Emma to Beretania, to Nuuanu to the Royal Mausoleum."[324]

Funeral

"On Saturday night, while a few fast friends of the dead chiefess [...] were in the funeral chamber, a special mourning service was arranged by natives. The finest large kahilis, 27 in number, were brought in and placed around the bier and in the corners of the room. The gass jets were turned low, the kahili wavers stood as if carved from stone, the natives crowded into the open hall ways, the few close friends sat silent, and on the westward porch a group of native singes began a series of meles to Pauahi's memory."[325] The formal funeral was brief, consisting of the Rev. H. Parker's "prayer and remarks in Hawaiian."[326] The procession went from the Bishop home on Emma Street to the Royal Mausoleum. After another short service, the coffin of Pauahi was placed between the coffins of Keʻelikōlani and Leleiohoku.[327] Today, coffin of Bernice Pauahi Bishop is located in the Kamehameha Tomb.

Queen Emma (1885)

Queen Emma, the widow of Kamehameha IV, who had opposed Kalākaua in the election of 1874, and boycotted his coronation along with Princess Ruth Keʻelikōlani and Bernice Pauahi Bishop, died during his reign on April 25, 1885, at her house at Nuʻuanu and Beretania streets. She was born in Honolulu on January 2, 1836, the daughter of Fanny Kekelaokalani and George Naea. She was the *hānai* daughter of Grace Kamaʻikuʻi Young and Thomas Charles Byde Rooke. She married Kamehameha IV on June 19, 1856.

LYING IN STATE

The lying in state integrated a mix of traditional Hawaiian and Western signs of mourning. As in ancient times, the lying in state for Queen Emma included elements that had not been banned by Keōpūolani. There were "wailing women and wailing men" and during the around the clock vigil, "kahili wavers stood or sat beside the dead Queen's coffin that lay in state in the same room where—28 years and 10 months before—she had been dressed for her royal nuptials."[328] The ancient traditions persisted, as a "white-haired old woman stood at the foot of the coffin and chanted the praise of the dead chief."

The Western elements, too, showed the extravangence of a royal funeral. Befitting Queen Emma and her role in establishing the Anglican church in Hawaiʻi, the "coffin was covered with a splendid pall. It had been made by the Anglican sisterhood in 1861, to cover the remains of the Prince of Hawaiʻi. A year later it was enlarged and lay on the coffin of Kamehameha IV. Now it reposes—with all its regal embroidery and all its royal pomp—over all that is mortal of Emma Kaleleonalani, the last link that binds the nation to the lineage of the conquering Kamehamehas."[329] Her ties with British royalty were reflected in the presence of "large silver vase presented to Queen Emma by Queen Victoria."[330] The lying in state also displayed elements of ancient pomp, especially in the presence of the ancient royal standards, the *kāhili*. The description of her lying in state included a detailed catalogue of the marks of Hawaiian royalty:

> The Queen's special kahilis, "Malulani," by name, two that had once been one titanic one, stood at the coffin's head. It was made from feathers taken from the oo bird. At the sides of the coffin stood two tall kahilis, enveloped in tapa, and mounted on kauwila staffs. They had also come down from the ancient days in which they heralded the approach of royalty or sovereign chieftaincy. Within those tapa folds were human bones 'twas said. When—in those good old days some people are so fond of lamenting—"common folk" saw those tapa folds approaching, gentlemen who repine about

116   1. Royal Deaths

The *Illustrated London News* showed Queen Emma lying in state at Rooke House.

these degenerate days—to prostrate themselves upon their faces and remain in that position until the royal presence had passed. Two smaller kahilis of red feathers stood by the two kalilis of tapa. At the foot of the coffin stood a large black kāhili, in token of mourning. [...] There were 44 kahilis of the Queen's own estate standing in the hall way when the preparations for removing the coffin to Kawaiahao Church were completed.[331]

Funeral

The funeral consisted of two services. The first by Henry H. Parker featured a eulogy. In his address Parker asked: "How did it come about that the late Queen Dowager held so supreme a place in the hearts of this people? I answer, she loved the people. Love begets love."[332] "If with All Your Heart," from Mendelssohn's *Elijah* was sung to conclude the service. The Anglican service started a 1 p.m.

Procession

Additions and deletions in the Order of Procession resulted in the distribution of a circular, dated May 11, 1885, from Walter M. Gibson, the Minister of Foreign Affairs, regarding "Certain Changes in the Arrangements for the Funeral of Her late Majesty the Queen Dowager Emma Kaleleonalani."

The Order of Procession published before the funeral and after differed in several places. The one printed following the obsequies[333] omitted the fraternal societies, the clergy and bishop of the Roman Catholic Church. It also explicitly referred to the first band as the Reformatory School Band and the second band as the Royal Hawaiian Band. It also added the Governor of Oahu Jail.

The final Order of Procession comprised:

Undertaker. | Deputy Marshal. | Police. | Marshal of the Kingdom. | Cavalry. | Band. | Queen's Own. | Mechanics' Benefit Union. | Honolulu Fire Department. | Governor of Oahu. | Governor's Staff. | Band. | Detachment of Sailors and Marines from | H.I.R.M.S. Corvette Djighit. | Honolulu Rifles. | Mamalahoa. | Prince's Own. | King's Own. | King's Guard. | Geo. W. DeLong Post No. 45, G.A.R. | St. Andrew's Priory Girls' School, with | Sisters. | Servants of the Deceased. | Protestant Clergy | The Clergy of the Roman Catholic | Church. | Monseigneur the Right Reverend Bishop | of Olba, Vicar Apostolic of the | Hawaiian Islands. | The Clergy of the Anglican Church. | The Right Reverend Bishop of | Honolulu. | Three boys carrying floral pillow, crown | and cross. | Officer Bearing Decorations and Jewels | of Her late Majesty. | Officer Bearing Crown. | Ahahui Pauwai Lokahi. | Ahahui Poola. | Escort of Cavalry. Large Kahilis. Small Kahilis. Pall Bearers. [cut of coffin] Pall Bearers. Small Kahilis. Large Kahilis. Escort of Cavalry. | Carriage of Chief Mourners. | Carriage of His Majesty. | His Majesty's Staff. | Carriage of Her Royal Highness Prin- | cess Liliuokalani. | Carriage of Her Royal Highness Prin- | cess Likelike. | Carriage of Her

Lack of a suitably sized Anglican location meant that the funeral service for Queen Emma took place at Kawaiahaʻo Church (courtesy Hawaii State Archives [PP-25-3-005]).

Hawaiian military members in the procession display the presentation of arms "in reverse," in this case their rifles over both shoulders (courtesy Hawaii State Archives [PP-25-3-013]).

Royal Highness Prin- | cess Pomai-kelani. | The Chancellor. | His Majesty's Ministers. | Diplomatic Corps, Admiral Upshur and | Staff. | Members of the House of Nobles. | Judges of the Supreme Court. | Privy Councilors. | Consular Corps. | Officers of H.I.R.M.S. Djighit | Circuit Judges. | Post Master General. | Collector General of Customs. | Sheriffs of the Different Islands. | Clerks of Government Departments. | Custom House Officers and Officers of | the Customs. | Members of the Bar. | Foreign Residents | Hawaiian Population Generally. | Police Force.[334]

The Hawaiian military displayed the use of arms "in reverse." Prominent in the procession were the fraternal and benefit societies. The Mechanic's Benefit Union made its tenth appearance. Another volunteer organization, the Honolulu Fire Department, was founded in 1850 by Kamehameha III and Alexander Cartwright.

The Improved Order of Red Men, ironically open only to the "free white male of good moral character and standing," descended from patriotic groups formed during the Revolutionary War.[335] The Ancient Order of

Foresters was a British friendly society started in Yorkshire in 1834. The Hawaiian Tribe No. 1 of the Improved Order of Red Men, started 1874, had several prominent individuals including Kalākaua, Dominis and John M. Kapena.[336]

The American Legion of Honor, not to be confused with the World War I veterans organization called the American Legion, was founded as a fraternal benefit society founded in Boston in 1878. The Order of Knights of Pythias was an international fraternal order founded in 1864 in Washington, D.C.[337] The Independent Order of Odd Fellows, with its motto of "Friendship, Love and Truth," was begun in the U.S. in Baltimore, Maryland, in 1819. The procession also included the first appearance of the George W. De Long Post of the Grand Army of the Republic for the funeral of Queen Emma. Relatively new, the organization of United States Civil War veterans had started in Hawai'i in September 1882.

Following the Governor of O'ahu, John O. Dominis, and his staff were the military component of the procession. First came the sailor and marines from the Russian corvette *Djighit*. In 1879 His Imperial Russian Majesty's Clipper *Djiguitt* had dropped torpedoes at the entrance of Honolulu Harbor to help deepen. Samuel G. Wilder expressed to Capt. K. de Livron: "It being at all times, to extend hospitality to the Officers of a Russian National Vessel."[338] A different officer, Capt. de Muller, commanded the ship in 1885. Next was the all-white Honolulu Rifles, which two years later would help persuade Kalākaua to sign the "Bayonet" Constitution.

The religious component of the procession featured the clergy from the Protestant, and Anglican churches including the bishop of the Anglican church. As a youth Queen Emma had studied under the Protestant missionaries at the Chiefs' Children's School; with her husband, Kamehameha IV, she had invited the Church of England to send clergy to Hawaii. Emma's funeral made the first conspicuous display of jewels, a presentation that would be repeated in the processions of Likelike, Keliiahonui, Kalakaua, Lili'uokalani and Elizabeth Kahanu Kalaniana'ole.

The distinctive mixture of traditional Hawaiian and Western forms of mourning received comment from the chronicler in the *Saturday Press*, who wrote: "The pageant was unique; it was a blending of savage rite and customs with the tinsel and insincerity of civilization. Such a funeral procession can be seen but in one place on earth—in Hawaii."[339]

BURIAL

The procession ended at the Royal Mausoleum at Mauna 'Ala. "The sombreness of Hawaii's royal tomb was relieved by the presence of quantities of exotic flowers, the delicate white petals, and feathery green ferns showing in startling contrast to the black palled coffins of former chiefs. The coffin rested in the anteroom, where the Bishop of Honolulu read the conclusion of the burial service."[340] The choir sang the final hymn, "Now the Laborer's Task is O'er." The hymn, written fifteen years before the queen's death by Anglican priest, John Ellerton, ends with the refrain: "Father, in Thy gracious keeping | Leave we now thy servant sleeping."

Cost

The expenses for the funeral of Queen Emma totaled $5,965.98 and were "paid by order of H.M. Government and Approved by H.M. Privy Council of State." The finance department files include a list of men and women "who were supplied with clothing on a/c of Funeral of Her Late Majesty Queen Emma." The clothes for men included 176 coats, 149 vests, 183 pairs of pants, 148 hats, and 122 pairs of shoes.[341]

The last rites of the popular Queen Emma even resulted in a publication: *Funeral Obsequies of the late Queen Dowager Emma Kaleleonalani, Relict of the late Kamehameha.*[342]

Princess Miriam Likelike (1887)

Likelike was born in Honolulu on January 13, 1851, the daughter of Kapaʻakea and Keohokālole. She married Archibald Scott Cleghorn at Washington Place, the residence of her sister, Liliʻuokalani, on September 22, 1870. She served as governor of the island of Hawaiʻi from March 29, 1879, to September 1880. Princess Likelike, sister of King Kalākaua and Princess Liliʻuokalani, and mother of Princess Kaʻiulani, died at ʻĀinahau in Waikīkī on February 2, 1887. Her funeral would be one of the most extravagant in Hawaiʻi history.

Lying in State

Likelike laid in state in the throne room of ʻIolani Palace.

Funeral

The Chamberlain's Office distributed invitations on February 22, 1885, for the funeral services of Likelike: "By command of the King, I have the honor to invite you to be present at the Funeral Services for Her Late Royal Highness Princess Likelike which will be held at Iolani Palace, on Sunday, the 27th instant, at 1 o'clock p.m."[343]

The actual funeral service was preceded by a special service at 9:30

The lying in state of Princess Likelike took place in the throne room of 'Iolani Palace (courtesy Hawaii State Archives [PP-26-4-001]).

a.m. at 'Iolani Palace with a special "verbal invitation" given to her friends. The usual Western aspects prevailed in the special service: "The coffin was covered with a black pall and there was a profusion of beautiful flowers." Indeed, the Church of England, dominated that morning: "The morning service of the Anglican ritual with special psalms was impressively read by the Rev. Alexander Mackintosh. The canticles and the hymn, 'Forever with the Lord,' were sung by the usual quartette choir, while the hymn, 'Nearer My God to Thee' was sung in Hawaiian by the Kawaihau Club."[344] The latter hymn was translated into Hawaiian by Laiana, the Hawaiian name for Lorenzo Lyons, who was called the "Isaac Watts of Hawaii." The first stanza went:

> E pili i ou la wau, E kuu Iesu
> Ina kue mai i'au Ko keia ao,
> Ku'u mele oia mau.
> E pili i ou la wau,
> E pili i ou la wau,
> E kuu Iesu.[345]

The funeral service took place in the Throne Room of 'Iolani Palace at 1 p.m. King Kalākaua, Queen Kapiolani, Princess Lili'uokalani, and

Princess Poomaikelani sat on the dais with the chief mourners, A.S. Cleghorn and Princess Kaʻiulani, at the head of the coffin.

The service music featured a chant composed by Liliʻuokalani as the setting for Psalm 90. The Kawaihau Club sang a hymn titled "Through All the Changing Scenes of Life," while several of them waved *kāhili* over the coffin.[346] The words of the hymn, from *A New Version of the Psalms of David*, fit Psalm 34 to "tunes used in churches."[347]

PROCESSION

The Adjutant General's Office issued the Order of Procession on February 21, 1887:

Order of Procession | for the | Funeral of Her late Royal Highness | Princess Likelike [rule] | Undertaker—Mr. C.E. Williams. | Platoon of Police. | Marshal—Hon. Frank Pahia [Deputy Marshal]. | St. Louis Band. | St. Louis College. | Royal School Cadets. | Cavalry. | Portuguese Band. | Portuguese Societies. | Honolulu Fire Department. Mechanics' Benefit Union. | Improved Order of Red Men. | Ancient Order of Foresters. | American Legion of Honor. | Knights of Pythias. | Geo. W. De Long Post, No.45, G.A.R. | Independent Order of Odd Fellows. | Reformatory School Band. | Church of the Latter Day Saints. | Hui Kau Lei [sp.] | Ahahui Opiopio Puuwai Lokahi. | Ahahui Poola. | Hale Haua Society. | Hoolu Lahui Society. | Nihoa Society. | Liliuokalani Mutual Benevolent Society. | Second Division, Liliuokalani Educational So- | ciety. | First Division Liliuokalani Educational Society. | Attending Physicians. | Konhikis of Crown Lands. | Konohikis of Private Lands of His Majesty. Konohikis of Private lands of Her late Royal | Highness. | Major General Commanding and Staff. | Royal Hawaiian Band. | Honolulu Rifles. | Mamalahoa. | Queen's Own. | King's Own. | Prince's Own. | King's Guards. | Servants of Her Royal Highness Princess Liliuo- | kalani. | The King's Household Servants. | Servants of Her late Royal Highness. | Protestant Clergy. | The Clergy of the Roman Catholic Church | Monseigneur the Right Reverend Bishop of Ol- | ba, Vicar Apostolic of the Hawaiian Islands. | Choir—Kawaihau Club. Organist—Wray Taylor. | The Clergy of the Anglican Church—Revs. Alex- | ander Mackintosh, George Wallace, W.H. | Barnes and H.H. Gowen. | The Right Reverend Bishop of Honolulu. | Alii bearing Decorations and Jewels of Her late | Royal Highness. | Alii bearing Coronet. | Escort of Cavalry. Large Kahilis. Small Kahilis. Pall Bearers. Catafalque. Pall Bearers. Small Kahilis. Large Kahilis. Escort of Cavalry. | Chief Mourners—Hon. A.S. Cleghorn and H.R. | Princess Kaiulani. | Her Royal Highness Princess Liliuokalani, and | Lieutenant General the Hon. John O. | Dominis.| Carriage of Her Majesty. | Her Royal Highness Princess Poomaikelani | The Chancellor—Hon. A.F. Judd. | Cabinet Ministers—Their Excellencies W.M. Gibson, L. Aholo, Paul P. Kanoa and An- | tone Rosa. | Diplomatic Corps. | President of the Legislative Assembly—Hon. J. | S. Walker | Judges of the Supreme Court, | Governors of the different Islands. | Nobles. | Privy Councillors. | Representatives. | Consular Corps. | Collector General of Customs. | Postmaster General. | Sheriffs of the different Islands. | Clerks of Government Departments | Custom House Officer and Officers of the Cus- |toms. | Members of the Bar. | Foreign Residents. | Hawaiian Population generally. | Police Force. |

1. Royal Deaths

The Procession will form at 1 o'clock p.m., Sunday, February 27th, on King Street, in front of Iolani Palace.

Those who precede the Catafalque will form on the West side of Richard Street, and those who are to follow, on the Waikiki side of the Palace gate.

The Procession will start at 2 o'clock p.m., precisely, proceed through King to Nuuanu Street, thence to the Royal Mausoleum.

Those parties to whom places are assigned on the Programme and who attend the Funeral in carriages, are respectfully requested to furnish their cards to the drivers in order that their carriages may be placed in proper position in the Procession.

The Procession will be under the direction of Major General C.P. Iaukea
Adjutant General's Office.
Honolulu, Feb. 21, 1887.[348]

The *Pacific Commercial Advertiser* gave a detailed description of the catafalque:

The catafalque was similar to that used in previous state funerals. The body was covered with black cloth, and from each corner was a pillar, also covered with black material, round which white silk ribbons were twined. The pillars supported a dome-shaped canopy, on top of which was a large crown. A black plume, the feathers tipped with white, stood on the top of the pillars at each corner. The catafalque was drawn to the

The burial service at Mauna 'Ala included the hymn, "Now the Laborer's Task Is O'er" (courtesy Hawaii State Archives [PP-26-4-002]).

mausoleum by means of two black and white twisted cords by about one hundred natives, each of whom wore a yellow cape.[349]

Burial

"The coffin was carried into the Mausoleum by the pall-bearers and placed on a bier specially prepared for it. The members of the Royal Family occupied seats on one side, and the Bishop and clergy stood at the foot. Very few people were admitted to this, the final service."[350] Once again, music played a central role in the service. "The Kawaihau Club sang the 23rd psalm, 'The Lord Is My Shepherd,' to a plaintive chant, after which the Bishop read the committal service. The Rev. Alexander Mackintosh offered up several prayers, the choir sang the hymn, 'Now the Laborer's Task Is O'er,' and the last sad rites were concluded."[351] The hymn had last been sung at the funeral of Queen Emma.

A broadside, published March 7, 1887, announced, "The return of Princess Kaiulani with her father to their residence at Waikiki, after a stay of some weeks at the Palace whilst the remains of her mother lay in state."[352] The court also received notice by broadside: "The full period assigned for the observance of the sorrowful event in regards to the death of Princess Likelike have been completed, the King and Queen and other Members of the Court have gone out of mourning."[353]

Cost

The cost for the state funeral for Princess Likelike dwarfed all preceding obsequies, prompting an investigation by a legislative finance committee. The committee found that claims for the funeral totaled $30,337.54. "We find from the evidence before us that bills were run up on account of this funeral that are unprecedented in the history of state funerals in this country, so far as we have been able to ascertain from the records. There was utter recklessness, lawlessness and lack of proper authorization in the expenditures incurred."[354]

The clothing included "813 suits of clothing for men and boys, 458 shirts, 740 hats, 716 pair shoes, 887 dresses, besides sundry other articles of apparel for both sexes, such as gloves, bonnets, etc., amounting to over $22,000 for clothing."[355] In contrast, Queen Emma's funeral expenses included 176 coats, 149 vests, 183 pairs of pants, 148 hats, and 122 pairs of shoes.[356] The report compared the expenses to the Prince of Hawai'i, Kamehameha IV, Victoria Kamāmalu, Kamehameha V, Lunalilo, Leleiohoku, Kekaulike and Queen Emma. The committee noted, "In the expenditures for funerals mentioned above, there does not appear to be any strikingly unwarranted and extravagant expenditures, as is the case of the late Princess."[357]

The committee expressed its support for state funerals; it emphasized in the report "that notwithstanding the illegality, and total want of proper authorization for these expenditures, that it is but right and proper for the country to pay tribute due the rank of Her Royal Highness."[358] The committee, "following the custom as near as possible for expenditures made for like state funerals in the past," made a recommendation that only $10,772.71 be paid for the expenditures.[359] As to the difference between their recommendation and the claims, the committee recommended the claimants, in the event that the legislature did not vote to pay the total amount, "obtain a full settlement from the Trustees of His Majesty's estate."[360]

Prince Edward Abel Keliiahonui (1887)

Edward Abel Keliiahonui, the nephew of King Kalākaua, died on September 21, 1887. Godfrey Brown, Department of Foreign Affairs, distributed a broadside circular that announced: "it is my painful duty to inform you of the death of His Royal Highness Prince Edward Keliiahonui, which took place at Iolani Palace, at 3 o'clock yesterday [Wednesday, September 21, 1887] afternoon."[361]

Lying in State

The lying in state took place, not in the formal 'Iolani Palace, but in the personal residence of the king: "The remains were lying in state last evening in the bungalow in the Palace grounds, and were viewed by a large number of Hawaiians and others."[362]

Funeral

The remains of Keliiahonui were moved from the less formal site to more ceremonial 'Iolani Palace for the funeral service. A broadside noted the change of venue: "The funeral of the late Prince will take place on Sunday the 25th inst. At 2 o'clock p.m. from Iolani Palace."[363]

Procession

Unlike the procession for Likelike, the participants lining up to honor Keliiahonui were much fewer. Coming less than seven months after much criticized funeral expenses of his aunt, the cost of his funeral would have received increased scrutiny. The sparse Order of Procession was reported in the *Pacific Commercial Advertiser*:

Undertaker. | Police. | Marshal of the Kingdom. | St. Louis Cadets. | Ohuas. | Major Commanding and Staff. | Royal Hawaiian Band. | Household Servants. | Clergy of the Anglican Church. | Bishop of Honolulu. | Bearer of Jewels. | Large Kahilis, Small Kahilis. Pall Bearers. The Hearse. Pall Bearers. Small Kahilis. Large Kahilis. | Chief Mourners. | Carriage of Her Majesty the Queen. | Carriage of H.R.H. Princess Liliuokalani. | Governor of Oahu and Staff. | General Public.[364]

Missing from the procession were the military units, government officials and organizations. Although not in the procession, Hale Naua, an organization in which Keliiahonui had participated, recognized his contribution: "As to death of the late Prince, though young, he was exceedingly energetic and zealous and in his contributions in the Archaeological branch of the Society. [...] His example is worthy to be followed by us all and especially by the younger members of our association."[365]

The *Pacific Commercial Advertiser* recorded the route used by procession: "The procession passed through King to Nuuanu street; thence to the Royal Mausoleum, and was viewed by a large number of people."[366]

BURIAL

The funeral of the young prince used the Anglican rite, and at "the mausoleum the committal service was read by the Bishop of Honolulu."[367] The next royal funeral would be observed in a vastly different manner.

King David Kalākaua (1891)

When King Lunalilo died childless and without naming an heir, an election between Kalākaua and Queen Emma would decide the demise of a dynasty or the birth of a new one. Kalākaua prevailed and reigned from February 12, 1874, until his death. He was born on November 16, 1836, in Honolulu, the son of Kapaʻakea and Keohokālole. Kalākaua had ably served the Kamehameha dynasty. He was a member of Privy Council from November 20, 1855, and the House of Nobles from 1859. He served as the King's Chamberlain from February 19, 1864. He was a colonel on the King's staff from January 20, 1873. During his reign Kalākaua negotiated a treaty of reciprocity with the United States that lowered sugar tariffs and allowed the United States exclusive use of Pearl Harbor for a coaling station. In 1881, he was the first head of state to circumnavigate the earth. Forced by critics to sign the Constitution of 1887, Kalākaua found his authority limited for the remainder of his reign.

Seventeen years separated the death of King David Kalākaua and his predecessor. His obsequies would reflect the grandeur befitting the progenitor of a new dynasty. But his death abroad would have a great impact on his funeral services.

The *Daily Alta California* explained in detail the preparation of the king's body following his death:

King David Kalākaua adopted the symbols of Western monarchs (courtesy Hawaii State Archives [PP-96-16-008]).

Soon after 6 o'clock access to the death chamber was denied to every one, as the undertakers had been instructed to embalm the body. This operation was performed in a very through manner and the whole night and part of yesterday morning were consumed in the work. In the ordinary process of embalming, or "cavity injection," as it is called, the process of decay is merely arrested for a few days or weeks, by puncturing the abdomen to let out the gas, and then injecting into the stomach, the intestines and all cavities which can be reached a preparation having the property of coagulating the albumen and preventing the access of air. But in the case of King Kalakaua, whose remains are to be transported over 2000 miles of ocean and then exposed to the view of his subjects in a topical climate, it was obvious that nothing but a complete embalming of the entire body would suffice. In the ancient practice this was done by steeping the remains in natron for several weeks and closing the pores of the skin with resinous preparations, pitch, spices, etc. Modern practice revolts at the result, which leaves the body so disfigured and mummified as to be painful to contemplate. By the process used in King Kalakaua's case the features retain their form and expression for months and years, while decomposition is absolutely arrested. If twenty years hence the body of the King should be exhumed, it will be found a little dried up and withered, but every feature readily recognizable. Under favorable conditions the remains will not molder into dust for fifty or a hundred years. The process used in such cases is first to remove all the blood from the veins by suitable incision, and then to inject, by the carotid or femoral artery a strong solution of sulphate of alumina, arsenite of potash, bichloride of mercury, or other agent having the property of entirely coagulating and "tanning" the albuminous substances of which the flesh chiefly consists. A body so tanned is, to all intents and purposes, converted into leather, and will last as long as leather would under similar conditions.

Those few who were permitted to see the face of the dead King immediately after the operation of embalming had been completed, expressed surprise and pleasure at the placid and natural appearance of the features. The contracted features had filled out with the embalming fluid, and all evidence of the death-struggle had passed away.[368]

The body of King Kalākaua was taken first to the "mortuary chapel of Trinity Church, on Post street, in the undertaker's closed wagon, accompanied by a detail of United States troops."[369] The lying in state in the chapel was described by the *Daily Alta California* reporter: "the casket had already been placed on the catafalque, and covered with a broad pall of royal purple, reaching to the ground and spreading out two or three feet."[370] The traditional colors of Hawaiian royal funerals—the red of the *ahu'ula* and yellow of the *pā'ū* of Nāhi'ena'ena—were replaced by the colors of Western royalty. Under military guard the body of King Kalakaua was watched by "six men of the Fifth Artillery, U.S.A. [United States Army] [...] under the command of Lieutenant McClellan, and it was understood that the men would not be relieved, but would pass the night in the chapel."[371] Thus, the around the clock Hawaiian vigil had its Western equivalent at the chapel. Instead of thousands seeing the body of their king, however, visitors in San Francisco read the notice: "The body of King Kalakaua cannot be seen. No one admitted to the mortuary chapel."[372] A few did get to pay their respects. The newspaper reported that "a few privileged ones were indulged, about 9 p.m., with a view of the dead King prior to the enclosure of the casket in an hermetically sealed metallic case, and this again in an outer case. The casket was draped with heavy black broadcloth, worked into fluting and paneling, and had octagonal ends. The top was composed of two large molded raised panels, the upper end having a heavy plate-glass insertion with beveled edges. The glass was large enough to permit a clear view of the body of the King down to waist."[373] A coffin made of *kou* and *koa* would have to wait until Hawai'i.

The reporter also commented on the royal visage: "The appearance of King Kalakaua was exactly that of a person sleeping and in a pleasant dream. There was a perceptible and agreeable smile on the lips."[374] His final outfit was described in detail: "The King was attired in a full-dress suit, with white kid gloves, white satin vest and a broad red sash from the right shoulder to the left side. On the sash were a large Maltese cross and a small circular jewel of triangular form. On the left breast was a large regal jeweled badge, and in the right hand was a lily, the emblem of purity." In death, Kalākaua wore the Western trappings of his royal station, along with the symbolism associated with the Western way of death. The interior of the coffin, too, included Western symbols "in oxidized silver: the familiar Christian emblems, the laurel and palm branch."[375] The laurel wreath given to the winner of an athletic competition represented victory; the palm branch, too, symbolized victory, and in the context of the Christian funeral, victory over death. The motto of the University of Southern California,

Palmam Qui Meruit Ferat, translates as "to the one who merits it goes the palm."

In recognition of the denominational membership of King Kalākaua in the church that had been invited to Hawai'i by Kamehameha IV and Queen Emma, the mainland funeral service was conducted according the rites of the Church of England and took place in Trinity Church, an Episcopal church in San Francisco, on January 22, 1891. The program was titled "In Memoriam | of the | Stranger-King | Kalakaua."[376] The two hymns sung at the service were "Jerusalem, the Golden" and "Rock of Ages."

The official death certificate, certified by a U.S. Navy medical inspector, G.W. Woods, gave the cause of death as "Bright's disease and uræmia."[377] The king's death overseas required three death certificates, "one to be used at the wharf, one on the Charleston and the third at Honolulu."[378]

Though obsequies in California were conducted and concluded, the lack of an undersea cable to Hawaii meant that no news could reach Hawai'i, except via the USS *Charleston*. Initially, the king's remains were slated to sit between the two guns at the stern of the USS *Charleston*, but the inability of the lighthouse tender *Madrono* to lower the casket there resulted in the positioning of the coffin amidship. After the transfer, at 4:25 p.m., the firing of the two guns announced the departure of the USS *Charleston*.[379]

Aboard the USS *Charleston* the traditional forms of mourning continued. On the trip back a mourner composed a dirge:

> Mourn ye sons of Hawaii,
>   Sad news to you we bring.
> No more you'll gaze with loving eye,
>   Upon your generous King.
> King Kalakaua's no more.

The first news of the king's death in Hawai'i came at 8:15 a.m., January 29, 1891, when the USS *Charleston* arrived offshore with its Hawaiian and United States flags at half mast. The USS *Charleston* itself entered port a half hour later.[380]

Because of his death in California, the Honolulu obsequies for King David Kalākaua started not with lying in state in the place of his death but with a procession from Honolulu harbor.

PROCESSION

Ida Pope described the transportation of the coffin containing the body of King Kalākaua from the USS *Charleston* to 'Iolani Palace:

> At five o'clock in the evening the remains of the King were placed on a barge. The barge was moved to the wharf by a boat followed by sailors from the different war

The coffin of King David Kalākaua arrives at Honolulu harbor from San Francisco (courtesy Hawaii State Archives [PP-25-5-001]).

ships. Admiral Brown landed first. He was followed by marines bearing the coffin. The coffin was put in the hearse drawn by four black horses. The line of march was down Fort to King and from thence to the Palace. The Charleston and led the procession. It was followed by marines with arms reversed, then by standard bearers with the American flag: then came one hundred and fifty sailors from the U.S. warships Charleston and Mohican and then forty sailors from H.B.M.S Nymphe, following these was the hearse, escorted by the Hawaiian police, then came the Hawaiian Ministers, officers of the war ships and clergymen. The Band played The Dead March in Saul, the natives wailed and it must have been a most gruesome spectacle. The streets were literally packed with people.

From the gate to the front entrance, lighted torches were placed. The Honolulu firemen were ranged either side of the entrance, also the Native Sons of Hawaii. At the right of the entrance were the Royal Guards and at the left the Royal Military Band. On the steps on either side of the entrance were the King's retainers with feather capes and waving kāhili wands. The members of the Supreme Court and the Chamberlain met the procession at the door and the coffin was carried into the throne room.[381]

FUNERAL

The correspondence of Mary Sophia Hyde Rice of the Ninth Company of missionaries sent by the ABCFM gives their perspective concerning

King David Kalākaua lay in state in the throne room of the palace that he had dedicated a decade earlier (courtesy Hawaii State Archives [PP-25-6-023]).

the king's death and funeral. She wrote on February 2, 1891: "Matters at the palace are conducted with great decorum. There are no heathenish doings, but some quiet wailing, so we hope the Queen will be a power for good."[382]

On February 9, 1891, Rice wrote: "The funeral is a wonderful pageant, with a sort of barbaric splendor. When we called at the palace the queen received us most graciously. She can appear so well. She—the queen—said what we feel, that the prayers and words of truth uttered around his [the king's] bed were something to be thankful for."[383]

"Paul R. seems well to enjoy the *Charleston*. He brought the Admiral here to call. We were very grateful for his—the Admiral's attentions to our poor king, especially for the words of faith, hope and love that were uttered around the king's dying bed. He [the king] knew all the way of salvation and though he could not speak he may have understood.| In the funeral the Kawaiahao girls were the crown of the procession, but the whole affair was beyond anything that I had seen. The hula women with their muffled drum and their gay colors was another picture, while the ninety towering kahilis, the catafalque draped with the feather cloaks were grand."[384]

The use of 'Iolani Palace as a venue for the funeral services once again necessitated the use of cards of admission. The communication from James W. Robertson, Vice-Chamberlain, announced: "The Religious Services on the occasion of the Funeral of His late Majesty Kalakaua, Will take place at Iolani Palace on Sunday the 15th instant, at 11 o'clock a.m."[385]

PROCESSION

As usual, the procession for the ruling monarch surpassed all other royalty in its pageantry and included the daylight kukui nut torches of Iwikauikaua, the hallmark of the funerals of his descendants.

> Order of Procession | for the | Funeral of His late Majesty| Kalakaua. | [rule] | Mounted Torch Bearers. | Police. | Marshal of the Kingdom and Aids. | Band. | Students of St. Louis College. | Kamehameha School. | Iolani College. | Public Schools. | Kawaiahao Female Seminary. | St. Andrew's Priory. | Oahu College. | Band. | Portuguese Societies. | Honolulu Fire Department. | Mechanic's Benefit Union. | Ancient Order of Foresters. | American Legion of Honor. | Knights of Pythias. | Geo. W. De Long Post, No. 45, G.A.R. | Independent Order of Odd Fellows. | Representatives of the Masonic Veteran Association of the Pacific Coast. | Free and Accepted Masons. | Members of the Medical Fraternity. | Attending Physicians to the late King. | Ahahui Opiopio Puuwai Lokahi. | Liliuokalani Educational Society. | Hoola and Hooulu Lahui Society. | Lei Mamo Society. | Hale Naua Society. | Konohikis of Crown Land. | Konohikis of Her Majesty's Private Lands. | Konohikis of the late King's Private Lands. | Colonel Commanding and Staff. Royal Hawaiian Band. | Band of the U.S.F.S. "Charleston." | Detachment of Marines and Blue Jackets from | U. S. Flagship "Charleston," | U.S.S. "Mohican," | H.B.M.'s S. "Nymphe." | King's Guards. | Her Majesty's Household Servants. | Servants of the Late King. | Protestant Clergy. | Clergy of the Roman Catholic Church. | The Right Reverend the Bishop of Olba. | Choir. | Officiating Clergy. | The Right Reverend the Bishop of Honolulu. | The late King's Charger. | His late Majesty's Chamberlains. | The Honorable Majors R.H. Baker and J.T. Baker | bearing the Crown Jewels | The Native Sons of Hawaii drawing the Catafalque. | Large Kahili Bearers, Small Kahili Bearers, Pall Bearers, Catafalque, Pall Bearers, Small Kahili Bearers, Large Kahili Bearers | Royal Carriage with Her Majesty the Queen Dowager [Kapiʻolani] and H.R.H Princess Poomaikelani | The State Carriage with Her Majesty the Queen [Liliʻuokalani] and His Excellency the Hon. J.O. Dominis, Consort. | Carriage of H.R.H. Princess Kaiulani bearing | Hon. A.S. Cleghorn | The Chancellor of the Kingdom. | The Cabinet Members. | The Diplomatic Corps and Rear Admiral Brown | and Staff. | Justices of the Supreme Court. | The President of the Legislature. | The Ladies of the Court | The Privy Councilors | Officers of the U. S.F.S. "Charleston," U.S.S. "Mohican," | and H.B.M.S. "Nymphe." | Consular Corps. | Members of the Bar. | Government Officials. | Foreign Residents. | The Public. | Police. |

The Order of Procession reveals a number of changing aspects of the royal Hawaiian way of death. Firstly, the diminished number of lesser chiefs

Poola (stevedores) pull the catafalque of King David Kalākaua (courtesy Hawaii State Archives [PP-25-5-016]).

who used to draw the catafalque were now replaced with "Native Sons of Hawaii." Secondly, the suddenness of the death of Kalākaua left Kaʻiulani absent from Hawaii when the funeral took place. With Kaʻiulani away at school in England, her father, Archibald S. Cleghorn, occupied her carriage in the procession, hence the language of the vehicle "bearing" him. The procession of Kalākaua also marks the first appearance of Hale Naua, a secret order founded by the late king. Although the king was a fifth degree member of the society, his procession did not follow the "Form of Funeral Procession" that included the "Almoner and Orator," "Annointer and Keeper of Ancient Fire" and "Annointer of Oil and Annointer of Fire."[386] The Bishop of Olba would make his last appearance in a funeral procession; he would die the following year. A growing portion of his flock, the Portuguese laborers, would be represented by the Portuguese societies that made their first appearance in the procession for Kalākaua. The Portuguese first started immigrating in large numbers in 1878 during the reign of Kalākaua.

BURIAL

Kalākaua was buried on Sunday, February 15, 1891, at the Royal Mausoleum. The Bishop of Honolulu officiated using the burial service of the Church of England. The choir sang the hymn that began "Now the laborer's task is o'er."[387] The hymn, numbered 533 appeared in the "Burial of the Dead" portion of the *Church of England Hymn Book*,[388] published in 1880, but not authorized by the Church of England. After the Anglican service, the Masons conducted their own ritual: "Mr. John Phillips as Master read the sermon, after the Masons had formed around the coffin. The Mr. David Dayton went on with the service, the Masons saying the responses, after which the brothers moved in procession round the body, each depositing a sprig of evergreen on the coffin. The grand honors were given three times."[389] At the end of the masonic service, members sang their own dirge: "Solemn strikes the fun'ral chime."[390]

Crowds thronged outside the Royal Mausoleum during services for King David Kalākaua (courtesy Hawaii State Archives [PP-25-5-014]).

COST

To make certain the expenses for the funeral of King Kalākaua remained under control, an official notice was published by Godfrey Brown, Minister of Finance, on the same day as the arrival of the king's body: "Notice is hereby given that all material, etc., required for the Funeral Ceremonies of His late Majesty Kalakaua is only to be furnished on requisitions signed by the Minister of Foreign Affairs."[391]

As required by Article 15 of the Constitution, the Council voted to concur "in the expenditure of money from the Public Treasury [...] not to exceed Fifteen Thousand dollars as may be necessary for the purpose of defraying the funeral expenses of His Late Majesty Kalakaua."[392] The funeral expenses eventually totaled $21,422.22. The "large Koa and Kou ornamental Casket" cost $1,200.[393]

John Owen Dominis (1891)

Prince Consort John Owens Dominis, husband of Queen Lili'uokalani, died on August 27, 1891, at their home called Washington Place. Thus the man who as governor of O'ahu had planned so many funeral obsequies became the subject of the same. Dominis was born 1832, in Schenectady, New York, came to Hawai'i with his parents, Capt. John and Mary Dominis, in 1840. He married the future queen of the Kingdom of Hawai'i in Honolulu on September 16, 1862. Dominis served on the Privy Council from December 24, 1863, to 1891. He was Governor of O'ahu from February 18, 1864, to October 4, 1886.

LYING IN STATE

Unlike observances that took place weeks after the death of royal personages, the lying in state for Dominis occurred the next day. The *Daily Bulletin* announced that "the body of the dead Prince Consort was laid in state this morning [August 28, 1891], in the beautiful Throne room of the Palace. The general public was received from 10 to 11, and representatives of the diplomatic and consular bodies and Government employees from 11 till 12 o'clock. The Household troops in full number lined the front of the Palace and the Royal Hawaiian Band occupied a position near the steps and played appropriate music during the hours of lying in-state. Callers were received at the entrance by Major James W. Robertson, Her Majesty's Chamberlain, and ushered into the chamber of death, passed by the dead Prince, and left by one of the mauka doors."[394]

The arrangement of the body of the Prince Consort called to mind past displays at royal funerals. The *Daily Bulletin* wrote of Dominis: "The body was dressed in the habiliments of a general and laid, uncoffined, on one of the famed feather cloaks which covered the resting place. At the head, on a cushion, were placed several insignia of rank and the sword of the deceased."[395] The rapid progress of the observances no doubt contributed to the body being "uncoffined" and that after the ceremony "preparations were soon made and completed for the temporary coffining of the Royal corpse."[396]

FUNERAL

The funeral services took place on Sunday, September 6, 1891.

PROCESSION

The Foreign Office issued a broadside with the Order of Procession:

Marshal of the Kingdom and Aids. | The Police. | Honolulu Fire Department. | Society de Santo Antonio. | Society Luzitana. | Native Sons of Hawaii. | Ahahui Hooulu Lahui. | Hui Kalaiaina Hawaii. | Hale Naua Society. | Liliuokalani Educational Society. | American Legion of Honor. | Geo. W. De Long Post No. 45 G.A.R. | Independent Order of Odd Fellows. | P.H. Brook's Div. No. 1, U.R.K. of P. | Free and Accepted Masons. | Colonel Commanding and Aids. | Royal Hawaiian Band. | Military Escort. | H.M.'s household Servants. | Physician to the late Prince. | Officiating Clergy. | The late Prince's Horse. | Aids-de-Camp to His late Royal Highness. | Bearers of the Sword and Decorations.| Kahili Bearers, Pall Bearers, [*image of coffin*] Pall Bearers. Kahili Bearers. | Her Majesty the Queen. | Their R.H. Princes Kawananakoa and | Kalanianaole, | The Chancellor of the Kingdom. | Her Majesty's Ministers. | The Diplomatic Corps. | Justices of the Supreme Court. | The President and Members of the Leg- | islature.| Members of the Pricy Council of State. | The Ladies of the Court. | The Consular Corps. | Government Officials. | Members of the Bar. | The Public. |[397]

The procession included the second, and last appearance of Hale Naua Society.

BURIAL

The burial of a high ranking member of the Masonic Lodge Le Progres was occasioned by full ceremonies by members of the fraternal order, including a detailed recording of the rites in the *Pacific Commercial Advertiser*: "After the members had taken their positions around the coffin, Bro. John Phillips, in distinct tones, commenced the service by reading 'Once more, my brethren, have we assembled to perform the last sad and solemn duties to the dead. The mournful notes which betoken the departure of a spirit from its earthly tabernacle have again alarmed our outer door, and another has been taken to swell the numbers in that unknown land whither our fathers have gone before us.'"[398]

The funeral for the husband of Queen Lili'uokalani marked the last state funeral under the monarchy.

Cost

The agreement for the government to advance the expenses took place on August 31, when the Cabinet Council resolved to pay for the funeral with an amount not to exceed five thousand dollars. Under the constitution the Privy Council was required to concur with the action, which it unanimously adopted on the same day. The funeral expenses totaled $5,001, included $800 for a koa and kou coffin and $240 for the coffin plate.

Royal Deaths During the Provisional Government and the Republic of Hawai'i

> *Ka i'a 'ula weli i ke kai.*
> The red fish that causes red color to show in the sea.
> The *'alalauwā*, a small red fish whose appearance in great numbers was regarded as a sign that a member of the royal family would soon die.[399]
> —Hawaiian proverb

The treatment of royal deaths would change following the overthrow of the monarchy and the establishment of the Provisional Government on January 17, 1893, and later the Republic of Hawai'i on July 4, 1894.

Virginia Kapooloku Po'omaikelani (1895)

No state funeral took place for the first royal death after the overthrow of the monarchy. Princess Virginia Kapooloku Po'omaikelani, sister of Dowager Queen Kapi'olani, died in Kalihi Valley around 6 p.m. on October 2, 1895, "after a few minutes illness."[400] Her body was immediately taken to Honuakaha, the residence of Queen Kapi'olani at Punchbowl and Queen streets, where it was embalmed.[401]

Poomaikelani was born in Pi'ihonua on the island of Hawai'i on April 7, 1839. She married a cousin of King Kalākaua, Hiram Kahanawai, in March 1855. She served as governor of the island of Hawai'i from January 21, 1884, until 1886. Starting February 16, 1887, Poomaikelani also headed the board of health.

Funeral

The funeral for Po'omaikelani took place the day after her death at St. Andrew's Cathedral, where the princess was a member. The location "was crowded in every part with the friends of the deceased, principally Hawaiians."[402] The article in the *Pacific Commercial Advertiser*, made the specific point of calling her "ex–Princess" and her nephews, Kawānanakoa and Kalaniana'ole "ex–Princes."[403] Unlike royal funerals of the past, the funeral service drew few governmental representatives, but included "Chief Justice Judd, Judge Whiting and Paul Neumann."[404] All three had ties with the monarchy. Albert Francis Judd had served as a 1st Lieutenant with the Hawaiian Cavalry during the reign of Kamehameha V, rising to the rank of Captain. He had served on the Privy Council for eighteen years starting in 1873. From 1881 he had served as chief justice of the Supreme Court. Although his ties were shorter, William Austin Whiting had served as Attorney General and been a member of the House of Nobles under Lili'uokalani. Like Whiting, Paul Neumann had served as Attorney General and as a member of the House of Nobles. He had also served on the Privy Council under Kalākaua.

The service was read in Hawaiian by the Anglican Bishop of Honolulu, Alfred Willis using the prayer book that had been translated into Hawaiian by Kamehameha IV.[405]

PROCESSION

No account of the funeral includes a description of a procession, and no order of procession was published by the government.

BURIAL

Her burial took place at Mauna 'Ala, where according to the *Pacific Commercial Advertiser*, "all the kings and queens are buried."[406] No longer the decision of the king, permission to have her body entombed in the Royal Mausoleum was granted on October 3, 1895, by James Anderson King, the Minister of the Interior,[407] who himself would be accorded a state funeral four years later.[408]

Ka'iulani (1899)

The obsequies for Princess Ka'iulani, who died on March 6, 1899, stood in marked contrast the observances of Princess Po'omaikelani. Whether it was the chronological distance from the failed Counter Revolution of 1895 or the popularity of Ka'iulani, the late princess received a state funeral.

Princess Victoria Kawekiu Ka'iulani Lunalilo Kalaninuiahilapalapa was born in a residence on Emma Street in Honolulu on October 16, 1875, daughter of Archibald S. Cleghorn and Princess Likelike. When she departed in 1889 from Hawai'i to attend school in England, Robert Louis Stevenson wrote a poignant poem for her:

> Forth from her land to mine she goes,
> The island maid, the island rose,
> Light of heart and bright of face:
> The daughter of a double race.
>
> Her islands here, in Southern sun,
> Shall mourn their Kaiulani gone,
> And I, in her dear banyan shade,
> Look vainly for my little maid.
>
> But our Scots islands far away
> Shall glitter with unwonted day,
> And cast for once their tempests by
> To smile in Kaiulani's eye.

She was named heir apparent by Queen Lili'uokalani. Ka'iulani went to Washington, D.C., after the overthrow to argue for the restoration of the Kingdom of Hawai'i.

Princess Ka'iulani was heir apparent of the last monarch of the Kingdom of Hawaii (courtesy Hawaii State Archives [PP-96-8-008]).

FUNERAL

March 12, 1899
(Order of Service for the Funeral of Her Royal Highness Princess Victoria Kaiulani, conducted by Bishop and Clergy of the Anglican Church at Kawaiaha'o Church, Sunday Mar 12, 1899.)
ORDER OF SERVICE
FOR
THE FUNERAL
OF
HER ROYAL HIGHNESS
Princess Victoria Kaiulani,
CONDUCTED BY
The Bishop and Clergy of the Anglican Church
AT
KAWAIAHAO CHURCH
(By Permission of the Rev. H.H. Parker)
Sunday, March 12th, 1899.

The funeral for Princess Ka'iulani presented a dilemma to planners of the obsequies, who wanted an Anglican service and the largest

Ka'iulani lies in state at Kawaiaha'o Church (courtesy Hawaii State Archives [PP-25-4-006]).

available sanctuary. The still uncompleted Anglican cathedral would not seat as many as Kawaiaha'o. The religious tensions between the two Protestant denominations were reflected in the program for services. The words on the cover were carefully parsed to indicate the service was "conducted by The Bishop and Clergy of the Anglican Church" at Kawaiahao Church (By Permission of the Rev. H.H. Parker)"

PROCESSION

A broadside gave the Order of Procession for participants:

Order of Procession | for the | Funeral of the late | Princess Kaiulani | [rule] | Marshal of the Republic and Officers. | Company of Police. | Band. | St. Louis College. | Oahu College. | Kamehameha School. | St. Andrew's Priory. | Band. | Fraternal Societies. | St. Antonio Beneficente Society. | Sociedade Lusitania Beneficente. | Aha Hui Kalaiaina. | Aha Hui Aloha Aina. | Aha Hui Aloha Aina O na Wahine. | Grand Marshal and Aides. | Band. | Second Battalion U.S. Volunteer Engineers. | Detachment of Blue Jackets from U.S.S. Scindia and Iriquois. | Band. | First Regiment National Guard of Hawaii. Protestant Clergy. | Clergy of the Roman Catholic Church. | The Right

1. Royal Deaths

Reverend the Bishop of Panapolis | Choir. | Officiating Clergy. | The Right Reverend the Bishop of Honolulu. | Large Kahilis. Small Kahilis. Pall Bearers. Catafalque. Pall Bearers. Small Kahilis. Large Kahilis. | Carriage with Hon. A.S. Cleghorn| and | Mrs. J.W. Robertson and Mrs. J.H. Boyd. | Carriage of ex–Queen, Liliuokalani. | Carriage of Her Majesty the Queen Dowager with Prince Kawananakoa, Prince Kalanianaole and wife. | The President [Dole] and Staff. | The Cabinet Ministers. | The Justices of the Supreme Court. | The Special Agent of the United States. | Officers of U.S. Army and Navy. | President of the Senate. | Speaker of the House. | Consular Corps. | Circuit Judges. | Government Officials. | Public. |

The Procession will form at 1:30 p.m., Sunday, March 12, on King Street.

The line of Procession preceding the Catafalque will be formed on King Street, with the right resting on Richards Street. All who follow will form on the Waikiki side of Punchbowl Street. The Procession will proceed along King Street to Alakea, thence by Alakea and Emma Streets to Vineyard Street, Vineyard Street to Nuuanu, thence to the Royal Mausoleum.

All attending the funeral in carriages are respectfully requested to furnish cards to their coachmen in order that positions may be assigned to them.

Procession will be under the direction of Maj. G.C. Potter, of the President's Staff.[409]

The catafalque of Ka'iulani had no canopy (courtesy Hawaii State Archives [PP-25-4-023]).

Just a short six years after the overthrow, the Order of Procession was careful to call the former ruler of Hawai'i "ex–Queen Liliuokalani." One of the copies of the Order of Procession in the Hawaii State Archives has penned insertions for "Mr Haywoods carriage" immediately following "The Special Agent of the United States," and "Senators | Representatives" following the "Speaker of the House." Harold Sewall was the special agent from the U.S. State Department.

Queen Kapi'olani (1899)

The Dowager Queen Kapi'olani died at her Waikiki home called Pualeilani on June 24, 1899. The granddaughter of Kaumuali'i, the last king of Kaua'i, Kapi'olani was born on December 31, 1834. She was the namesake of the Hawai'i island chiefess who defied Pele. She married Bennett Nāmākēhā, uncle of Queen Emma, and served as governess of the queen's son, the Prince of Hawai'i. Following the death of Nāmākēhā, she married David Kalākaua on December 19, 1863, and became queen when her husband was elected king on February 12, 1874.

FUNERAL

Even though Hawaii had already been annexed by the United States on August 12, 1898, the territorial government was not established until the passage of the Organic Act on April 30, 1900. Thus, the Minister of Foreign Affairs, a position that would disappear when the territorial government was established, would announce the funeral of Queen Kapi'olani in 1899. A note, signed by E.A. Mott-Smith, sent June 29, 1899, to foreign consul informed them: "The Religious Services on the occasion of the Funeral of the late Queen Dowager Kapiolani will take place on Sunday next, the 2nd proximo, [July 2, 1899] at the Kawaiahao Church, at 2 o'clock p.m."410

Kapi'olani, married to the uncle of Queen Emma, cared for the Prince of Hawai'i. She later married David Kalākaua, becoming queen when he ascended to the throne (courtesy Hawaii State Archives [PP-97-15-017]).

1. Royal Deaths

Kapi'olani lies in state at Kawaiaha'o Church (courtesy Hawaii State Archives [PP-25-10-015]).

PROCESSION

The Order of Procession was published "By Authority," given official government sanction.

Order of Procession | ...... for the ...... | Funeral of Her Late Majesty, | The Queen Dowager. | [*rule*] Torch Bearers. | Marshal of the Republic and Officers. | Company of Police. | Oahu College. | Kamehameha School. | St. Andrew's Priory. | Fraternal Societies | St. Antonio Beneficente Society. | Sociedade Lusitana Beneficente, | Ahahui Kalaiaina. | Ahahui Aloha Aina. | Ahahui Aloha Aina o na Wahine. | Matron Kapiolani Home and Aides. | Konohikis and Tenants of the late Queen | Dowager's Private lands. | Grand Marshal and Aides.| Band. | Battalion Sixth Artillery, U.S.A. | Detachment of Blue Jackets from U.S.S. | Iroquois. | Band. | First Regiment National Guard of Ha- | waii. | Servants of the Late Queen Dowager. | Physicians in Attendance. | Protestant Clergy. | The Right Revered [*sic*] the Bishop of Pano- | polis. | Choir. | Officiating Clergy. | The Right Reverend the Bishop of Ho- | nolulu.| Staff Officers of His late Majesty Kala- | kaua, | Hon. J.T. Baker, Bearing Decorations of | the Late Queen Dowager. | Native Sons of Hawaii drawing the | Large Kahilis, Small Kahilis, Pall Bearers [rectangle around CATAFALQUE] Pall Bearers, Small Kahilis, Large Kahilis. | Carriage with Prince Kawanakoa [*sic*] | Prince Kalanianaole and wife, | and

L. Kamakala. | Carriage of Her Majesty, Ex-Queen Liliu- | okalani. | Carriage with Mrs. G.H. Fairchild and | Mr. Fairchild. | Carriage with Mrs. Stella Cockett and Mr. | Cockett.| Carriage with Hon. A.S. Cleghorn. | The President [Dole] and Staff. | The Cabinet Ministers. | The Justices of the Supreme Court. | The Special Agent of the United States. | Consul-General of the United States. | Officers of the U.S. Army and Navy. | President of the Senate. | Senators. | Speaker of the House. | Representatives. | Consular Corps. | Circuit Judges. | Government Officials. | Public.[411]

The order of Procession was also published in Hawaiian:
PAPA KUHIKUHI | O KA | HUAKAI HOOLEWA | MOIWAHINE KANE-MAKE | ————:O:———— | Na Paa Kukui o Iwikanikaua. [sic] | Ilamuku o ke Aupuni amen a Hope | Puali Makai | Kula Nui o Punahou | Kula o Kamehameha | Kula Kaikamahine o Sana Anaru. | Na Ahahui Puuwai Lokahi. | Ahahui Manawalea St. Antonio o na Pukiki | | Ahahui Manawalea Lusitana o na Pukiki. | Ahahui Kala-iaina. | Ahahui Aloha Aina. | Ahahui Aloha Aina o na Wahine. | Makuahine o ka Home Hoohanau Kapiolani ame na Kokua. | Ahahui Hooulu a Hoola Lahui. | Kono iki amen a Ohua o na Aina o ka Moiwahine i Make. | Hamuku o ka La ame na Hope. | Bana. | Bataliona Koa, Mahele Eono o na Koa Pukaa Amerika. | Pualikoa o ka Mokukaua Iroquois. | Bana. | Regimena Ekahi. Pualikoa o Hawaii. | Na Kawa a ka Moiwahine i Make. | Na Kauka Lawelawe. | Na Kahunapule o ka Hoomana Hoole-

Poolas line up in front of 'Iolani Palace to pull the catafalque of Queen Kapi'olani (courtesy Hawaii State Archives, [PP-25-10-021]).

pope. | Na Kahunapule o ka Hoomana Katolika. | The Reverend Bishop o Panopolis o ka Hoomaaa Katolika. | Na Kahunapule o ka Hoomana Anegalikana. | The Right Reverend Bishopa o Honolulu. | Na Ukali o ka Moi Kalakaua i Make. | Hon. J.T. Baker e hii ana i na Kea Hoohanohano o ka Moi | wahine i Make. | Na Keiki Oiwi o Hawaii e Huki ana i ke Kaa Kupapau.| Kahili Nui. Kahili Liilii. Hapai Pahu. [rectangle around PAHU KUPAPAU] Hapai Pahu. Kahili Liilii. Kahili Nui. | Kaa o na Keikialii Kawananakoa, ame Kalanianaole ame | Kana Wahine, L. Kamakaia. | Kaa o ka Moiwahine Liliuokalani. | Kaa o Mrs. G.H. Fairchild ame Mr. Fairchild. | Kaa o Mrs. Stella Cockett ame Mr. Cockett. | Kaa o ka Mea Hanohano A.S. Cleghorn. | Ka President amen a Ukali. | Na Kuhina o ke Aupuni. | Na Lunakanawai Kiekie. | Na Agena Kuikawa o ke Aupuni o Amerika. | Kanikela Kenerala o ke Aupuni o Amerika. | Peresidena o ka Aha Senate. | Na Hoa o ka Senate. | Lunahoomalu o ka Hale o na Lunamakaainana. | Na Lunamakaainana. | Na Knikela o na Aina E. | Na Lunakanawai Kaapuni. | Na Luna Aupuni. | Ka Lehulehu. | ————:O:————[412]

As with the funeral of her husband, King Kalākaua, the torchbearers led the funeral procession for Queen Kapiʻolani, by virtue of her marriage to him.

Missing from the procession were the Konohikis of Crown Lands, lands that had been taken by the government. James A. King, who would die four months after the observances for Kapiʻolani, served as Commissioner of Crown Lands.

Two Portuguese societies were represented by name. The San Antonio Beneficente Society had started in 1877; the Sociedade Lusitana Beneficente in 1882. The spiritual shepherd for many of the Portuguese, the Roman Catholic bishop, the Rev. Gulstan F. Ropert, took as his title the Bishop of Panapolis. The extinct see of Panapolis was in what today is southern Egypt. Panapolis today is called Akhmim, Egypt.

Royal Deaths During the Territory of Hawaii

Pio ke kukui, pōʻele ka hale.
When the light goes out, the house is dark.[413]
—Hawaiian proverb

On April 30, 1900, Hawaii became an organized territory of the United States of America, a country that in its constitution rejected the awarding of titles to its citizens. On that day, the president of the Republic of Hawaii, Sanford Ballard Dole, became the first governor of the territory of Hawaii. Although many members of government had served under the Kingdom of Hawaiʻi (Dole had been an associate justice of the Supreme Court), the treatment of royal deaths in the newest territory of the United States had not been tested.

Albert Kūnuiākea (1903)

The death of Albert Kūnuiākea on March 10, 1903, provided the first instance of the passing of royalty during the territorial period. The timing of the death of Albert Kūnuiākea could not have been more fortuitous; it allowed for an action that might not have occurred outside the dates of the Regular Session of the Second Legislature of the Territory of Hawaii, which ran from February 18 to April 28, 1903. The Speaker of the Territorial House of Representatives, Frederick William Beckley, was himself descended from royalty. The action by the House of Representatives, on March 11, 1903, resolved "that the Clerk of this House is hereby instructed to notify the family of the deceased that this Hall will be at their disposal on Sunday, March 15, 1903, and if they so desire, the remains of the Late Prince may lie in State so that the community may have a chance to view the remains." The resolution, introduced by Samuel Keliinoi of the Third District, made no reference to the Throne Room of 'Iolani Palace as the location of the lying in state, instead referring to "this Hall." Thus, Kūnuiākea had his lying in state take place in the traditional site. He had initially lain at his Kapālama residence, his casket in the midst of "all the ancient Hawaiian insignia of royalty. [...] Day and night the chants of ancient days are heard in solemn and weird tones, the chants which tell of the noble lineage of the dead Prince. On each side of the bier at all times stand rows of kahili-bearers, waving the beautiful feathered symbols of royalty in unison over the casket."[414]

OBSEQUIES

Although Dole mentioned Kapi'olani and Ka'iulani in his address to the first territorial legislature, the observances for Albert Kūnuiākea represented the first instance under the territory of honoring an *ali'i*. Kūnuiākea, the son of Kamehameha III and Jane Lahilahi Young Ka'eo was considered by many to be the last of the Kamehamehas. Representative Keliinoi introduced House Resolution No. 180, calling for a state funeral:

> *Whereas*, it is proper for this people to pay due respect to one of the last representatives of an honored hero, and,
> *Whereas*, the late Prince Kunuiakea, was himself a member of a former Legislature, and a man greatly respected by Hawaiian Americans.[415]

Keliinoi chose his words carefully. It was "proper for this people," not the territory, to honor a member of royalty, an honor "due" not for the attainments of Kūnuiākea, but as a proxy for Kamehameha the Great. The "former Legislature" makes no reference to it being the legislature of the overthrown kingdom. The resolution, introduced by a newly minted U.S. citizen, noted the respect of "Hawaiian Americans."

The House action "resolved that the Speaker is hereby instructed to order this Hall properly prepared for Sunday [March 15, 1903] to receive the remains of the late Prince."[416]

Lying in State

The change in government had little impact on what took place during the lying in state of Kūnuiākea. The description in the *Pacific Commercial Advertiser* of the throne room could have easily been written of Kingdom-era activities:

> The casket was carried into the throne room and deposited upon a bier overspread with a beautiful pall of heavy black velvet faced with yellow silk. At the head was a magnificent candelabra authorized by the Roman Catholic church. Four huge kahilis, the tabu marks of the royal presence, designated the sacred enclosure and within this, six chiefs, three on each side of the bier, were placed upon watch, waving small kahilis in unison over the casket. From the old throne of the Kalakauas the crown flag of Hawaii was suspended and over the entrances the Hawaiian colors were draped. [...] The waving of the kahilis, and the chanting of the genealogy of the Prince were continued through the night and will be part of the weird ceremony until the casket is borne from the palace.[417]

Funeral

The funeral services for Kūnuiākea were conducted by Pro Vicar Libert (Libert H. Boeynaems), a Roman Catholic prelate. Kūnuiākea had attended the Roman Catholic school at ʻĀhuimanu in Kāneʻohe as a youth.

Procession

Although Albert Kūnuiākea had never been considered for the throne, he was the son of King Kamehameha III and Jane Lahilahi Young, and his funeral procession displayed the accouterments due his royal lineage. The *kāhili*, standards of royalty, flanked the pall bearers escorting the catafalque, small *kāhili* closest to the coffin and large ones next. The Order of Procession was as follows:

> Band | St. Louis College. | Young Men's Institute. | Kamehameha School. | Alumni Kamehameha School. | Fraternal Societies. | Hawaiian Societies. | Marshal and Aides. | Col. Commanding N.G.H. and Staff. | Government Band. | First Regiment, N.G.H. | Clergy. | Officiating Clergy. | Pro Vicar Libert. | Mrs. Kunuiakea, widow of the late Prince, and Mrs. Grace Kahooalii. | Mrs. Malulani Piinaia and Mrs. Keomailani Cockett. | Mrs. Kaonaeha and Mr. Kahooalii. | Prince and Princess D. Kawananakoa. | Prince and Princess J. Kalanianaole. | Mrs. Peleuli Amalu and Mrs. Theresa Wilcox. | Mrs. Taylor and Miss Kekauanohi. | Mrs. Lucy K. Peabody and Mrs.

P. Mikona. | Mrs. Elizabeth Booth and Mrs. Lucy K. Henriques. | Mrs. Kahaawelani Kahea and Mrs. Annie Kaikioewa. | Mrs. K. Nahaolelua and Mrs. Kekai Kuihala Mahaulu. | Mr. and Mrs. Willie Simonson. | Mrs. Kahakuhaakoi and Mrs. Maluhi Reis, | Mrs. E.S. Boyd and Miss Kamaiopili. | George Rooke. | Governor and Staff. | Secretary of Territory and Chief Justice. | President and Vice President of Senate. | Speaker of House of Representative and Vice-Speaker. | Justices Supreme Court. | Heads of Territorial Departments. | Officers, U.S. Army and Navy. | Federal Officials. | Members of Senate and House of Representatives. | Consular Corps. | Circuit Judges. | The Rt. Rev. Restarick. | Hon. John Cummins. | Mrs. Julia Afong and Mrs. M. Montano. | Mrs. Kamaka Stillman, etc. | Members of Committees. | Public. |

The *Pacific Commercial Advertiser*, dated March 16, 1903, carried a photograph by Davey showing Albert Kūnuiākea lying in state in the throne room of ʻIolani Palace, then called the "Assembly Hall, Capitol Building."

The Order of Procession also gave directions for the participants. Predating the widespread use of the automobile, the procession depended on carriages and coachmen for transportation. The directions read:

> The procession will form at 1 p.m. on King street. The line of procession preceding the catafalque will be formed on the mauka side of King street with right resting on Alakea street. All who follow will form in Waikiki entrance to Capitol grounds. The procession will proceed along King street to Alakea, thence by Alakea and Emma streets to Vineyard; Vineyard street to Nuuanu; thence to the Royal Mausoleum.
>
> All attending the funeral in carriages are respectfully requested to furnish cards to their coachmen in order that positions may be assigned.
>
> The procession will be under the direction of the Marshal, Major J.W. Pratt, of the Governor's staff.
> Alexander G. Hawes,
> Secretary to the Governor
> Executive Chamber, March 14, 1903

Conspicuously absent from the procession was Queen Liliʻuokalani, who was still in Washington, D.C., pursuing her claim for the crown lands when the funeral took place. She returned from the nation's capital to Hawaii on March 23, 1903.[418] Still, the Kalākaua Dynasty was ably represented by Princes Kalanianaʻole and Kawānanakoa and their wives. The "Palace" grounds were now called the "Capitol" grounds.[419]

BURIAL

The body of Kūnuiākea would rest initially with the members of the dynasty that supplanted the Kamehameha rulers. The *Pacific Commercial Advertiser* explained the reason: "The Kamehamehas lie in a vault in the Mausoleum premises and are covered with a huge slab of stone, appropriately inscribed. It is understood that permission will be asked to have this vault opened at some future time so the remains of Prince Albert can be laid away with those of his own line."[420] Initially put in the anteroom of the Royal Mausoleum, his body would later be reunited with at least part of his family: "At some future time the casket will be taken into the main room of the Mausoleum and deposited near those containing the remains of Prince Albert's mother [Jane Lahilahi] and twin brother."[421]

The editorial writer at the *Pacific Commercial Advertiser* noted the extraordinary nature of the state funeral for a royal scion taking place in the newly established territory of the United States. The opinion piece, titled "Time's Changes," contrasted the treatment of Kūnuiākea in life and in death:

> All that was once mortal of the late Prince Albert Kukailimoku Kunuiakea was laid away yesterday afternoon in the Royal Mausoleum, of those of our monarchs and chiefs that have gone before him, in all the splendor of the days that have passed, making a grand spectacular display. He received all the honors, and more too, than was due to his rank, practically an unknown quantity while living. Yet we consider the Government's action most graceful. His parents, aunts, uncles, and brother never received like consideration, yet the respect shown him after death was more than he received in life. We have nothing to say against the dead alii, and we are pleased that he received such a recognition from those now in power. "Peace be to his ashes."[422]

Robert W. Wilcox (1903)

A state funeral for Robert Wilcox, first delegate to Congress for Hawai'i, would have been an appropriate honor for highest national office holder from the newly established Territory of Hawaii. Wilcox, however, had also tried in 1889 to overturn the "Bayonet Constitution" and fought in the 1895 Counter-Revolution that had attempted to restore the monarchy. Not surprisingly he received no state funeral. His death also took place outside the legislative session that could have brought on political pressure to honor him.

FUNERAL

The funeral, instead, took place at the Roman Catholic cathedral on Fort Street on November 9, 1903. The *Hawaiian Gazette* reported: "The coffin was handsomely draped with Hawaiian flags and floral wreaths. The face of the dead leader was not exposed. [...] About 3:30 the organ pealed in the doleful strains of Cor Jesu, and as the choir sang the selection, Bishop Libert, accompanied by the acolytes, choir boys, censer bearers and cross bearer, entered the chancel and then descended the steps to the space occupied by the casket, where the impressive ritual of the church was said."[423] Like the funeral of Albert Kūnuiākea, the Roman Catholic bishop presided over the service.

PROCESSION

Unlike the procession of Kūnuiākea to the Royal Mausoleum, the procession for Wilcox went from the cathedral down Fort Street to King Street where it continued to the Catholic cemetery. The Order of Procession for Wilcox was not published "By Authority." To avoid the question of royal titles, the newspaper was careful to note that it printed the "titles as given by those in charge of the arrangements."[424] The Order of Procession was:

> Marshal of the Day | Platoon of Police | S.C. Dwight, leader, and the Hui Hookuonoono, Oiwi Hana. | William Kaleihuia, leader, and the Hui Puuwai Aloha. | Members of the Home Rule Party. | Executive Committee of the Home Rule | party. | Dr. Walters. | Bishop Libert. | Hui Poolas, under Wm. Olepau, drawing the hearse. | Catafalque. | Honorary and Active Pallbearers. | Princess Theresa Owana Wilcox, Prince | Keoua Wilcox, Princess Kaohi Ka- | pumahana Wilcox. | W.S. Wilcox, Mrs. W.F. Sherratt and | child. | Chas. Wilcox and children. | Mrs. Gohier, E Wilcox and R. Wilcox. | John Napua. | Mrs. E. Johnson and Stone. | William White and wife. | Mrs. J.A. Akina and family. | Sam Aki and family. | Mrs. Taylor. | The Rev. Mr. and Mrs. Manase.| High Chiefess E.K. Kekaaniauokalani.| High Chiefess Lucy K. Peabody. | High Chiefess Kalani Kiekie Henriques | High Chief O. Makainae. High Chief A.K. Palekaluhi.| Princess Mary Kunuiakea. | Princess Kekaikuihala. | Princess Hoonanea Simerson. | Princess Malaea Kahaawelani. | Princess Mary Kinoole Ailau. | Princess Methau Beckley. Princess Kahapula Beckley. | Princess Kahinu. | Princess Hannah Boyd and sister. | Sam Kamaiopili and wife. | Princess Kahalelaukoa Booth. | Princess D. Hoapili. | Princess Kalinonoa. | President D. Kalauokalani and wife. | Vice-President J.P. Makainai and wife. | Rep. D.M. Kupihea and wife.| J.M. Kealoha and wife. | Members of the Legislature. | Public.[425]

Though not considered a state funeral under the Territory of Hawaii, and certainly not a "royal" funeral in the American republic, the order of procession included the names of fourteen princesses, a prince, three high chiefesses and two high chiefs. The royal titles were derived from descent in Kamehameha dynasty. High Chiefess Elizabeth Keka'aniauokalani had been designated eligible for the throne by Kamehameha III and attended the Chiefs' Children's School. In the Wilcox procession his wife was called "Princess Theresa Owana Wilcox"; in Kunuiakea procession, "Mrs. Theresa Wilcox." Even the wife of Albert Kūnuiākea, who had been called "Mrs.

Kunuiakea widow of the late Prince," in her husband's Order of Procession, was called "Princess Mary Kunuiakea" in the Wilcox procession. Lucy K. Peabody and Lucy K. Henriques were called by their titles of High Chiefess in the Wilcox procession. At least four of the women listed as "Mrs." in the Kūnuiākea list were called "Princess" in the one prepared for the Wilcox procession.

Party officials and the democratically elected members of the legislature followed behind. David Kalauokalani was a state senator and president of the Home Rule Party. Makainai was vice president and assistant clerk of the House of Representatives. David Malo Kupihea represented the Fifth District in the House.

The "attentions given on behalf of the government"[426] at the funeral of William Hulilauakea Coney in 1904, called into question why Wilcox had not received appropriate honors from the government. In an editorial titled "Attentions Beyond Reason," the *Independent* noted: "When the late Hon. R.W. Wilcox died and was buried, the man who was the recognized leader of the majority of the Hawaiian people and who was the first choice of that people, by electing him, to first represent this new American outpost in the halls of Congress, he never got such honors bestowed over him and in his memory. No soldiers turned out for him, although the band played at the cemetery the Government making less of him than what was his due."[427] The *Independent* indicated the possible politics behind the snub, pointing out that "Dole was Governor then, and the present Governor was then Secretary of State."[428]

Mary Kūnuiākea (1904)

Although she was called "Princess Mary Kunuiakea" in the procession of Robert Wilcox, the widow of Prince Albert Kūnuiākea did not receive the honors accorded her husband. She died at the residence of Mr. Kanakanui[429] on April 6, 1904, after a swim at Waikīkī.[430] Her funeral took place just two days later at the Roman Catholic Cathedral, at 4:30 p.m., April 8, 1904.[431] The *Hawaiian Star* reported that the interment would be in the King Street Catholic Cemetery.[432] The Hawaiian language newspaper, *Ke Aloha Aina*, called the location Koula Cemetery.[433]

David Kawānanakoa (1908)

In line for the throne after Princess Ka'iulani, Prince David Kawānanakoa was one of three brothers named by King Kalākaua as eligible to rule. Although in life David Kawānanakoa never had the opportunity to occupy the throne room of 'Iolani Palace, in death he would repose there.

David Kawānankoa lying in state at 'Iolani Palace (courtesy Hawaii State Archives, [PP-26-2-003]).

FUNERAL

The Roman Catholic liturgy once again took center stage for the obsequies for the recently converted Roman Catholic, David Kawānanakoa. The Latin chants of drew comparisons with the traditional Hawaiian *oli* of the past.[434] As he had at the services five years earlier for Kūnuiākea, Libert, now called bishop, presided over the Roman Catholic rite "wearing the full vestments for such solemn functions, assisted by numerous priests and sanctuary boys."[435]

PROCESSION

The Order of Procession for the funeral of Prince Kawānanakoa once again brought up the topic of precedence. On June 22, 1908, A.S. Cleghorn wrote from 'Āinahau regarding "much nonsense talked and written in regard to precedence"[436] related to the omission of the carriage of Elizabeth Keka'aniau Pratt and Princess Theresa Wilcox from the funeral procession for David Kawānanakoa. Before the funeral, Wilcox had written a letter to the governor's secretary, D.L. Conkling, on June 18, 1908, stating that "our carriage was left out, I mean The High Chiefess Elizabeths Kekaaniau Pratts of which she and myself ought to occupy."[437]

Addressing her as Princess Theresa Wilcox, Conkling replied on the same day, June 18, 1908: "Allow me to say that this office is endeavoring to do everything desired by the personal representative of the deceased. Colonel Iaukea having been given charge of the funeral arrangements by the relatives of the deceased furnished this office with a list of and arranged the order of precedence of those who were to attend as mourners at the funeral. I am sorry that any question has been raised affecting the feelings of anyone desiring to attend the funeral, but feel that this office is only carrying out the wishes of the relatives as conveyed by Colonel Iaukea."[438]

Cleghorn provided a copy of the order of precedence used by King Kalākaua at his coronation and that had he said remained unchanged during the reign of his successor. Cleghorn noted: "There should now be added to the list the late Prince's wife [Abigail Campbell Kawānanakoa] and three children [David Kalākaua Kawānanakoa, Abigail Helen Kapiʻolani Kawānanakoa, and Lydia Liliʻuokalani Kawānanakoa] and the wife of Prince Kalanianaole [Elizabeth Kahanu Kaʻauwai], and as Republics do not create princes or princesses there can be no further additions."[439] The funeral of Prince David Kawānanakoa took place on Sunday, June 21, 1908, with the carriage of Pratt and Wilcox absent.[440] Both women claimed descent from Keōua, and had made a rival claim to that of Liliʻuokalani for the crown lands.[441]

Procession

The final Order of Procession as published "By Authority" appeared in *Pacific Commercial Advertiser* on Sunday, June 20, 1908.

Order of Procession | for the Funeral of | the late | Prince David Kawananakoa. [rule] | Funeral obsequies of the late Prince | David Kawananakoa will take place | from the Capitol on Sunday, June 21st, | at 1 p. m. | Order of procession will be as fol- | lows: | Mounted Police | Marshal and Aids | Kamehameha Aquatic Club | Labors Union o na Poola | Hui Kokua ame Manawalea o na Poola | Kalama No. 1, Order of Kauikeaouli | Ahahui Poo, Order of Kauikeaouli | Hui Kokua a Hookuonoono o na Oiwi | Hawaii | Hui Kokua a Hookuonoono o na Wahine | Oiwi Hawaii | Hui Kaahumanu | 20th Infantry, U. S. A. | U. S. Marines | Detachments from U. S. S. Maine and | U. S. S. Alabama | 1st Infantry and detachments, N. G. H. | Physician to the late Prince | Retainers of the late Prince | Cross Bearer | Choir | Sanctuary Boys | Officiating Clergy | Rt. Revd. Bishop Libert | 100 Poolas drawing the Catafalque | Large Kahilis. Small Kahilis. Pall Bearers. Catafalque. Pall Bearers. Small Kahilis. Large Kahilis. | Carriage bearing Princess Kawanana- | koa and Prince Kalanianaole | Carriage bearing Princess Kalanianaole | and Mrs. Fairchild | Carriage of Her Majesty ex–Queen | Liliuokalani | Colonel and Mrs. Samuel Parker | Secretary of Territory and Governor's | Staff | Chief

Royal Deaths During the Territory of Hawaii 155

Carriages in the funeral procession of Prince David Kawānanakoa. Absent from the procession was the carriage of Theresa Owana Wilcox and Elizabeth Kekaʻaniau Pratt, excluded by the organizers of the funeral (courtesy Hawaii State Archives [PP-26-2-006]).

Justice of the Supreme Court | President of Senate | Speaker of House | Justices of Supreme Court | Heads of Territorial Government | Officers U. S. Army and Navy | Federal Officers | Members of Senate | Members of House of Representatives | Members of Consular Corps | Circuit Judges | Territorial and County Officials | Public

The procession will form at 2 p. m.

The line of procession preceding the catafalque will be formed on the mauka side of King Street with the right resting on Bishop Street. All who follow will form at the Waikiki entrance to the Capitol grounds.

The line of march will be from the Capitol grounds along King Street to Nuuanu Avenue; thence to the Royal Mausoleum.

All attending the funeral are requested to furnish cards to their coachman in order that positions may be assigned.

The procession will be under the on of the Marshal, Colonel C. P. Iaukea.

By direction of the Secretary of
Hawaii.
D. L. CONKLING,
Chief Clerk.[442]

Missing from the procession were the fraternal societies present in the procession of Albert Kūnuiākea. The procession for Kamehameha V and Lunalilo had included the Good Templars, Knights of Pythias, Odd Fellows, and Free Masons. Kawānanakoa, after joining the Roman Catholic Church in 1907, had given up his Masonic connections.[443]

The ancient Hawaiian features were even more prominent in the now American territory. *Pacific Commercial Advertiser* reported: "There were 107 kahilis in the procession, more than have ever been carried at a royal funeral in Hawaii."[444] The article also described the disposition of the *kāhili* after the obsequies: "The kahili were taken back to Prince Kalanianaole's residence at Waikiki last night. Each separate feather will be dusted with powdered native tobacco and then wrapped in a piece of tapa, the whole kāhili then being wrapped in tapa. The sticks, according to custom, will be wiped off and covered with camphor to prevent the ravages of borers."[445]

BURIAL

The burial once more featured an element of nature expected at royal funerals: "Again it rained, though not heavily, as the widow alighted from her carriage and approached the entrance to the tomb and again it brightened after the coffin had been deposited."[446]

Archibald Scott Cleghorn (1910)

Archibald Scott Cleghorn, husband of Princess Likelike and brother-in-law of Queen Lili'uokalani, died November 1, 1910, at 'Āinahau in Waikīkī. A native of Edinburgh, Scotland, Cleghorn had arrived in Honolulu on June 17, 1851. His daughter, Princess Ka'iulani, had been heir apparent under Lili'uokalani.

The *Hawaiian Star* reported on the preliminary discussions about the obsequies: "It is probable that the funeral will not strictly speaking, be a state one, but it will be a public one."[447] Instead, Cleghorn was accorded a state funeral with full participation of the territorial government and U.S. military. The Imperial Japanese Navy, represented by Rear-Admiral Rokuro Yashiro, also participated in the obsequies. In 1881, Kalākaua proposed a marriage between a Japanese prince and Cleghorn's daughter, Ka'iulani.

LYING IN STATE

The lying in state of Cleghorn took place, not at 'Iolani Palace, where it occurred for Kūnuiākea and Kawānanakoa, but at his beloved residence at 'Āinahau, on November 5, 1910.

FUNERAL

Scottish by birth, Cleghorn was a member of the Anglican church, which by the time of his death had been replaced by the Protestant Episcopal Church of the United States of America. The Rev. Canon William Ault conducted the services at St. Andrew's Cathedral on Sunday, November 6, 1910.

PROCESSION

Territorial Secretary Ernest A. Mott-Smith announced the order of procession on Saturday, November 5, 1910:

> Order of Procession | for the funeral of | the late | Honorable A.S. Cleghorn. | Mounted Police | Band | Military Companies | Eight uniformed foot police | Six grandsons of the deceased. | The Rev. Canon Ault | Hon. S.B. Dole, Mr. C.P. Iaukea, Rear-Admiral Corwin P. Rees, U.S.N., Hon. Cecil Brown [*cut of coffin*] Hon. A.S. Hartwell, Mr. T. Clive Davies, Hon. W.O. Smith, Mr. E.I. Spalding | Mourners | The Governor [Walter Francis Frear] and Secretary of Hawaii [Ernest A. Mott-Smith]. | The Governor's Staff. | The Delegate to Congress [Jonah Kūhiō Kalanianaʻole]. | United States District Judges. | The Justices of the Supreme Court. | Speaker of the House [Henry Lincoln Holstein] | Rear-Admiral R. Yashiro, I.J.N., and staff. | Brigadier General Tasker H. Bliss, U.S.A. | Colonel W.S. Schuyler, U.S.A., and Staff. | Members of the Consular Corps. | The Mayor of the City and County of Honolulu. | Master of Hawaiian Lodge. | Officers of Pacific Club. | Public. The line will be formed at 2 p.m., Sunday, November 6, 1910, on the Waikiki side of Emma Street with the right resting near Vineyard Street.
>
> The line of march will be from St. Andrew's Cathedral along Emma to Vineyard to Nuuanu to the Royal Mausoleum grounds.
>
> The conveyances of those participating in the official program will assemble on Emma Square during the services and will there be assigned their places by an officer.
>
> By direction of the Secretary of Hawaii.[448]

Seven carriages comprised the mourners in the procession, including Queen Liliʻuokalani in the first carriage.[449] The presence of automobiles made the reference to carriages no longer wholly accurate, hence the use of "conveyances."

BURIAL

Ault conducted the graveside service from the *Book of Common Prayer*, and Cleghorn joined his wife, Princess Likelike, and daughter, Princess Kaʻiulani, in the Kalākaua Crypt. His niche has a simple inscription: "Gov. A.S. Cleghorn | Born 1835 Died 1910."[450]

Charles Reed Bishop (1915)

The death in Berkeley, California, of Charles Reed Bishop, husband of Princess Bernice Pauahi, delayed the ceremony as his remains were brought back to Hawai'i on the SS *Matsonia*. Unlike the arrivals of Kamehameha II, Kamāmalu, and Kalākaua after their deaths abroad, residents of Hawai'i knew of his death long before the arrival of the ship, courtesy of the Trans-Pacific cable. Observances began with flags at half-staff on June 7, 1915, the day of his death.[451]

Bishop was born in Glens Falls, New York. He was naturalized as a Hawaiian citizen February 27, 1849. He served as collector general of customs from March 1, 1849, to March 31, 1853. He was named to the House of Nobles in 1859 and served until 1886. He was a member of the Privy Council from 1859 to 1891. The firm he started in 1858 eventually became Bank of Bishop, later renamed First Hawaiian Bank.

Lying in State

His ashes lay in state for two days, June 22 and June 23, 1915, at Kawaiaha'o Church,[452] unlike his wife, whose funeral ceremonies took place in Keōua Hale. By the time of his death, the site of his wife's funeral had been sold to the state, in 1895, and served as Honolulu High School.

As at the obsequies of his wife, kāhili bearers waved over his ashes, an act usually reserved for royalty, and only extended once before to a *haole*—John Young.

Funeral

The funeral took place at 3 p.m., June 23, 1915, led by the pastor of Kawaiaha'o, H.H. Parker. Among the floral offering, Queen Lili'uokalani sent a wreath of orchids.

Burial

Though not a member of the founding dynasty, Prince Jonah Kūhiō Kalaniana'ole was given the responsibility of putting the urn containing the ashes of Bishop onto the coffin of Bernice Pauahi in the Kamehameha Tomb. His cremation, the first and only for any burial at Mauna 'Ala, allowed his remains to be interred in the Kamehameha Tomb.

Lili'uokalani (1917)

The last ruling monarch of the Kingdom of Hawai'i, Queen Lili'uokalani died on November 11, 1917, at Washington Place, the royal standard still fluttering on the staff in front of her residence. Now the very men who had overthrown her kingdom and raised the flag of the United States above her palace—taken all from her in life—were called upon to honor her in death.

Royal Deaths During the Territory of Hawaii

On the day of her demise, Gov. Lucius E. Pinkham issued a proclamation:

> It is with profound sadness the Governor of Hawaii announces the death of Her Majesty Ex-Queen Lilioukalani [sic], the last reigning monarch of the Hawaiian Islands.
>
> I have been witness of some of her sorrows. I have found her tender and kind to her own race, thoughtful and helpful to others and a valuable and appreciative friend. Her last days have been devoted to aiding the Red Cross work with marked sympathy and liberal financial assistance.
>
> Her Majesty has linked more strongly than ever, the Hawaiian and American races, who will join each other in paying their respects in this, her final rest.
>
> May all the people of Hawaii join in these last ceremonies.
>
> The Hawaiian and American flags on Public Buildings will be at half mast during the time of the lying in state and proper military guards perform their duties.
> /s/
> Governor of Hawaii.
> Honolulu, November 11, 1917.[453]

Lili'uokalani was born in Honolulu on September 2, 1838, the daughter of Kapa'akea and Keohokālole. She married John Owen Dominis on September 16, 1862. Following the death of her brother, King David Kalākaua, she became queen on January 29, 1891, until the monarchy was overthrown on January 17, 1893.

Perhaps the funerals of two princes, Kūnuiākea and Kawānanakoa, helped set the precedent for such honors, for in death Lili'uokalani received the respect due her rank in a kingdom now passed. The *Hawaiian Gazette* noted: "She was laid to her final rest in beautiful Nuuanu Valley Sunday with all the impressive honors that would have been hers had she when she died been ruler of Hawaii."[454] It was the mixture of royalty and republic that presented what the editorial writer of the *Hawaiian Gazette* called "the strangest

Lili'uokalani was the last monarch of the Kingdom of Hawai'i (courtesy Hawaii State Archives [PP-98-13-019]).

ceremony ever to be held, for it was not only a Hawaiian queen, but an American queen."455

Even before the death of Liliʻuokalani, the politics surrounding her funeral played out in letters. Lorrin Andrews, a scion of American missionaries, informed Curtis P. Iaukea, William O. Smith, S.M. Damon, and J.K. Kalanianaʻole, in a letter dated two days before the queen's death, of the appointment of John F. Colburn as executor and noted: "No one would wish any unseemly controversy at this time over this matter; but, under the Will, it is imperative that Mr. Colburn should act as representative of Her Majesty's estate, and he has expressed his desire to work with you in all matters connected with the obsequies of Her Majesty." The letter ended in a conciliatory tone: "Trusting this notification will be received by you in the spirit in which it is written and that there will be no necessity for an unpleasant legal controversy in regard to the last rites to be performed for Hawaii's last queen."456

For the former queen of the Kingdom of Hawaiʻi, the observances surrounding her death marked a strange mixture of allegiances. The government that had aided in her overthrow, through President Woodrow Wilson, requested the Hawaiʻi congressional delegation to represent it in "an official capacity." At the same time, authorities of the museum founded in honor of another member of royalty, Princess Bernice Pauahi Bishop, refused to allow the pāʻū of Nāhiʻenaʻena, the "royal feather cloak of ancient Hawaii [to] drape the body of the late Queen Liliuokalani, during the period of lying-in-state, or on the day when the final obsequies are held."457

LYING IN STATE

The royal standard that had first flown during the funeral of Nāhiʻenaʻena played a symbolic role in the funeral of the last monarch: "the royal standard which had hung at half-mast there [Washington Place] was hurriedly lowered and carried into the mansion, where it was wrapped around the Queen's remains, and thus the body was carried into the church, the flag of the monarchy of Hawaii being removed only when the Queen was placed upon the bier for lying-in state."

Liliʻuokalani was taken to Kawaiahaʻo Church with an auto-hearse for her lying-in-state. Instead of the yellow feathers of pāʻū of Nāhiʻenaʻena, the body of Liliʻuokalani "rested upon a pall of yellow plush adorned with the Queen's monogram; the brilliant coloring contrasting beautifully with the chaste hue of the shroud."458 The royal trappings only added to the regal demeanor of the late monarch. "The Queen's countenance was covered with a filmy tulle through which the features were easily discernable, show-

Lying in state for Lili'uokalani took place in the Kawaiaha'o Church. The casket lay on several '*ahu'ula* or feather cloaks (courtesy Hawaii State Archives [PP-26-5-031]).

ing them in repose and yet with the dominant strength of former days not altogether missing."[459] Also visible were the jewels she had worn in life, most notably an emerald ring and a diamond solitaire. Her lying-in-state continued until Saturday evening when Lili'uokalani was transported to the throne room of 'Iolani Palace by auto-hearse "flanked on either side with flaring kukui torches."[460] Once again, as at the funerals of her brothers, the symbol of Iwikauikaua provided a link with the ancient funerary practices.

FUNERAL

The funeral would take place at 10 a.m. on Sunday, November 18, 1917. Even the program made reference to the overthrow. The service "for the funeral of | Her Late Majesty | Liliuokalani" was "Held in | The Throne Room | of | Iolani Palace | *now the Executive Building* [*italics* mine]."[461] The officiants were the Rt. Rev. Henry B. Restarick, Bishop of Honolulu;

The funeral for Liliʻuokalani took place in the throne room of ʻIolani Palace (courtesy Hawaii State Archives [PP-26-5-023]).

his assistant, the Rev. Leopold Kroll, Priest in Charge of St. Andrew's Hawaiian Congregation; and the Rev. Henry H. Parker, pastor of Kawaiahaʻo, who read the lesson.[462]

The solemn pace of George Frideric Handel's "Dead March in Saul" opened the funeral service of Queen Liliʻuokalani. Immediately following the music, the Episcopal Bishop of Honolulu, the Right Rev. Henry Bond Restarick, opened the service with the familiar scripture: "I am the resurrection and the life, saith the Lord; he that believeth in me, though he were dead, yet shall he live; and whosoever liveth and believeth in me, shall never die."[463] Henry Hodges Parker, son of missionaries and pastor of Kawaiahaʻo since 1863, read 1 Corinthians 15:20 in Hawaiian: *"Aka, ua ala io no o Kristo, mai ka make mai, a ua lilo oia i hua mua o ka poe i moe"*[464] (But now is Christ risen from the dead, and become the first fruits of them that sleep. Authorized [King James] Version).

After the Apostles Creed was read, the final hymn was sung, beginning

The coffin of Lili'uokalani was lowered into the Kalākaua Crypt (courtesy Hawaii State Archives [PP-26-8-003]).

with the words: "Now the laborer's task is o'er; | Now the battle day is past; | Now upon the farther shore | Lands the voyager at last," sung to the tune "Requiescat" by J.B. Dykes. The final hymn, from *The Hymnal* of the Episcopal Church, was written by John Ellerton in 1870 and published for the church's convention in 1892. Numbered 248, the hymn appears in a section titled "The Church—Burial of the Dead." The hymn had been sung at the burial service for her brother, King David Kalākaua.

ROYAL PROTOCOLS

The death of a royal person initiated communication regarding the decorations of orders bestowed upon Queen Lili'uokalani by Her Britannic Majesty, the late Queen Victoria, and the necessity for their return "on the death of the holder." The British consul expressed his willingness to "take charge of them after the funeral is over."[465] In reply, Iaukea requested the protocol regarding medals, and received a reply from the British consul: "I shall leave the Jubilee Medal bestowed on the late Queen in the possession of the Executor."[466]

PROCESSION

The Order of Procession for the trip from 'Iolani Palace to the Royal Mausoleum was still being negotiated in a series of conferences on Friday, November 16, 1917, just two days before the funeral on Sunday, November 18, 1917. Major Francis Green, aide to the governor, met with representatives of the U.S. Army, Navy and the Hawaiian National Guard on Friday, having met with Prince Kalaniana'ole the previous day.[467] Despite the last minute preparations, the procession took place expeditiously.

The symbolic significance of the pall bearers formed the basis of a letter from John F. Colburn, executor of the estate of Liliuokalani, to Jonah Kūhiō Kalaniana'ole and Curtis P. Iaukea. Colburn expressed his interest in naming three of the pallbearers: "I desire to be one of such and name the other two Chas. B. Wilson and James K. Merseberg. The former, with myself, are survivors [...] of those who with the late Queen were deposed on January 17, 1893, upon the overthrow of the monarchial form of government in this land. The latter is the son-in-law and brother-in-law of the late John Cummin who was, during his lifetime, the loyal friend and supporter of the Aliis of this land and who was one of those foremost in devoting his time and efforts to the pleasure and comfort of Royalty."[468]

The final list of pall-bearers included fourteen individuals, but none requested by Colburn: F.W. Beckley, Jesse P. Makainai, David Hoapili, Albert K. Hoapili, David Maikai, William Simerson, G.K. Kealohapauole, Fred H. Iaukea, J.H. Boyd, Henry F. Bertleman, A.N. Alohikea, T.P. Cummins, Edwin Kea, A.K. Nahaolelua and H.P. Beckley.[469]

ORDER OF PROCESSION

The *Pacific Commercial Advertiser* called the procession a "Great Spectacle" in its headline of the article that listed the order. The cortege included:

Mounted and Foot Police | Grand Marshal and Aides. | Hawaiian Band. | Kamehameha School Cadets | Queen's Own Troop Boy Scouts. | Hawaiian Societies. | St. Louis College Band. | Hawaiian Societies. | Second U.S. Infantry Band. | Squadron, Fourth U.S. Cavalry. | Battalion, First U.S. Field Artillery. | Second U.S. Infantry. | Detachment of U.S. Marines. | Detachment U.S. Navy. | Coast Artillery Band. | Detachment H.I. J. M.'s Tokiwa. | Provisional Battalion National Guard. | Physician of the late Queen. | Retainers of the late Queen. | Choir. | Clergy. | Honorary Pall Bearers. | Poolas drawing the Catafalque. | Bearers of Hawaiian Decorations. | Bearer of Japanese Imperial Decoration. | Catafalque, Kahili and Pall Bearers. | Prince Kalanianaole and Princess | Kalanianaole. | Carriage of Princess Kawananakoa representing Prince Kalakaua, and Princesses Kapiolani and Liliuokalani. | Governor and Aides. | Commanding Officer, Hawaiian De- | partment and Aides. | Commandant Pearl Harbor Naval | Station and Aides. | Adjutant General Territory of Ha- | waii and Aides. | The Congressional Party. | Secretary of the Territory of Hawaii | Governor's Staff. | Staff of Department Commander. | Staff of Commandant Naval Station. | Chief Justice. | President of the Hawaiian Senate. | Speaker of the House of Repre- | sentatives | Justices of the Supreme Court. | Heads of Territorial Departments. | Officers U.S. Army and Navy. | Federal Officers. | Members of Hawaiian Senate. | Members of House of Representatives. | Members Consular Corps. | Circuit Judges. | County Officials. | Board of Supervisors. | Various Societies, not Hawaiian. | Punahou Cadets. | Cadets Honolulu Military Academy. | Schools.[470]

ROUTE OF PROCESSION

The procession moved down King Street to Nuuanu, up Nuuanu to the Royal Mausoleum.[471]

BURIAL

The burial service concluded with the following hymn:

> Peace, perfect peace, in this dark world of sin?
> The blood of Jesus whispers peace within.
> 2. Peace, perfect peace, with sorrows surging round?
> On Jesus' bosom naught but calm is found.
> 3. Peace, perfect peace, our future all unknown?
> Jesus we know, and He is on the throne.
> 4. Peace, perfect peace, death shadowing us and ours?
> Jesus has vanquished death and all its powers.
> 5. It is enough: earth's struggles soon shall cease,
> And Jesus call us to heaven's perfect peace.[472]

Written by the Rt. Rev. Edward Henry Bickersteth in 1875, the hymn appeared as number 667 in a section titled "Home and Personal Use" in the 1892 version of the Episcopal hymnal. Only verses 1, 3, 5, 6 and 7 in the hymnal, renumbered 1 through 5 in the program, were sung.

FUNERAL EXPENSES

The timing of the death of Liliuokalani after the legislative session meant that a request could not be made for expenses prior to the funeral. In lieu of action by the government, eight individuals (J.K. Kalaniana'ole, C.F. Chillingworth, H.L. Holstrin, C.P. Iaukea, W.O. Smith, E. Faxon Bishop, R.W. Brekons and R.W. Shingle) borrowed money from Bank of Hawaii to cover for expenses.[473] The funeral expenses totaled more than $8,500. The largest amounts were $2,000 for the undertaker, H.H. Williams, $1,600 for Honolulu Planing Mill for the casket, and $1,520 to Silva's Toggery and $995.50 to the Clarion, Gent's Furnished Goods, for the funeral clothing.[474] The bill from Williams included $100 for making a death mask of the late queen and 160 pounds of 2¼ inch Manila rope for the drawing of the catafalque. W.O. Smith made himself personally responsible if the bills were not paid within three months for the payment of expenses for the "necessary clothing for not to exceed sixty kahili bearers, and two hundred ten persons drawing the Royal catafalque."[475]

Another expense not incurred in past funerals was for a film of the funeral of Queen Liliuokalani by W.F. Aldrich. Sen. Desha introduced Senate Bill 31 to provide for the purchase of the motion picture, but the bill was tabled.[476]

The Hawai'i government formally remembered Queen Lili'uokalani during a special session in 1918, called not for her but because of the impact of World War I on the state economy. On May 14, 1918, Gov. Lucius Pinkham noted the funeral that had taken place in the absence of the legislature: "In her throne room and your assembly room we together extended to thousands of the people the courtesies we felt, and Democracy gave way so far as possible that Her Majesty might once more touch the hearts of her people. No occasion that could promote this friendliness was omitted."[477] The legislature honored Lili'uokalani with a memorial service at Kawaiaha'o Church on May 26, 1918. The memorial service opened with "Ka Makua Mana Loa, played by what was now called the Hawaiian Band instead of the Royal Hawaiian Band. Next the choir and audience sang Hawai'i Pono'i, once the national anthem of the Kingdom of Hawai'i, but retained by it successor Territory of Hawaii." "Nearer my God to Thee," a Shubert Quartette, followed. The eulogy was delivered by Rep. Lorrin Andrews. Handel's "Largo" and Lili'uokalani's own "Queen's Prayer" came before another eulogy, this one by Sen. S.L. Desha. An anthem, "The Lord Is My Shepherd," followed, sung by the Kawaiaha'o Choir. Although Lili'uokalani disliked her love song, "Aloha Oe," being sung at funerals, ironically it was sung at her own memorial service. The singing of the "Star-Spangled Banner" was a necessity for the governmental body. The benediction by the Rev. H.H. Parker brought the memorial service of Lili'uokalani to an end.[478]

Jonah Kūhiō Kalaniana'ole (1922)

The timing of the death of Prince Jonah Kūhiō Kalaniana'ole, almost three decades after the overthrow of the monarchy, and after the death of its last monarch, provided sufficient distance to allow for a state funeral. Unlike the funeral for the first delegate to Congress, Robert Wilcox, the observances for the second delegate had the imprimatur of the state, replete with the military that had supported the overthrow of the kingdom over which he had been destined never to rule. Kalaniana'ole served as the second delegate from the Territory of Hawaii.

LYING IN STATE

Kalaniana'ole lay in state at Kawaiaha'o Church on Saturday, January 14, from 10 a.m. to 3 p.m. A Hawaiian service, lead by Akaiko Akaka, took place at Kawaiaha'o from 10 p.m. to midnight, after which his coffin was moved from the church to the throne room of 'Iolani Palace.[479]

FUNERAL

On Sunday, January 15, 1922, at 10 a.m., a second funeral service took place at the throne room.[480] Bishop John La Mothe conducted the burial service of the Episcopal Church. After the benediction the casket of the prince was carried from the throne room.[481]

The funeral service at Kawaiaha'o remembered Jonah Kūhiō Kalaniana'ole, the last prince named by King Kalākaua to die (courtesy Hawaii State Archives [PP-25-7-016]).

1. Royal Deaths

PROCESSION

The government issued a broadside of the funeral cortege of Prince Jonah Kūhiō Kalaniana'ole:

Order of Procession | For the Funeral of the late Delegate to Congress | Prince Jonah Kuhio Kalanianaole | [*rule*] | Mounted Police | Funeral Director | Twenty-first Regiment, U.S. Infantry | Second Battalion and Band, 13th Field Artillery | Provisional Battalion, Hawaiian Anti-Aircraft Regiment, | consisting of Battery A (75 mm. guns), | Battery D (searchlight) | Provisional Battalion, U.S. Coast Artillery, and 55th U.S. Coast | Artillery Band. | U.S. Naval Battalion | Combined Mine Squadron and Naval Station Band | One Company U.S. Marines | One Company U.S. Navy Mine

A stereoscopic photograph of the procession allowed individuals with a viewer to see the scene in three dimensions (courtesy Hawaii State Archives [PP-25-8-040]).

Royal Deaths During the Territory of Hawaii 169

Squadron Two | One Company U.S. Navy Division 14, Submarine Force | two Battalions 1st Infantry, H.N.G. | One Howitzer Company, H.N.G. | St. Louis College Band | University of Hawaii R.O.T.C. | Punahou Cadets | Honolulu Military Academy | Kamehameha School Cadets | British Veterans | Boy Scouts | Concordia Band | Civic and Fraternal Organizations | (tab) Order of Owls | [tab] Lunalilo Circle No. 279 | [tab] Court Lunalilo No. 6600 | [tab] Chiefs of Hawaii | Grand Marshal and Aides | Foot Police | Royal Hawaiian Band | Hawaiian Societies: | [tab] Kamehameha Alumnae| [tab] Longshoreman's Mutual Aid | [tab] Kamehameha Alumni | [tab] Hale o na Alii o Hawaii | [tab] Hui Opio L.D.S. | [tab] Hui Ona Manawalea | U.S. Army Band | [tab] Hui Oiwi o na Wahine| [tab] Hui Oiwi o na Kane| [tab] Hui Kalama| [tab] Hui Kaahumanu| [tab] | Kapiolani Maternity Home | Retainers of the late Prince | Physicians of the late Prince | Clergy of All Denominations | Officiating Clergy | Adjutant General of Hawaii and Custodian of the Body of the late Prince | Bearer of Decorations | Daughters and Sons of Hawaiian Warriors | Poolas drawing the Catafalque | Torch Bearers, Order of Kamehameha, Large Kahilis, Small Kahilis, Honorary Pall Bearers, Pall Bearers, CATAFALQUE, Pall Bearers, Honorary Pall Bearers, Small Kahilis, Large Kahilis, Order of Kamehameha, Torch Bearers | Carriage bearing | PRINCESS KALANIANAOLE, PRINCESS KAPIOLANI | and High Chiefess Keomailani | Princess Kawananakoa and Chiefess Maria Maiopili Piikoi Parker | Governor of Hawaii | Commandant 14th Naval District and Aide | Commanding General, Hawaiian Department, and Chief of Staff | Commanding General, Hawaiian Division, and Aide | Chief Justice and Associate Justices of Supreme Court | President of the Senate | Speaker of the House of Representatives | Secretary of Hawaii | Consular Representatives | Governor's Staff | Mayor of the City and County of Honolulu | Heads of the Territorial Departments | Members of the Legislature | Federal Officials | Circuit Judges | Board of Supervisors | Public Officials | Public.[482]

The procession began at 11 a.m., with thousands participating in the procession and tens of thousands lining the route from 'Iolani Palace to the mausoleum.

BURIAL

Once again the torches of Iwikauikaua brought ancient tradition to the burial of royalty. The torches lined the pathway to the burial crypt.[483] The burial service continued at Mauna 'Ala, with the Bishop of Honolulu officiating.

As with the funeral of Lili'uokalani, a film record of the obsequies once existed. The *Honolulu Advertiser* congratulated the Liberty Theatre on the "film of the ceremonies incident to the death and burial of Prince Kalanianaole, which formed one of three features on the program" on January 22, 1922.[484] The film was a collaboration between E.K. Fernandez and W.A. Aldrich, using five cameras to film the Sunday funeral.[485]

Ironically, the state funeral was not what Prince Kalaniana'ole desired. The *Honolulu Advertiser* reported: "he [Kalaniana'ole] expressed a desire that his body be cremated and that a simple funeral service be said over

Episcopal Bishop John La Mothe recited the burial service in the presence of a veiled Princess Kalaniana'ole at Mauna 'Ala (courtesy Hawaii State Archives [PP-25-9-006]).

his ashes at 'Pualeilani' and that the urn be taken to the mausoleum in their motor car, with the Princess driving him to his last resting place."[486]

Elizabeth Keka'aniau (1928)

Elizabeth Keka'aniau, daughter of high chief Gideon La'anui and high chiefess Owana, was one of the students of the Chiefs' Children's School, named eligible to the throne. Born in Waialua, O'ahu, on September 14, 1834, she was 94 when she died.[487] She married Frank S. Pratt. The high chiefess died at 9 a.m. on December 20, 1928, at the residence of her grand-niece, Mrs. Dwight Styne, in Honolulu.[488]

LYING-IN-STATE

The traditional Hawaiian practice surrounding the lying-in-state continued with Keka'aniau: "Throughout Saturday night the Daughters and Sons of Hawaiian Warriors and the Hui Kaahumanu kept watch over the bier. Mrs. J.F. Woods, formerly Princess Kalanianaole, moi of the Warriors' society, and Mrs. Emma Ahuena Taylor, premier of the Warriors, directed watches." Although Keka'aniau was not given an official state funeral, the mourners came from the highest ranks of government: "Governor and Mrs. Wallace R. Farrington were among the distinguished mourners" as was "Ex-Governor Walter F. Frear."

FUNERAL

Her funeral took place at Kawaiaha'o Church on Sunday, December 23, 1928, at 3:30 p.m.[489] The Rev. Akaiko Akana conducted the litany.[490] Called "simple and brief," the funeral lasted just half an hour.[491]

PROCESSION

No formal procession took place for the high chiefess, though the newspaper account noted: "Those who attended the service at the church accompanied the body to Nuuanu cemetery [now called O'ahu Cemetery] where with solemn ceremonies the casket was lowered into the grave of the last of Hawaii's great aliis."[492]

BURIAL

Also conducted by the Rev. Akana, the burial service was read in Hawaiian. The newspaper account noted the body was "interred in historic Nuuanu valley—resting place of many of the nobles of the Hawaii of old."[493] Keka'aniau, however, was buried apart from the other nobles, not in the Royal Mausoleum at Mauna 'Ala, but across Nuuanu Avenue in O'ahu Cemetery.

Elizabeth Kahanu (1932)

Joined in marriage with Prince Jonah Kūhiō Kalaniana'ole, Elizabeth Kahanu was not destined to be joined with him in death. She had married Frank J. Woods after the death of her husband, Jonah Kūhiō Kalaniana'ole. Nevertheless, the woman born Elizabeth Kahanu, continued to be known by her title Princess Kalaniana'ole. The rites following her death on February 19, 1932, however, included no state funeral.[494]

LYING IN STATE

Starting at noon on Saturday, February 20, 1932, the body of Princess Kalaniana'ole lay in state at her Pacific Heights house under the watch of several Hawaiian societies. Though not a state funeral, the emblems of royalty accompanied the obsequies: "Stately kahilis, symbols of royalty, stood on either side of the casket." In addition the "famous jewels of the Order of Kapiolani and the feather cloak of the princess. The cloak was draped over the casket and the jewels were pinned to the dress of the princess, where they remained until a few minutes before the casket was sealed."[495]

FUNERAL

Services were conducted at her Pacific Heights residence by Episcopal Bishop S. Harrington Littell, resulting in a delay of the dedication of St. Andrew's Cathedral by an hour. Col. Curtis P. Iaukea read Psalm 37 in Hawaiian.[496]

PROCESSION

The procession of automobiles, led by the Royal Hawaiian Band, numbered in the dozens, a mile in length. The band played Chopin's Funeral March.[497] An already scheduled concert by the Royal Hawaiian Band was also delayed.[498]

BURIAL

The burial took place, not at the Royal Mausoleum where her first husband, Jonah Kūhiō Kalanianaʻole, was interred a decade earlier, but across the street, beside her second husband, Frank J. Woods, at Nuʻuanu Cemetery. The graveside music consisted of two songs written by royal composers—"Aloha Oe," by her first husband's aunt, Queen Liliʻuokalani, and "Hawaiʻi Ponoʻi," written by her first husband's uncle, King David Kalākaua.[499]

The question of whether she had given up her royal title upon her marriage to Woods was clearly answered by the skies: "Many held that the heady downpour of rain that fell throughout the afternoon was significant of the ancient Hawaiian tradition which says the heavens weep at the passing of an alii."[500]

As it had in so many previous funerals, the *Honolulu Advertiser* characterized the present one as the final one: "So passed the last of the Alii. It was such a funeral as a nation might properly offer to its last monarch, such a funeral as might move the most idle bystander, certainly such a funeral as the Princess herself might have desired, as the last expression of respect and every proper emotion from a loyal people; picturesque, simple, splendid to the last degree sincere and solemn in the uttermost measure."[501] One more princess, the wife of a prince, however, still lived.

Abigail Wahiʻikaʻahuʻula Campbell (1945)

Abigail Wahiʻikaʻahuʻula Campbell would be the last princess of Hawaiʻi by virtue of her marriage to a titled prince, although their nuptials occurred after the end of the monarchy. By the time she married Prince David Laamea Kahalepouli Piʻikoi Kawānanakoa in San Francisco, California, on January 6, 1902, Hawaiʻi was already a territory of the United States. The daughter of James Campbell and Abigail Kuaihelani Maipinepine, she was born in Honolulu on January 1, 1882.

Once again, timing may have had an impact on the funeral observances for Abigail Campbell Kawānanakoa. Her death on April 12, 1945, took place after martial law in Hawaii ended in October 1944. Similar to the timing of the death of Albert Kūnuiākea, the death of Kawānanakoa took place during the Regular Session of the Twenty-Third Legislature of the Territory of Hawaii, which ran from February 21, 1945, to May 4, 1945.

Gov. Ingram Macklin Stainback issued a proclamation on April 13, 1945, calling upon all businesses to close on Saturday, April 14, 1945, but not for Kawānanakoa. The proclamation instead was issued so Hawaiʻi could "join the rest of the nation in mourning for the President [Franklin Delano Roosevelt]." Although written for an American president, the proclamation did have at least an indication of a monarchical past; it was signed "Done at Iolani Palace, Honolulu, Territory of Hawaii."[502] Secure as part of the United States, the government allowed the name to revert back to its original name after being called the "Executive Building" immediately after the overthrow.

The honor for Princess Kawānanakoa would wait another two days after the one for Roosevelt. On April 16, 1945, the Senate of the Territory of Hawaii passed Senate Resolution 46 honoring Princess Abigail Wahikaahuula Kawananakoa, which noted, "in her death, Hawaii has lost the last link with the Hawaiian Crown."[503] The same day the House of Representatives passed H.R. 78, which acknowledged "her generous contributions of time and talents and personality and of material things."[504]

LYING IN STATE

Lying in state would not take place at Iolani Palace. Instead, the residence of the late princess on Judd Street would serve as the venue for visitation. The newspaper noted the traditional sign of the royal funeral: "Nuuanu skies wept during Saturday when the body of the Princess lay in state at her Judd Street home and on Sunday when it was escorted with regal ceremony to its last resting place."[505]

FUNERAL

The minister of the Protestant church that served as the backdrop for the first Western funeral for royalty presided over the funeral ceremony for the last titled member of the Kalākaua dynasty. Edward Kahale, pastor of Kawaiahaʻo Church, comforted the gathered with words that noted the royal nature of the princess regardless of the status of the monarchy: "Within her great and generous heart, within her amazing breadth of mentality, her infinite sympathy, her dauntless courage and her unshakeable constancy in the wise leadership of the people of her race lay her most significant patent of royalty; hers by Divine inspiration."[506] The service displayed the traditional sign of a royal funeral. The newspaper account noted: Graceful kahilis, symbols of royalty, tufted with priceless feathers from now extinct indigenous birds, swayed gently as though nodding affirmation of the words."[507]

In contrast, another ceremony on Sunday morning drew more than 4,000 military personnel to Hickam to offer their final respects to President Franklin Delano Roosevelt.[508]

Procession

Among the pallbearers was Sheriff Duke Kahanamoku. The honorary pallbearers included Gov. Ingram M. Stainback; the chief justice of the supreme court of Hawaii; the president of the territorial senate; a former house speaker; two former Honolulu mayors; and the former delegate to the U.S. Congress, Capt. Victor S.K. Houston. With uniformed cadets from Kamehameha School for Boys serving as *kahili* bearers, the hearse made its way up Nuuanu Avenue the short distance to Mauna 'Ala.[509]

Burial

With "appropriate ceremony" the remains of Kawānanakoa were "placed beside those of her princely husband."[510] With the death of Abigail Campbell Kawānanakoa, the last spouse of an individual proclaimed Prince or Princess by King Kalākaua had died and the Kalākaua Crypt received what was then considered its last burial. The *Honolulu Advertiser* acknowledged: "Descendants of the blood line of the Kamehameha and Kalakaua dynasties remain, but none now lays claim to royal title in this *American* community" (*italics* mine).[511]

Although at the time Kawānanakoa was considered to be the last eligible to be entombed, the *Honolulu Advertiser* pointed out the presence of an empty niche at Mauna 'Ala: "One more crypt in the vault dedicated to the Kalakaua dynasty is empty and will remain so in accordance with the designated disposition of space in the royal tomb. This is the niche that had been intended for the repose of the late Princess Elizabeth Kalanianaole, who elected to forgo her right to burial there when she abandoned her royal title upon her marriage after the death of Prince Kuhio."⁵¹²

David Kalākaua Kawānanakoa (1953)

Though he had not received a royal title from his namesake, David Kalākaua Kawānanakoa was the last male descendant of a prince named eligible for the throne of the Kingdom of Hawai'i. The son of Prince David Kawānanakoa and Princess Abigail Campbell Kawānanakoa would occupy the last niche at Mauna 'Ala.

He was born at the Kawānanakoa residence on Pensacola Street (now the campus of Hawaiian Mission Academy), on March 10, 1904.⁵¹³

Despite the controversy that marked his life, the obsequies observed at his death followed the traditional protocols that had accompanied the funerals of his parents and his namesake.

Lying in State

Arrangements for the obsequies for Kawānanakoa were delayed "pending the arrival of Mrs. Clark Lee [his sister, Lydia Lili'uokalani Kawānanakoa]. He was "survived by his wife, Cecelia Lake Kawananakoa, who he married October 27, 1949, on Bethel Island, California."⁵¹⁴

The funeral service at the church began 2:30 p.m.

Funeral

"In a short funeral sermon, the Rev. Edward Kahale paid tribute to the royal blood of the deceased, saying that "the very name connects us with the memory of King Kalakaua."⁵¹⁵

Procession

Because it was not a state funeral, no formal publication of an Order of Procession appeared in newspapers. The procession, nevertheless, displayed elements of the march of mourners. The route went from Kawaiaha'o Church, down King Street, and up Nu'uanu Avenue to the Royal Mausoleum. The music for at least one portion of the march was recorded: "As the procession moved slowly in the hot afternoon sun past the gates of Iolani Palace, the band played 'Nearer My God to Thee.'"⁵¹⁶

Lacking the military of an independent monarchy, or the status of a state funeral, the procession used uniformed students from the Reserve Officer Training Corps at the school founded by Bernice Pauahi in the role reserved for "soldiers." The *Honolulu Star-Bulletin* reported the order of procession:

An honor guard of R.O.T.C. students from Kamehameha School followed the band and seven police motorcycles that helped clear the way ahead. More than 50 men and women of Hale O Na Alii Society, wearing red and gold capes, marched behind the honor guard. Mr. Kawananakoa was Regent of Hale O Na Alii after the death of his mother Abigail Kawananakoa, its founder.

Behind the marcher, about 50 cars moved slowly carrying older members of the society, black clad ladies of the Kaahumanu Society and the active and honorary pallbearers led by Governor King and John C. Lane.[517]

The procession also featured an element found exclusively in royal funerals: "Kahilis made of feathers of now extinct Hawaiian birds [...] together with with tabu sticks which are the mark of Hawaiian royalty."[518]

Instead of a horse-drawn carriage, the kāhili now marked the motorized hearse that carried the coffin of the deceased: "Members of Hale O Na Alii carried four large and six small feather kahili next to the hearse, while Manuel Silva walked immediately ahead giving the traditional chants of the Kalakaua family."[519] The four *kāhili* paled in comparison to the more than one hundred paraded in the procession of his uncle more than two decades earlier, but nevertheless reflected the presence of royalty. Accounts do not mention whether the other aspect of Kalākaua dynasty obsequies—the daylight kukui nut torches—appeared during the observances for the grandnephew and namesake of last king of Hawai'i.

BURIAL

On Saturday, May 24, 1953, the remains of David Kalākaua Kawānanakoa, the son of a prince, but never himself named a prince, were brought to Mauna 'Ala to rest with the king, queens, princes and princesses of the Kalākaua dynasty. David Bray, a *kahuna*, delivered the final chant as the gray casket of Kawānanakoa went down the stairs into the underground tomb. In what would have gone against the wishes of Queen Lili'uokalani, her composition about parting lovers, "Aloha Oe," was played "in final farewell"[520] at what many considered the last royal funeral.[521]

2

Burial Places

> Ka hale koʻekoʻe o ka pō.
> The cold house of darkness.[1]
> —Hawaiian proverb

After the introduction of Western burial practices for *aliʻi*, a series of tombs were constructed for Hawaiian royalty: the tomb at Honolulu Fort, tomb at Halekamani, tomb at Mokuʻula on Maui, the Royal Cemetery at Pohukaina, and the Royal Mausoleum at Mauna ʻAla. Mauna ʻAla consists of four tombs and a memorial: John Young Tomb, Kamehameha Tomb, Wyllie Tomb, Kalakaua Tomb and Charles Reed Bishop Memorial.

The hiding of the bones of Kamehameha the Great to prevent the expropriation of his spiritual power or *mana* by his rivals stands in stark contrast to the burial of his son, Liholiho, in a known place, the royal tomb at Pohukaina. "Mausoleum" in Hawaiian is "*ilina*," the Royal Mausoleum being called *Ka ilina o nā aliʻi*. A cemetery is pā ilina.

The royal burial sites that preceded the Western burials were Hale o Līloa and Hale o Keawe. Historian S.M. Kamakau listed the names twenty-seven chiefs put in *kāʻai*: Haholani, PalenaniuiaHaho, HanaaPalena, LanakawaiaHana, Laau, Pili, Koa, Loe, Kukohoulani, Kanipahu, Kalapana, Kahai (Kakaimoeleaikaaikapupou), Kalau (Kalaunuiohua), Kuaiwa, KahoukapuKauhola, Kihanuilulumoku, Liloa, UminuiaLiloa, Kanaloa or Kukailani, Makakaualii, Iwikauikaua, Lono, Keaweikekahiaaliimomoku, Kalaniaeaumoku (Keeaumoku), Kalanikupuapaikalaninui (Keoua) and Kalaniaihienaena.[2] Malcolm Naea Chun speculated that "these chiefs may be those whose bones were interred at Hale o Liloa."[3] The twenty-three names of the chiefs from Hale o Keawe were also recorded, this time by missionary Levi Chamberlain[4]: "Keawe, Kumukoa, Lonoikahaupu, Hukihe, Kakoamano, Keaweakanuha, Niula, Kowainiulani, Lonoamoana, Lonohonuakini, Ahaula, Kanaloaikaiwilewa, Keohokuma, O Kua/Kua, Umioopa,

Keaweluaole, Keaeakapeleaumoku, Kuaialii, Kaaloa, Lonoakolii, Laleioku, Kalaimamahu, and Kaoleioku."[5]

Here is a chant associated with the *kāʻai* of King Keawe:

> ʻO Keawe kea aliʻi,
> ʻO Manawainapoʻo ka ʻaha
> ʻO Kahuluiaiku kāholo ka ʻaha maloko,
> ʻO Kaolemaiheʻeluʻukia,
> ʻO Luʻukia ka ʻaha lanalana,
> ʻO Kekapo ma waho,
> Paʻa ʻia Keawe a kū i kāʻai.
> Keawe was the chief,
> Manawainapoʻo was the (name of his sacred) cord,
> Kahuluiaiku was the cord inside,
> Kaolemaiheʻeluʻukia,
> Luʻukia was the cord for lashing,
> Kekapo was the cord outside,
> And bound was Keawe in the *kāʻai*.[6]

In 1829 Kaʻahumanu took the bones of the chiefs from the Hale o Keawe (and Hale o Līloa) and had them sent to Kaʻawaloa.[7] The missionary letters to the American Board of Commissioners for Foreign Missions described the transfer: "Kaahumanu and other chiefs accompanied by Mr. Ruggles, removed from this house to Kaawaloa the bones of 24 ancient kings and princes. The bones were put into two coffins and after funeral services deposited into the common burying place."[8] Kamakau recorded the reason for the move: "When she [Kaʻahumanu] heard that some chiefs and people had been deifying the bones of chiefs deposited in the Hale-o-Keawe at Honaunau, Kona, and at Waipiʻo in Hamakua, she gathered up the bones and deposited them in the cliffs of Kaʻawaloa and burned the debris. Her name was heaped with abuse for this deed, but what she really did was place the bones where they would be undisturbed."[9] Ultimately, the remains would be disturbed. The two large containers in which the kāʻai had been stored were taken from the caves of Pali Kapu o Keoua and moved to Honolulu on the British man-o-war *Vixen* after its visit to Kaʻawaloa in 1858.

W.D. Alexander commented in the *Maile Wreath*, an often handwritten set of missives that was circulated among members of the Hawaiian Mission Children's Society, about Hale o Keawe: "After the completion of the present mausoleum in Nuuanu, on the night of October 30, 1865, the coffins of the former royal personages of Hawaii nei, including those brought from Kaawaloa were removed to it in an imposing torch-light procession. It is to be hoped that their repose will not be disturbed again."[10]

The *iwi* or bones kept at Hale o Keawe were transported by Kaʻahumanu to caves at Kaʻawaloa to prevent people from deifying them (courtesy Hawaii State Archives [PP-29-8-017]).

Fort Tomb

A Western style royal burial site was created for Kauwai at the Honolulu Fort. The disposition of her remains after their original interment is unknown; the fort was demolished starting in January 1857. The *Pacific Commercial Advertiser* reported: "The work of demolishing this great eyesore has commenced."[11] Whether she was moved to the Royal Tomb after it was built at Pohukaina is unknown; she does not appear on the list transferred to Mauna 'Ala.

Tomb Near Halekamani

The next royal burial site was located in Lahaina near the residence of Nāhiʻenaʻena. The Interior Department noted on Feb. 16, 1854, that the "tomb is situated on the S.E. side of the Halekamani premises."[12] The building was the final resting place for Queen Keōpūolani, Kaumualiʻi and Nāhiʻenaʻena. Their remains were later transferred to Mokuʻula Tomb.

Mokuʻula Tomb

Sometime after the burial of Nāhiʻenaʻena, the remains interred at the tomb near Halekamani were transferred to a tomb at Mokuʻula. In 1884 some were later transferred from the tomb to Mauna 'Ala and others to the tomb at Waineʻe cemetery.

Waiola Cemetery (Waineʻe Cemetery), Lahaina, Maui

Individuals known to be buried at Waineʻe Cemetery, now called Waiola Cemetery, are:

Hoapili, trusted advisor of Kamehameha I
Keopuolani, wife of Kamehameha I
Kaheiheimalie, wife of Kamehameha I, later wife of Hoapili, also known as Kalakua and Hoapiliwahine. Mother of Kamāmalu and Kīnaʻu
Kekauonohi, granddaughter of Kamehameha I, wife of Kamehameha II, later wife of Kealiihonui and Levi Haalelea
Liliha, Wife of Boki, daughter of Hoapili
Nahienaena, sister of Kamehameha III

Royal Tomb at Pohukaina, Honolulu (1825)

Constructed in 1825 to house the remains of King Kamehameha II and Kamāmalu, the Royal Tomb at Pohukaina served for four decades as the primary burial site for *ali'i*. The site of the tomb and enclosure are marked as "Royal Cemetery" on an 1825 map by Lt. C.R. Malden of H.M.S. *Blonde*, the ship that had returned the bodies of Kamehameha II and Kamāmalu to Hawai'i.

The royal couple were joined in the Pohukaina tomb by Nāmāhāna six years later in 1829. The remains of Ka'ahumanu next entered the Royal Tomb in 1832.

In 1836, Levi Chamberlain noted in his journal: "his [John Young's] remains were deposited in the enclosure of the Royal Cemetery."[13] Chamberlain also noted that Young was "buried with military honors."[14] Unlike the other members of the royal family, John Young was not entombed in the Royal Tomb itself, but on the grounds of the Royal Tomb within the enclosure.

Whitewashed walls without windows and a single heavy door distinguish the Royal Tomb at Pohukaina (middle left) (courtesy Hawaii State Archives [PP-38-1-009]).

2. Burial Places

The coffin of Queen Kīnaʻu was put in the Royal Tomb in 1839.

The burial in the Royal Tomb of Haʻalilio, the first envoy from Hawaiʻi, marked an early instance of inclusion of individuals, who were not royalty but had provided special service to the kingdom.

The coffin of Kekāululohi was deposited in the Royal Tomb with military honors in June 1845. The Royal Tomb was located on the grounds of her house.

At the June 7, 1848, meeting of the Privy Council, Kanaʻina, the husband of the late Kekāuluohi, "brought forward a motion for an appropriation for repairs to the Royal Cemetery." The condition of the royal tomb prompted suggestions in the Privy Council for a new location for the deceased chiefs. "Mr. Judd suggested that it would be better to transfer the coffins to the Vaults underneath Mr. Armstrong's Church [Kawaiahaʻo]. Mr. Wyllie was of the same opinion, but as Judge Lee stated some doubts, whether pestiferous exhalations could be prevented, it was agreed to postpone the question for further consideration."[15]

"Reminiscences of Honolulu" published in 1882 described the original Royal Mausoleum simply as "a coral stone building, situated in Kekauluohi's premises, (since incorporated in the Palace grounds)."[16]

On December 19, 1849, the Privy Council approved payment of $169 to Kanaʻina for repairing the "Royal Mausoleum."[17] On January 24, 1850, Privy Council approved $27 to Kanaʻina "for shingles to be employed on the Royal Cemetery."[18]

A report in the April 1855 *Sailors' Magazine and Naval Journal* described the Royal Tomb at Pohukaina:

> In the Royal Sepulchre rest the mortal remains of Kihoriho [*sic*] Kamehameha II, and his Queen, who died in England in 1824, but which were brought hither in 1825, on board the frigate "Blonde." There rest also the remains of Kaahumanu, Kinau, the Rev. Wm. Richards and several others, whose names are well known to the religious community in the United States.[19]

A July 1865 issue of *Hours at Home* depicted the interior of the Royal Tomb. Based on a February 1865 visit to Honolulu, the detailed account read:

> Next to the palace grounds are those of a high chief [Kanaʻina], within which stands the royal tomb. This is a small stone building with only one room. On a table in the center, lying on a crimson velvet cushion, is the Hawaiian crown. On either side are frames supporting enormous coffins. Here lies the dust of kings and queens. No one seems to know where the remains of Kamehameha I., the founder of the present dynasty, were deposited, but here are Kamehameha II., and his queen, who died on a visit to England ; and here are those of the third Kamehameha. The most interesting of all is the coffin of Kaahumanu, the favorite queen of the conqueror. When the first

missionaries landed, she was an imperious pagan; afterward she became a lowly Christian.[20]

The next couple of decades filled the coral sepulcher at Pohukaina.

Royal Tomb at Pohukaina Filled

Cabinet appointments were delayed following the death of Kamehameha IV because the funeral required a suitable burial site. The *Pacific Commercial Advertiser* reported the circumstances regarding the postponement:

> The delay is caused by the necessity of erecting a new royal tomb, the building used for that purpose in the palace grounds being full. The new tomb is located in the vacant lot opposite the residence of Judge Andrews, in Nuuanu. It is now in process of erection, and numerous workmen are busy hurrying on the work, but it will require at least a month to complete it. When finished, the remains of the late King, those of the Prince and of all the deceased Sovereigns and chiefs now in the royal tomb, are to be removed thither. The site chosen is admirably suited for the purpose, and with liberal outlay and taste in embellishing, it can be made a most beautiful spot as it will surely be a sacred one.[21]

On October 30, 1865, eighteen caskets were transferred to Mauna 'Ala from the Royal Tomb at Pohukaina.

In preparation for building the current 'Iolani Palace the grounds were expanded to include the property that once contained the Royal Tomb. In 1881, Kalākaua put up a mound to mark the spot where the former sepulcher stood: "In Pohukaina lot, within the enclosure of the palace yard, stood the tomb-house of former kings and chiefs; garden mound erected by King Kalakaua."[22]

In 1883, "An Unpublished Chapter of Hawaiian History" from *Harper's Monthly*, reprinted in the *Pacific Commercial Advertiser*, revealed another use that had been made of the royal tomb during the loss of sovereignty in in 1843: "The papers were drawn up by Dr. Judd and a confidential clerk at midnight, in the royal tomb in Honolulu, with a king's coffin for a table."

Gorman D. Gilman, who had arrived in Honolulu in 1841, gave in 1904 a brief description of the royal tomb: "There was one very modest building, of very plain construction without a window; the only light entering was through a heavy door which was the only opening. This was the tomb of the royal family, kings and queens."[23] A photograph of the building shows that the door faced *makai*.

By 1909, the widespread memory of the site had dimmed and Gilman, then living in Boston, was called upon once again to answer an inquiry about "a mound at the corner of Punchbowl and King streets thought by some to be a relic of the old tomb of royalty."[24] Gilman confirmed the identification of the site and gave a description of the former sepulcher: "The tomb of the royal family, Liholiho and wife, Kaahumanu and Kinau, was a small structure built of coral which stood alone, some way from any street, in the palace grounds, on the right-hand side of the main drive to the entrance to the palace from King street. At that time, 1842, it was quite a distance from any street."[25] Gilman also suggested why Dr. Judd had used the tomb to write his diplomatic papers: "As I remember it, it had no window; hence any light inside could not be seen on the outside. Thence Dr. Judd retreated in the Lord George Paulette reign of English rule over the Islands."[26]

Fifteen years later, A.P. Taylor, head of the Archives of Hawaii, was once again answering the question: "Where was the old royal tomb located?"

Just as the remains of John Young were buried just outside the Royal Mausoleum and the grave of Auhea Kekauluohi sits on the Waikīkī side of the Lunalilo Mausoleum, burials may still exist on the grounds of the Royal Cemetery at Pohukaina. A lead coffin was discovered in 1931 that was believed to be that of Princess Kekupuohi, a wife of Kamehameha I.[27] Kekupuohi died on February 8, 1836, in Kailua on the island of Hawai'i.[28] A historical sketch about the royal tomb written more than a decade later concluded: "Many Hawaiians claim that the remains of several high chiefs are still beneath the former crypt."[29]

Henry P. Judd continued the call made seventeen years earlier for a marker for the royal tomb in *makai*-Waikīkī corner of 'Iolani Palace grounds.[30]

Today, the former location of the royal tomb sits surrounded by a low brick wall topped by an iron fence. A plaque reads: "Site of | First Royal Mausoleum and Crypt | Built in 1825 to House the Remains of | King Kamehameha II | and | Queen Kamamalu | Who Died in England in July 1824 | Used as a Royal Tomb until 1865." Another plaque reads: "KAPU | Only Authorized Persons Are Allowed | In This Historic Burial Mound. Please | Do Not Enter."

Mauna 'Ala, Royal Mausoleum at Kawānanakoa, Nu'uanu, Honolulu

At the meeting of the Privy Council, on December 3, 1863, a motion was made to construct a new Royal Tomb at Kawānanakoa, in Nu'uanu, for an amount not exceeding $2,000.[31] A letter from Heuck requested an appropriation of $6,000.[32]

On December 3, 1863, the "Privy Council approved the "recommendation of the Cabinet for the erection of a Mausoleum, and approve of the recommendation to furnish necessary Coral, and labour for the purpose."[33]

"Mon. Varigny addressed his Majesty begging permission to read a letter from Mr. Heuck addressed to the Minister of Finance in regard to the Completion of the Mausoleum. Praying that an immediate consideration be taken in finishing the other part of the mausoleum, as the old tombs that contain the body of the old Kings and Chiefs were in a very unfit condition. Estimating the sum of $6,000 to be appropriated and expended to complete the said work."[34]

"Mr. Allen, in accordance to the suggestions of His Majesty moved that the matter be referred to the committee to whom were appointed to the building the Mausoleum. The Motion was seconded by M. Wyllie and unanimously passed."[35]

The Royal Mausoleum at Mauna 'Ala opened in 1865 (courtesy Hawaii State Archives [PP-50-10-010]).

2. Burial Places

On February 1, 1864, the minister of the interior requested that Anglican Bishop Thomas Nettleship Staley dedicate the Royal Mausoleum at Mauna 'Ala.

On February 16, 1864, the Privy Council passed a resolution "the further sum of fifteen hundred dollars more, to close the present expenses incurred for the building of the Royal Mausoleum."[36]

Under the supervision of T.C. Heuck work on the Royal Mausoleum started again in early June 1865 using $8,000 appropriated by the legislature of the Session of 1864 that ended January 10, 1865.

On March 4, 1874, the *Hawaiian Gazette* listed twenty-six sets of remains entombed in the Royal Mausoleum.[37] The number included Lunalilo who was temporarily placed there until his own mausoleum could be constructed at Kawaiaha'o. The 1874 roster in the *Hawaiian Gazette*, comprised:

1.—Kamehameha II, who died in England, July 14, 1824.
2.—Queen Kamamalu, wife of the above, who died in England, July 8, 1824.
3.—Queen Kaahumanu, Regent under Kamehameha III., and Premier under Kamehameha III. Died June 5, 1832.
4.—Queen Kinau, daughter of Kamehameha I., wife of Kekuanaoa, and mother of Kamehameha IV. and V. Died April 4, 1839.
5.—Kamanele, daughter of Gov. Kuakini, of Hawaii.
6.—Kamehameha III., died December 15, 1854.
7.—Kamehameha IV., died November 30, 1864.
8.—The Prince of Hawaii, son of Kamehameha IV., and Queen Emma, died Aug., 1862.
9.—David, son of Kinau and Gov. Kekuanaoa. Died in 1837.
10.—Moses, another son of the above, died in 1848.
11.—Wm. Pitt Leleiohoku, Governor of Hawaii, died in 1848
12.—A. Paki, father of the Hon. Mrs. Bishop, died June 13, 1855.
13.—L. Konia, wife of Paki, and mother of Hon. Mrs. Bishop, died July 2, 1857.
14.—Keaweaweula, infant child of Kamehameha III.
15.—John Pitt Kinau, son of Gov. Leleiohoku of Hawaii.
16.—Keola, infant child of the Governess of Hawaii [Ke'elikōlani].
17.—Remains of Liloa and Lonoikamakahiki, two ancient kings of Hawaii.

18.—Dr. T.C.B. Rooke, died Dec. 28, 1858.
19.—Keoni Ana, son of John Young the pioneer, Premier under Kamehameha III., died in 1857.
20.—B. Namakeha, died in 1860.
21.—Jane Young, daughter of the elder John Young.
22.—Robert C. Wyllie, for many years Crown Minister; died Oct. 30, 1865.
23.—Princess Victoria K. Kaahumanu, sister of Kamehameha IV., and V., died May 29, 1866.
24.—Queen Kalama, wife of Kamehameha III., died Sept. 20, 1870.
25.—M. Kekuanaoa, Governor of Oahu, and father of Kaemhameha IV. and V.
26.—King Lunalilo, died February 3, 1874.[38]

A joint resolution of the U.S. Congress dated May 31, 1900, withdrew the "Royal Mausoleum premises from sale, lease or other disposition under the public land laws of the United States."[39]

Although originally entombed in the building now designated as the chapel at Mauna 'Ala, the royal remains today are contained in four different locations: the John Young Tomb, the Kamehameha Tomb, the Wyllie Tomb, and the Kalākaua Crypt.

John Young Tomb

The tomb of John Young[40] is inscribed: "Beneath this Stone are deposited the remains of JOHN YOUNG (of Lancashire in England) the Friend and Companion in Arms of KAMEHAMEHA who departed this life December 17, 1835 in the 93rd year of his age and the 46th of his residence on the SANDWICH ISLANDS." He was interred May 16, 1866. Also buried in the tomb are Ka'ōanā'eha[41] (also known as Melie or Mary Kuamoo, second wife of John Young), interred May 16, 1866, and possibly James Young Kanehoa[42] (son of Namokuelua and John Young).

Kamehameha Tomb (1887)

Twenty coffins of the Kamehameha Dynasty were moved "with fitting solemnity"[43] to the Kamehameha Vault from 7:30 p.m. on November 9, 1887, to 2 a.m. the following day.[44] The names listed in the *Pacific Commercial Advertiser* comprised "Kaahumanu I, Kamamalu I, David Kamehameha, Kaahumanu II (Kinau), Kekuanaoa, Kamehameha V, Kamehameha IV, Victoria Kamamalu, Moses Kekuewa, Keola Paki Bishop, William Pitt

2. Burial Places

The Kamehameha Vault separated the Kamehameha Dynasty remains from those of the Kalākaua Dynasty (courtesy Hawaii State Archives [PP-50-10-009]).

Leleiohoku, Keaweaweula, John William Pitt Kinau, Queen Kalama, Queen Emma, Prince of Hawaii, Paki and Konia, parents of Hon. Mrs. B.P. Bishop, Ruth Keelikolani, Hon. Mrs. Bernice Pauahi Bishop."[45] The list does not include Kamehameha II and Kamehameha III. It was dedicated June 19, 1904.

A monument now tops the tomb listing the individuals interred below. The *makai* face lists:

    1. Kamehameha II[46,47] ['Iolani Liholiho, son of Keōpūolani and Kamehameha I] He is listed as "1" in the November 4, 1865, list.

    2. Kamehameha III[48,49] [son of Keōpuolani and Kamehameha I] He is listed as "2" in the November 4, 1865, list.

    3. Kamehameha IV[50] [Alexander, son of Kīna'u and Kekūanāo'a] Interred February 3, 1864.[51] He is listed as "3" in the November 4, 1865, list.

    4. Kamehameha V[52,53] [Lot, son of Kīna'u and Kekūanāo'a]

    5. Kahaku o Hawaii[54,55] [Albert Edward Kauikeaouli] Interred February 3, 1864. The *Hawaiian Gazette* calls him "Prince of Hawaii." He is listed as "4" in the November 4, 1865, list.

    6. Emma Kaleleonalani[56,57] [Also known as Emma Rooke, wife of Kamehameha IV; *Hawaiian Gazette* calls her "Queen Emma"]

The *mauka* face lists:

7. Kaahumanu R.[58,59] [Kaʻahumanu, wife of Kamehameha I; "R." is the abbreviation for Regina, Latin for Queen.] She is listed as "6" in the November 4, 1865, list.

8. Kamamalu R.[60,61] [Kamāmalu, wife of Kamehameha II; she is listed as "5" in the November 4, 1865, list]

9. Kalama R.[62] [Wife of Kamehameha III]

10. Leleiohoku[63] [husband of Harieta Nāhiʻenaʻena and Ruth Keʻelikōlani, son of Kalanimoku]

11. Keaweaweula[64,65] [Keaweaweʻula, son of Kalama and Kamehameha III]

12. W.P. Kinau[66] [John William Pitt Kīnaʻu, son of Leleiohoku and Ruth Keʻelikōlani; *HG* lists him as "Wm. Pitt Leleiohoku"]

The ʻEwa face lists:

13. Kinau[67,68] [Kīnaʻu, mother of David Kamehameha, Moses Kekūāiwa, Kamehameha IV, Kamehameha V and Victoria Kamāmalu; *Hawaiian Gazette* calls her "Queen Kinau"]

14. Kekuanaoa[69,70] [Kekūanāoʻa, father of Keʻelikōlani, David Kamehameha, Moses Kekūāiwa, Kamehameha IV, Kamehameha V, Victoria Kamāmalu; *Hawaiian Gazette* calls him "Gov. M. Kekuanaoa"]

15. D. Kamehameha[71,72] [David Kamehameha, son of Kīnaʻu and Kekūanāoʻa]

16. Kekuaiwa[73,74] [Moses Kekūāiwa, son of Kīnaʻu and Kekūanāoʻa; *Hawaiian Gazette* lists as "Moses Kekuaiwa"]

17. Victoria Kamamalu[75,76] [Victoria Kamāmalu, daughter of Kīnaʻu and Kekūanāoʻa; *Hawaiian Gazette* calls her "Victoria K. Kaahumanu"]

18. Keelikolani[77,78] [Ruth Keʻelikōlani, daughter of Pauahi and Kekūanāoʻa]

The Diamond Head face lists:

19. Paki[79,80] [Abner Paki, father of Bernice Pauahi Bishop; *Hawaiian Gazette* lists as "A. Paki"]

20. Konia[81,82] [Laura Kōnia, mother of Bernice Pauahi Bishop; *Hawaiian Gazette* lists as "L. Konia"]

21. Bernice Pauahi[83,84] [daughter of Paki and Kōnia, wife of Charles Reed Bishop; the 1997 brochure lists her as Bernice Pauahi Bishop]

22. Keola [son of Ruth Keʻelikōlani and Isaac Young Davis Davis (married 1856–1868), *hānai* son of Bernice Pauahi Bishop and Charles Reed Bishop; *Hawaiian Gazette* lists as "Keola, son of Governess of Hawaii"]. The *Pacific Commercial Advertiser* has "Keola, infant child of the Governess of Hawaii, adopted by Mrs. Bishop."[85] The 1997 brochure lists him as Keolaokalani.

23. Keolaonalani.[86,87] Not mentioned in November 4, 1865, *Pacific Commercial Advertiser* list. According to David Parker: "He was a son of Leleiohoku and Princess Ruth Keʻelikōlani. He died as an infant."[88] Leleiohoku and Princess Ruth Keʻelikōlani were married between 1841 and 1848. The 1997 brochure omits Keolaonalani.

Not listed on monument but buried in Kamehameha Tomb:

24. Charles Reed Bishop[89] [husband of Bernice Pauahi]

Wyllie Tomb (1904)

The construction in 1904 of what today is called the Wyllie Tomb, but was originally called the Queen Emma Tomb, removed the remainder of individuals related to the Kamehameha dynasty from Royal Mausoleum building. The tomb cost $15,000 to construct.[90] The dedication took place under the auspices of the church that Queen Emma and her husband had invited to Hawaiʻi. The *Independent* announced: "Next Sunday afternoon [June 19, 1904], beginning at 4 o'clock, Bishop Restarick, assisted by clergy under him, as well as some of the other denominations, will dedicate the Royal tombs in Nuuanu valley. The vaults to be dedicated are those known as the Kamehameha and the Queen Emma [now called Wyllie] tombs. Queen Emma's remains are laid away in the Kamehameha tomb, but the tomb known after her contains the remains of nine members of her family."[91] At the dedication Restarick delivered an address that noted: "It is an instinct of the human race that has led men everywhere to select and build places of burial for those who have been great above their fellows, and the Hawaiian people have always been careful as to the burial places of their chiefs."[92] The *Pacific Commercial Advertiser* described the newly built burial vault: "Upon the grassy arch of the tomb proper is a heavy concrete block about ten feet long and two feet in height. From the four corners, low, thick pillars of concrete rear themselves as supports for an immense slab of concrete which in turn is topped by another with Grecian facades. A ball of concrete surmounts the whole, this last ornament typifying a tabu ball. The concrete was made from broken stone brought from the island mountains and therefore resembles the familiar dark-mouse-colored lava stone."[93] The monument combines the Western elements of Grecian architecture along with the indigeneous symbol of the aliʻi. The four faces have inscribed, gilded names:

The *makai* face lists the names of Queen Emma's cousin, Albert K. Kunuiakea; her aunt, Jane K. Lahilahi; and her cousin, Peter Young Kekuaokalani:

    1. Albert K. Kunuiakea[94] [son of Kamehameha III and Jane Lahilahi; the 1997 brochure does not have his middle initial][95]
    2. Jane K. Lahilahi[96] [daughter of John Young and Kaʻōanaʻeha; the 1997 brochure does not have her middle initial][97]
    3. Peter Y. Kekuaokalani[98,99] [Peter Young Kaeo. Kaeo, son of Jane Lahilahi and Kaeo; *Hawaiian Gazette* lists as "Peter Y. Kaeo, brother of Queen Emma"][100]

The *mauka* face of the monument lists Queen Emma's uncle, John Kaleipaihala Young; and her key advisor, Robert Crichton Wyllie, whose name is curiously misspelled "Wylie."

    4. J. Kaleipaihala Young[101,102] [Keoni Ana, John Young 2nd, son of John Young and Kaʻōanaʻeha] Interred May 16, 1866, in John Young Tomb.[103] *Hawaiian Gazette* calls him "Keoni Ana (John Young)."
    5. R.C. Wylie [*sic*][104] [Robert Crichton Wyllie][105,106]

The ʻEwa side of the monument is inscribed with the names of the uncle of Queen Emma, Bennet Y. Namakeha, and her mother, Fanny K. Kekelaokalani,

    6. Bennet Y. Namakeha[107] [brother of George Naea (father of Queen Emma); the 1891 *Hawaiian Gazette* lists "Namakaeha, a prominent chief."[108] Namakaeha is most likely Bennet Nāmākēhā. The 1997 brochure does not have his middle initial][109]
    7. Fanny K. Kekelaokalani[110,111] [mother of Queen Emma, daughter of Kaʻōanaʻeha and John Young; the 1997 brochure does not have her middle initial][112]

The Waikīkī face lists Queen Emma's *hānai* parents:

    8. T.C.B. Rooke[113] [Thomas Charles Byde Rooke, *hānai* father of Queen Emma][114,115]
    9. G. Kamaikui Rooke[116] [Grace Kamaʻikuʻi Rooke, *hānai* mother of Queen Emma; 1997 has G. instead of Grace][117]

The names on the sides most likely refer to the location of the individuals in the cruciform crypt below the monument.

Kalakaua Crypt (1910)

The building of the Kalākaua Crypt, the last resting place of Queen Liliʻuokalani, ironically came through the efforts of William Owen Smith, a member of the Committee of Safety that overthrew the last monarch of the Kalākaua dynasty and also a member of the Annexation Commission that brought about the establishment of the United States Territory of Hawaii. On the Ides of March, 1907, Smith, a senator representing the third senatorial district of Territory of Hawaii, introduced Concurrent Resolution No. 4 for an appropriation of $20,000 "for the purpose of interring the Remains of some of the Kings and High Chiefs of Hawaii."[118] The resolution was referred to the Senate ways and means committee. The committee on public expenditures considered the resolution and reported "while the object sought is commendable, the financial condition of the of the Territory of Hawaii is such that we cannot recommend the insertion of the item."[119] Smith moved to table the report and refer the resolution to the judiciary committee where he was a member. The judiciary committee subsequently reported favorably on the resolution, and Smith inserted its contents into Senate Bill 106, introduced late in the session, on April 15, 1907, "under suspension of the Rules."[120] Governor George Robert Carter vetoed the bill on April 26, 1907, stating that approval would require "sacrificing of many items of more immediate importance."[121] The governor's brother, Charles Lunt Carter, had been the only casualty in the counter-revolution of 1895. The senate overrode the veto with more than a two-thirds majority the same day, and the house by the same margin four days later.[122] Ten months later Marston Campbell, superintendent of public works, sent a letter to Queen Liliʻuokalani asking that she appoint a representative and "furnish a list of the remains of the sovereigns and high chiefs which [...] should be placed within the new vault."[123] Liliʻuokalani responded to Campbell's request by naming A.S. Cleghorn as her representative. By June 1909 the preparations for the Kalākaua Crypt were well underway. What was originally planned as a white marble column was replaced with a "a column with a crown thereon of [...] dark colored granite"[124] Jonah Kūhiō Kalanianaʻole also wrote Campbell a couple of days later, noting that he was "in favor of such suggestions as I believe it to be best and lasting."[125]

A year later Campbell announced the completion of the crypt to the mayor of Honolulu, giving him a timetable for the completion of the relo-

The Kalākaua Crypt displayed royal symbols, *kāhili* and *kapu* sticks in January 1922 for the burial of Prince Jonah Kūhiō Kalanianaʻole (courtesy Hawaii State Archives [PP-25-9-010]).

cated fence on Nuuanu street: "On the night of the 24th of this month [June] the bodies of the sovereigns and high chiefs of Hawaii now reposing in the Mausoleum will be removed to the new vault lately constructed."[126] Although Campbell thought the laying of the cornerstone would take place a "few weeks later," Campbell informed Liliʻuokalani in late August 1910 that "everything will be ready for the laying of the Corner Stone of the new Mausoleum on October 1st."[127] Although Campbell was confident in the completion, he received a request on September 29, 1910, from the Hawaiian Iron Fence and Monument Works for an extension of the time to complete interior vault work.[128] The next day Campbell granted a thirty-day extension.

Liliʻuokalani's representative, A.S. Cleghorn, would not see the dedication of the Kalakaua Crypt. He died November 1, 1910, and Campbell requested the simple inscription be placed on the slab: "Gov. A.S. Cleghorn Born 1835 Died 1910."[129] The ceremony still had not taken place when Liliʻuokalani wrote to Campbell on July 24, 1912:

2. Burial Places

I am very anxious that steps be taken before you leave office to have the one remaining casket in the Mausoleum conveyed to its last resting place in the tomb and the services of dedication held at an early date.

I feel that we owe this duty to the dead, and as the living representative of the last dynasty of Hawaii, I make this personal appeal to you in the hope that you may see your way to carry out and fulfill the work entrusted to your care.[130]

The individuals interred in the Kalākaua Crypt are listed as:

1. King Kalakaua | Born Nov. 16, 1836. | Died Jan. 20, 1891[131,132,133] [King David Laamea Kamananakapu Mahinulani Naloiaehuokalani Lumialani Kalākaua, Mauka Top]

2. Queen Kapiolani | Born Dec. 31, 1834. | Died June 24, 1899.[134,135] [Queen Kapiʻolani, wife of Kalākaua, Mauka Bottom]

3. Queen Liliuokalani | Last Sovereign of Hawaii | Born 1838–Died 1917[136,137] [Queen Liliʻuokalani, sister of Kalākaua. Diamond Head Wall, Waena Column, Middle Row]

4. Gov. J.O. Dominis | Born 1832–Died 1891[138,139] [John Owen Dominis, husband of Queen Liliʻuokalani, Diamond Head Wall, Mauka Column, Middle Row]

5. H.R.H. Like Like | Born 1851–Died 1887[140,141,142] [Miriam Likelike, sister of Kalākaua, Diamond Head Wall, Mauka Column, Bottom Row]

6. Gov. A.S. Cleghorn | Born 1835–Died 1910[143,144] [Archibald Scot Cleghorn, husband of Princess Likelike. Diamond Head Wall, Makai Column, Bottom Row]

7. H.R.H. Kaiulani | Born 1875 Died 1899[145,146] [Kaʻiulani, daughter of Princess Likelike and Archibald Cleghorn. Diamond Head Wall, Waena Column, Bottom Row]

8. H.R.H. Leleiohoku | Born 1855–Died 1877[147] [brother of King Kalākaua, *hānai* son of Princess Ruth Keʻelikōlani Diamond Head Wall, Makai Column, Middle Row]

9. Kaiminaauao | Born 1845–Died 1848[148,149] [daughter of C. Kapaakea and A Keoholalole. Diamond Head Wall, Makai Column, Top Row]

10. H.H. Keohokalole | Born 1818–Died 1869[150,151] [Ane Keohokālole, mother of King Kalākaua. Diamond Head Wall, Waena Column, Top Row]

11. C. Kapaakea | Born 1817–Died 1866[152,153] [Caesar Kapaʻakea Kaluaiku Kamakaehukai Kahana Keola, father of King Kalākaua. Diamond Head Wall, Mauka Column, Top Row]

12. H.R.H. Princess | Abigail Wahiikaahuula | Kawananakoa |

Jan 1, 1883-Apr. 12, 1945[154] [wife of David Kawananakoa, daughter of Abigail Kuaihelani Maipinepine and James Campbell, Ewa Wall, Mauka Column, Bottom Row]

13. Keaweaheulu[155] [Great-grandfather of Kalākaua. Ewa Wall, Waena Column, Bottom Row]

14. H.R.H. Keliiahonui | Born 1869–Died 1887[156,157,158] [Edward Abel Keliʻiahonui, son of David Kahalepouli Piikoi and Kinoiki Kekaulike. Ewa Wall, Makai Column, Bottom Row]

15. Prince Kalanianaole | Delegate to Congress | Born 1871–Died 1922[159,160] [Jonah Kūhiō Kalanianaʻole, son of David Kahalepouli Piikoi and Kinoiki Kekaulike. Ewa Wall, Waena Column, Middle Row]

16. David Kalākaua | Kawanananakoa | Mar. 10, 1904–May 20, 1953[161,162] [David Kalākaua Kawānanakoa, son of David Kawananakoa and Abigail W. Kawananakoa; Chapman also has father David interred. Ewa Wall, Makai Column, Middle Row]

17. Keliimaikai Naihe[163] Keliʻimaikaʻi. [Chapman identifies him as the brother of Kamehameha I. R.W. Wilcox disputed Liliʻuokalani's contention that Keliʻimaikaʻi had no issue.[164] Nāihe[165] [son of Keaweaheulu (great grandfather of Kalākaua), husband of Chiefess Kapiʻolani]. Thrum's 1909 *Hawaiian Annual* "Naihe et al., casket containing remains of Kalakaua's grandfather and great grandfather and Kailimaikai [*sic*], brother of Kamehameha."[166] Ewa Wall, Mauka Column, Top Row]

18. H.R.H. Pomaikalani | Born 1838–1895[167,168] [Virginia Kalanikuikapooloku Kalaninuiamamao Poomaikalani, sister of Queen Kapiʻolani. Ewa Wall, Waena Column, Top Row]

19. H.R.H Kekaulike | Born 1843–Died 1884[169,170] [Kinoiki Kekaulike, sister of Queen Kapiʻolani, mother of David Kawananakoa, Edward Abel Keliiahonui and Jonah Kuhio Kalanianaole. Ewa Wall, Makai Column, Top Row]

20. H.R.H. Kawananakoa | Born 1868–Died 1908 [David Laamea Kawanakoa Kahalepouli, son of David Kahalepouli Piikoi and Kinoiki Kekaulike, Ewa Wall, Mauka Column, Middle Row]

Ewa Wall			*Mauka Wall*	*Diamond Head Wall*		
Makai	Waena	Mauka		Mauka	Waena	Makai
H.R.H. Kekaulike	H.R.H. Pomaikalani	Keliimaikai Naihe	King Kalakaua	C. Kapaakea	H.H. Keohokalole	Kaiminaauao

Ewa Wall			Mauka Wall	Diamond Head Wall		
David Kalakaua Kawananakoa	Prince Kalaniannaole	H.R.H Kawananankoa		Gov. J.O. Dominis	Queen Liliuokalani	H.R.H. Leleiohoku
H.R.H. Keliiahonui	Keaweaheulu	H.R.H. Princess Abigail Wahiikaahuula Kawananakoa	Queen Kapiolani	H.R.H. Like Like	H.R.H. Kaiulani	Gov. A.S. Cleghorn

Thrum's *Hawaiian Annual* adds a curious note to the transfer of the caskets to the Kalākaua Crypt. The paragraph, within quotation marks, but without attribution reads:

"But one casket remained in the mausoleum, not honored by interment in the [Kalakaua] tomb. This casket containing remains which were once accredited by royal favor with being those of Kamehameha the Great. The casket, however, bears another name."[171]

The article does not record whose name is on the casket, although accounts record the presence of several individuals who are not listed on the inscriptions on the Kamehameha, Wyllie or Kalakaua crypts.

The "royal favor" is recorded in an account told by Bill Maioho: "'In 1918, there are still three sets of remains inside the mausoleum building,' says Bill Maioho. 'These were the ka'ai: Liloa, and Lonoikamakahiki, and there was a bundle of bones wrapped in kapa and red silk, and had King Kalakaua's signet ring. King Kalakaua believed that those iwi were the bones of Kamehameha the Great.'"[172]

The *kā'ai* were transferred to Bishop Museum:

1. Liloa[173]
2. Lonoikamakahiki[174]

OTHERS NOT LISTED IN THE INSCRIPTIONS

The inscriptions on the tombs indicate clearly the burial location of many of the members of the royal families of Hawai'i, but a number of chiefs reported to have been buried at the Royal Mausoleum do not have their names inscribed on the markers. The individuals lacking inscribed markers include: Kamanele, Chiefess Kapiolani, Ha'alilio, Alapai, Naea, Kaeo, Kapookawelo, Nunu and Kakohe.

Kamanele. The most prominent among these individuals is Kamanele.

She is listed as "8" in November 4, 1865, list in the *Pacific Commercial Advertiser*. The entry reads: "Kamanele, daughter of Governor Kuakini *alias* Governor Adams. She was affianced to Kamehameha III, and died aged about 20."[175] The 1891 *Hawaiian Gazette* lists her as "Kamanele, daughter of Gov. Kuakini, April 4, 1839."[176] She is not in the 1997 roster.

During the time when all the caskets were contained in the chapel, when it served as the royal mausoleum, the presence of Kamanele was not issue. With the construction of the Kamehameha Tomb, Wyllie Tomb and Kalakaua Crypt, that divided the dynasties and families, her burial spot became more problematic. Kamanele was not a descendant of Kamehameha, nor had she married a descendant and, therefore, would not be placed in the Kamehameha Tomb. She also is not related to Queen Emma and would not have been placed in the Wyllie Tomb, originally called the Queen Emma Tomb. She is also not part of the family of King Kalākaua. She, nevertheless, was the daughter of Kuakini, an advisor of Kamehameha I, and also the granddaughter of Keʻeaumoku Papaiahiahi, half-brother of Kameʻeiamoku and Kamanawa, the twin advisors of Kamehameha I, who appear on the seal of the Kingdom of Hawaiʻi. She also was niece of Kaahumanu, who was buried in the Kamehameha Tomb.

Chiefess Kapiʻolani. Chiefess Kapiʻolani was buried at the Royal Tomb at Pohukaina, but was not in the list of caskets transferred to Mauna Ala. The 1891 *Ko Hawaii Pae Aina*, however, includes "Kapiolani I"[177] as one of the aliʻi at Mauna ʻAla. Since Queen Kapiʻolani died in 1899, the reference must refer to Chiefess Kapiʻolani for whom the queen was named. The Kalākaua Crypt does contain Naihe, the husband of Chiefess Kapiʻolani.

Haʻalilio.[178] The 1891 *Hawaiian Gazette* lists "Haalilio, ambassador to London." Today, Haʻalilio is most likely not buried at Mauna ʻAla. An enclosure in Kawaiahaʻo Cemetery, makai of the Lunalilo Mausoleum, contains a marker for "Richard Haalilio, 1808–1844." The stone also bears the names of his brother Levi Haalelea and the wife of Haalelea, Ululani A.A. Haalelea.

William L. Lee.[179] The 1891 *Hawaiian Gazette* also lists " Wm. L. Lee, Chief Justice of Hawaii." A marker in Union Cemetery, Fort Edward, Washington County, New York, implies the body was moved there: "Here rest the remains of William L. Lee. Died May 28, 1867, aged 36 years, at Honolulu, Sandwich Islands, where he had resided for over ten years as Chancellor and Chief Justice of the Hawaiian Nation."

Alapai, Naea, Kaeo, Jane Lahilahi, Maikui, Kapookawelo, Nueu and Kakohe. The *Hawaiian Gazette* also reported on February 17, 1891: "Besides the above, the coffins of the following chiefs are said to be in the Mausoleum: Alapai, Naea, Kaeo, Jane Lahilahi, Maikui, Kapookawelo, Nueu and Kakohe."[180] An earlier, February 14, 1891, list in *Ko Hawaii Pae Aina*, helps to better identify the chiefs by giving the gender, either (w) for *wahine* or female or (k) for *kane* or male, and pairing the names with their spouses. (Juliana) Alapai (w) is paired with her husband, Keoni Ana (k); (George) Naea (k) is paired with his wife, (Fanny) Kekela (w); (Joshua) Kaeo (k) with his wife (Jane) Lahilahi (w), followed by their son P.Y. (Peter Young) Kaeo. Although Namakaeha (Bennet Nāmākēhā) is listed next to Maikui (Grace Kamaikui Young) (w) in the roster, she is not his wife. The wife of Nāmākēhā, Kapiʻolani, did not die until 1899, and therefore is not paired with his name. Although the husband of Maikui, Thomas C.B. Rooke, died in November 28, 1858, and could have been paired with her in the list, he is instead recorded as "C.B. Rooke" at the end of the list with the other two non–Hawaiians on the roster, W.L. Lee and R.C. Wyllie.[181] Of the remaining three chiefs, the spelling of "Nueu" from the *Hawaiian Gazette* as "Nunu" in *Ko Hawaii Pae Aina* would better allow the identification of Nunu and Kakohe as the two brothers of Kaleioku, high priest of Lono. Kapookawelo is the only remaining unidentified individual reported in accounts as possibly being buried at Mauna ʻAla.

BISHOP MEMORIAL

The Bishop Memorial is inscribed on the *makai* face with the name Charles Reed Bishop, but the site does not contain his remains. The inscription on the *mauka* face of the cenotaph reads: "Charles Reed Bishop | Born in Glens Falls, New York January 25, 1822 | Arrived in Honolulu, Hawaii October 12, 1846 | Married Bernice Pauahi June 5, 1850 | Died in Berkeley, California June 7, 1915." The base includes the words: "Builder of the State—Friend of Youth—Benefactor of Hawaii | His Ashes Rest in the Tomb of the Kamehamehas." Together the fifty-one words on the Bishop Memorial comprise the longest inscription for any individual buried at Mauna ʻAla.

Kawānakoa Tomb at Mauna ʻAla

With the last niche in the Kalākaua crypt filled by David Kalākaua Kawānanakoa, no additional burials have taken place at Mauna ʻAla since 1953. A proposal dated December 17, 2012, however, has opened the possibility for burials in the future.

A proposal by nonagenarian Abigail K. Kawānanakoa, *hānai* daughter of Prince David Kawānanakoa and Abigail Wahiikaahuula Campbell,[182] and *hānai* sister of David Kalākaua Kawānanakoa, would establish a Kawānanakoa Tomb at Mauna 'Ala. Although she does not have the official title of princess, Kawānanakoa has served as president of the Friends of 'Iolani Palace. Her mother and *hānai* sister, Lydia Lili'uokalani Kawānanakoa, started the organization that helped restore the palace built by the last king of Hawai'i to its former glory. She was one of the heirs to the estate of her *hānai* grandfather, James Campbell. In a letter to William J. Aila, Jr., chairperson of the Hawaii State department of land and natural resources, she wrote:

> I request to construct a burial structure at Mauna Ala to be used for the disposition of my remains.
> The design, engineering, and construction would be entirely at my expense. I will make provision for its care and maintenance in perpetuity.
> I also request that the structure be situated on the makai side of the property in the open area behind the flagpole. The approximate location is indicated on the enclosed site plan.
> I have also enclosed conceptual drawings with this letter.
> Thank you for your consideration.

The letter concluded with a handwritten personal note under her signature: "Mahalo Bill Merry Christmas."

Enclosed with the letter were a summary sheet, a site plan showing the location of the proposed tomb, comparisons with existing tombs, and artist renderings of what the Kawānanakoa Tomb would look like.

The summary sheet includes placement, size, design as well as a list of the square feet covered by each of the tombs.

When originally designed, the Royal Mausoleum sat in the center of the site, with two wings of the building aligned with the Nu'uanu Street entrance. When the Kamehameha Tomb was built it was sited at the mauka edge of the property, as was the Wyllie Tomb when it was constructed. The Kalakaua Crypt did not balance the design, but was centered on the axis that extended through the gate. The summary sheet gave the rationale for the placement of the new tomb: "It is located with purpose to offer additional enhancement in the natural balance and proportion of the site plan, through placement directly in line with, and perpendicular to the Willie [*sic*] Tomb, while also giving respect in its alignment to the original Mauna 'Ala Cross site plan."

Although not discussed on the summary sheet, the location of the Kawānanakoa Tomb sits in the appropriate location relative to the other tombs. When the *kahu* of Mauna 'Ala planned for the burial of the ancient *kā'ai*, a site was selected *mauka* of the Kamehameha Tomb, indicating the superiority of rank.

2. Burial Places

Artist rendering of the Kawānanakoa Tomb presented to the Board of Land and Natural Resources.

The size of footprint of the proposed Kawānanakoa Tomb is smaller than all other tombs at Mauna ʻAla. The size of the proposed burial site is no accident. The summary sheet explained: "The proposed size, both in footprint and scale, pays respect to the existing tombs, memorial, and burial site on the grounds, and its placement with respect to site balance." In regards to the size of the different burial locations at Mauna ʻAla, interestingly, the comparison of the various footprints does not include the Kalākaua Crypt that roughly equals the surface area of all the other tombs combined. Although the summary includes the footprint for the Bishop

Memorial with the other tombs, it is strictly a cenotaph since the ashes of Charles Reed Bishop are located with Bernice Pauahi in the Kamehameha Tomb.

The comparison, using measurements to the half-inch, showed the size of the proposed and existing tombs:

Existing and proposed Kawananakoa Tomb:

Kamehameha Tomb	13'1-½" × 24'1-½"	316.50 square feet
Willie [sic] Tomb	18'-0" × 21'-7"	388.50 square feet
Bishop Memorial	5'-10" × 8'6"	49.50 square feet
Young Burial Site	16'-6" × 22'-0"	363.00 square feet
Proposed Kawananakoa Tomb	15'-0" × 15'-0"	225.00 square feet

Although architectural renderings were included, the proposal noted the included design was "intended only for illustrative purposes, in that the proposed design concept reflects the Willie [sic] Tomb with resect to its elements, its stepped base, its four columns, and its roof." The size of the Young Burial Site also takes on added dimensions because of four cannon used to form an outer boundary. The actual stone base that sits below the slab has smaller dimensions. The dimensions also do not reflect the size of the underground portions of the Kamehameha Tomb and Wyllie Tomb that most likely have cruciform wings related to the inscriptions on the above ground monuments.

The proposal was considered at the April 26, 2013, meeting of the board of land and natural resources. Daniel S. Quinn, state parks administrator, submitted the request with background, discussion and a recommendation, dated April 26, 2013.

The recommendation first sought to establish that the board had the authority to approve the request. The federal government transferred the Royal Mausoleum property to the Territory of Hawaii. Executive Order 998 put the property under the control of the superintendent of public works. The State of Hawaii department of accounting and general services subsequently assumed the responsibility. In 1967 an act transferred "all state historic areas and buildings" to the department of land and natural resources, with a subsequent executive order specifically assigning the Royal Mausoleum to the department's state parks division. The recommendation further noted that no statute specifies "who can be interred on the Royal Mausoleum State Monument premises." An opinion letter from the attorney general, dated March 8, 1956, concluded: "it seems reasonably clear that the Royal Mausoleum premises were dedicated and preserved as a burial ground for members of the Royal family of Hawai'i, which included the sovereign and chiefs of the kingdom and their family members."

Quinn recommended that board of land and natural resources:

Authorize the construction and use of a burial tomb to house the remains of Abigail K. Kawananakoa on the grounds of the Royal Mausoleum State Monument and delegate authority to the Chairperson to issue, negotiate and approve a construction Right of Entry for said tomb subject to the following:
  a. The final review and approval for the precise location and design of the tomb as well as a plan for maintenance shall be subject to the Chairperson's approval;
  b. The costs of the design, construction and maintenance in perpetuity shall be paid for by Ms. Kawananakoa;
  c. The standard terms and conditions of the most current right of entry form, as may be amended from time to time;
  d. Review and approval by the State Historical Preservation Division as required by law; and,
  e. Such other terms and conditions as may be prescribed by the Chairperson to serve the interests of the State.

The chair of the board called William "Bill" John Kaiʻehe Maioho, *kahu* or curator of Mauna ʻAla, as the first to testify at the meeting. Maioho was a descendant of Hoʻolulu, who with his brother, Hoapili, was charged by Kamehameha I to hide his bones. The minutes of the meeting included the rationale and position of Maioho: "Kawananakoa is a descendant of Kaumualiʻi, an Aliʻinui of Kauaʻi whose grandchildren were Queen Kapiʻolani, Kekaulike, and Poʻomaikelani. The distinction of being a descendant of Kaumualiʻi, an Aliʻi bloodline, and Queen Kapiʻolani, as Queen Counselor and descendant of Kaumualiʻi, carried the mana. The Kahu supports Ms. Kawananakoa's request to be buried with her family at Mauna ʻAla." The argument focuses on descent rather than royal status.

The testimony of Nanette Napoleon, onetime director of the Cemetery Research Project and author of *Oahu Cemetery: Burial Ground & Historic Site*, opposed the request based on the lack of expertise of the board in determining "genealogical lineage for each family and which family took precedence over another family" (130426-minutes, 4). She also shared an email she had received from a relative of the Wilcox family suggesting that "criteria for burial include limiting burial to descendants of members of the Chief's Children (*sic*) School who were the highest Aliʻi children of the land trained by missionaries to become leaders and kings and queens of Hawaii" (130426-minutes, 4). Such a criteria would preclude the burial of Kawānanakoa because King Kalākaua and Queen Liliʻuokalani were the only representatives of the Kalākaua Dynasty who attended the Chiefs' Children's School, and both died without issue.

Kai Markell, compliance officer with the Office for Hawaiian Affairs, brought up "Western context" of Maioho being an employee of State Parks, a division under the land board. Aila "emphasized that the Kahu was there as a person with traditional and genealogical background and was culturally appropriate." After an exchange with Markell concerning "administrative rules and procedures," Aila noted the "conflict he was dealing with between the Western contexts with the Hawaiian context" (5).

All other testimony opposed approving the request on various grounds. Dana Naone Hall asked for "a wider discussion and consultation from the Hawaiian community on who should be the decision makers and from DLNR's own in-house experts of cultural history branch staff, State Historic Preservation Division (SHPD) and the ethnography and archeology staff" (6).

The original motion by John Morgan was amended by him to include a requirement that "Ms. Kawananakoa must complete an Archeology Inventory Survey." The board unamimously approved the amended motion.

A front page article in the *Honolulu Star-Advertiser*, a little over a month after the decision, noted that the request had "been received with both acceptance and vitriol."[183] Aila explained why the request was approved when most of the testimony, other than that of William Maiʻoho, was opposed to the proposal. He said of the *kahu*: "their testimony, their answers, their thoughts are given a higher weight and standing because that's what they've been trained for. They've been trained for answering the question: Does she have the genealogy to be (buried there)? ... For them the answer was yes, she has the genealogy to be there."[184]

An opponent to the approval, Lela Hubbard of Na Koa Ikaika, requested a contested case hearing, questioning whether the board has the authority to make the determination. The state attorney general, in turn, needed to establish whether Hubbard had standing to make the request for the contested case hearing.

Although much of the testimony at the hearing opposed an additional burial at Mauna ʻAla, an article titled "Mauna ʻAla: A proper memorial to Kawananakoa's legacy" endorsed the approval of the burial plan by the state board. The opinion piece by Daniel K. Akaka, Kamaki Kanahele and Ivan M. Lui-Kwan on the editorial pages of the *Honolulu Star-Advertiser* appeared on July 1, 2013:

> Welina Kakou I ka Ohana O Hawaii Nei.
> We support the decision of the state Board of Land and Natural Resources in approving the construction and use of a burial tomb at Mauna ʻAla for Princess Abigail K. Kawananakoa. The BLNR's decision complies with the March 8, 1956, opinion letter of acting Attorney General Richard Sharpless.
> The attorney general opined that "the Royal Mausoleum premises were dedicated and preserved as a burial ground for members of the Royal Family of Hawaii, which included the sovereign and chiefs of the kingdom and their family members."

> Princess Abigail is the granddaughter of Abigail Wahiikaahuula Campbell and Prince David Kawananakoa. Prince David Kawananakoa is the adopted son of King Kalakaua and Queen Kapiolani. The princess' royal grandparents also adopted Abigail, resulting in her being the daughter of Abigail Wahiikaahuula Campbell and Prince David Kawananakoa. Princess Abigail's alii genealogy clearly establishes her as a "member of the Royal Family of Hawaii."
>
> It is the duty of alii to advance the well-being of their people. Princess Abigail has emulated this royal duty through her significant contributions to Native Hawaiian health, education and culture. Her capital contribution enables the practice and perpetuation of traditional healing practices at the Dr. Agnes Kalanihookaha Cope Native Hawaiian Healing Center in Waianae. Cope refers to Princess Abigail as the Queen Emma of modern times.
>
> Over the past 40 years, Princess Abigail has supported the Merrie Monarch Festival. In recent years, she has provided significant annual stipends to participating halaus. Since the 1990s, she has provided steady support for the Hawaiian language through 'Aha Punana Leo.
>
> Princess Abigail cherishes the vision of her great grand-uncle and uncle by adoption, Prince Jonah Kuhio Kalanianaole, the principal architect of the Hawaiian Homes Commission Act of 1920. Embracing Prince Kuhio's vision, she has regularly shared her personal resources to improve the quality of life of the residents of the Hawaiian Homelands communities throughout Hawaii.
>
> Recognized as the symbol behind the Hawaiian nation, Iolani Palace has been nurtured back to grandeur by Princess Abigail's caring. Kippen de Alba Chu, executive director of Friends of Iolani Palace, has described her as the prime force for restoration of the palace, and for recovery of palace artifacts from around the world. The princess' capital contribution toward refurbishment of Hawaiian Hall at the Bishop Museum has enabled sharing with the rest of the world the cultural history of our alii from King Kamehameha I through Queen Liliuokalani. Princess Abigail annually provides funds for scholarships and financial aid to the students at St. Andrew's Priory, na pua o ke Alii Emmalani.
>
> O ko'u ola, alaila lawe aku oe ia'u ike alo o Ke Akua…. We thank Ke Akua for life, and seek to be in His Presence in the next life.

The individuals who supported Kawānanakoa in print represented leaders in the Hawaiian community: Akaka, a former U.S. Senator; Kanahele, director of the Waianae Coast Comprehensive Health Center; and Lui-Kwan, former vice chairman of the Queen Emma Foundation and chair emeritus of St. Andrew's Priory School.

The contested case hearing requested by Hubbard was denied on August 23, 2013, allowing the action of the board to go forward.

In May 2006, the ali'i trusts—Bernice Pauahi Bishop Estate, Queen Lili'uokalani Trust and Lunalilo Trust in a memorandum of understanding with the department of land and natural resources—joined together to fund the renovation of Mauna 'Ala. The Queen's Health Systems, Charles Reed Bishop Trust and Abigail Kawānanakoa Foundation also contributed to the effort. The $2 million effort was completed in May 2016.[185]

Lunalilo Mausoleum (1875)

Although the remains of King Lunalilo were located for a time at Mauna 'Ala, at his request a separate mausoleum was established for him on the grounds of Kawaiaha'o Church. The *Pacific Commercial Advertiser* described the new royal tomb for King Lunalilo:

> In the church-yard of Kawaiahao has recently been erected by the order of his Highness the father of the late King, a beautiful mausoleum of concrete, which when completed will be a fitting monument to the lamented Lunalilo, and a handsome ornament to that part of the city. The architect is Mr. Robert Lishman, and the design and execution do credit to his taste and skill. The building is in the form of Greek cross, with four aisles, each 10 feet by 4 feet 9 inches; 24 feet 4 inches extreme length outside of buttress; 20 by 20 feet inside, with 4 recesses and cement floor. The porch in front is 9 feet 2 inches in width; the height of the structure from the foundation to the finial top is 81 feet. There are four gable ends, surmounted with crosses; in three of the gables are two windows each, with small ventilators. The mausoleum is situated in front and to the westward of the church building. It is to be enclosed, on the mauka side by an iron fence nearly 100 feet in length, (ordered from England) of the same pattern with the fence around the Royal Mausoleum in Nuuanu Valley; on the Waikiki and makai side by a handsome stone wall, 274 feet in length, which is to be continued at the cost of His Highness on the sides of the churchyard facing Punchbowl and King streets, where will be erected two spacious gates for carriages, with concrete pillars of an elaborate pattern. On each side of the gates will be entrances for foot-passengers.
>
> The venerable Kanaina evidently feels a laudable pride and spares no expense in thus providing a fitting tomb for his Royal son, who was the last of a family of chiefs of high rank. There also, ere many years have passed, he himself expects to be laid to rest by the side of Kekauluohi, long since gone before.[186]

Interred at the tomb were:
King Lunalilo[187]
Charles Kanaina[188] (father of Lunalilo)
Kekauluohi[189]

Hawaiian Gazette lists "Kekauluohi, Mother of Lunalilo, died June 7, 1845." The *Hawaiian Gazette* also reported the location and contents of the Lunalilo Mausoleum: "The remains of King Wm. C. Lunalilo and those of his father Charles Kanaina, rest in a mausoleum specially built for them, that stands at the right of the front entrance to Kawaiahao churchyard, near the corner of King and Punchbowl streets. Lunalilo died, Feb. 3, 1874. Kanaina died March 13, 1878."[190]

In 1878, the trustees of the estate of Lunalilo demanded the keys to the Lunalilo Mausoleum. The government "declined to deliver the keys."[191] The refusal resulted in a Supreme Court decision on a "bill in equity to determine the right of possession, care and control of the mausoleum which was erected in the year 1875, in the church yard of the Kawaiahao church

2. Burial Places

The remains of King William Charles Lunalilo and his father, Charles Kanaʻina, rest in the Lunalilo Mausoleum on the grounds of Kawaiahaʻo Church (courtesy Hawaii State Archives [PP-50-11-016]).

in Honolulu, and which now contains the remains of His late Majesty Lunalilo." The trustees of the Lunalilo estate prevailed in their complaint against the Interior department.[192] The court determined that the government's payment for the keeper did not constitute justification for taking control of the mausoleum.

The 1879 Department of the Interior included the budgets for the keepers of the royal tombs. The budget for the Keeper of Royal Mausoleum was $600; the Keeper of Lunalilo's Tomb was $400.[193]

Others have attempted entry without the keys. In 1941 vandals opened the Lunalilo Mausoleum at Kawaiahaʻo.[194]

The last king of the Kamehameha dynasty continues to be honored at the Lunalilo Mausoleum. The *Honolulu Star-Bulletin* reported in 1967 that the mausoleum is "ordinarily opened once a year on Sunday closest to Jan. 31, his birthday, when the church has a commemorative service."[195]

Lanikeha

George Naea (father of Queen Emma) may have been temporarily buried at Lanikeha. Lanikeha was the name of the residence of Kamehameha III in Lahaina.[196] On October 4, 1854, Bennet Nāmākēhā wrote to Emma from Lanikeha: "We buried him on Tuesday, and was placed under Lanikeha, it being Fanny's purpose that when her bereavement for him has ended, to carry it to another place."[197] Naea was most likely brought to Mauna 'Ala for he appears in the list of chiefs "said to be in the Mausoleum" according to the *Hawaiian Gazette* in 1891.[198]

UNKNOWN

Several close relatives of individuals buried at Mauna 'Ala are not buried there.

Boki. Lost on his trip to the New Hebrides.

Robert Young (son of Namokuelua and John Young). Lost near Bermuda.

Polly Pa'a'aina (daughter of Fanny Kekelaokalani and Henry Lewis, half-sister of Queen Emma).

Pauli Kaoleioku (son of Kamehameha I and Kanekapolei, father of Pauahi and Kōnia, therefore grandfather of Kamehameha IV and Bernice Pauahi Bishop). Died prior to the arrival of missionaries and presumably was buried in the traditional manner for ali'i. Kaoleioku is one of the names of chiefs that may have been in a *kā'ai* at Hale o Līloa in Hamakua.

James W. Kaliokalani (brother of Kalākaua). Died at Lahaina, Maui. Body returned to Honolulu on May 5, 1852.[199] He is not listed among the inscriptions on the Kalākaua Crypt.

John Adams Kuakini. John Adams Kuakini, brother of Kaahumanu and father of Kamanele, died December 9, 1844. Little is written concerning the obsequies for Kuakini. The *Friend* reported: "On Sabbath afternoon, the 15th instant [January 15, 1845], the Rev. Mr. Armstrong preached a funeral sermon at the stone chapel [Mokuaikaua Church], and read also a letter from David Malo, who was present at the time of the Governor's decease."[200] Malo had written to Baldwin in a letter dated November 4, 1844, that Kuakini was quite ill.[201]

Kaikio'ewa. The guardian of Kamehameha III, Kaikio'ewa suppressed a revolt on Kaua'i and then served as governor of the island until his death in 1839. He was the father of Likelike, wife of Kalanimoku.

Emilia Keaweamahi. The wife of Kaikio'ewa, Emilia Keaweamahi served as governor of Kaua'i following the death of her husband, Kaikio'ewa. On November 24, 1848, Levi Chamberlain wrote in his journal that she died "a few days ago."[202]

Kalanimoku. The prime minister of Hawai'i under Kamehameha I and Kamehameha II, Kalanimoku died in Kailua on the island of Hawai'i on February 7 or 8, 1827. Richard Charlton uses the date February 7 in communication to Joseph Planta, Jr., Esq, to provide information for the Rt. Hon. George Canning that "Karimoku Regent of these Islands died at Owyhee on the 7th [February] Instant"[203]; Lorrin Andrews gives February 8, 1827, as the date Kalanimoku died in his Chronological Table of Remarkable Events appended to his *Dictionary of the Hawaiian Language*[204]; Hiram Bingham put February 8 in his *Residence of Twenty-one Years in the Sandwich Islands*. Levi Chamberlain, in his journal entry for February 12, 1827, wrote: "A native Schooner arrived from Lahaina bearing the mournful intelligence of Kalaimoku's death which had been received there yesterday from Kailua. It appears he died on the afternoon of Thursday the 8th and that a vessel was despatched next day to Lahaina to carry the news." The notice was received here with demonstrations of sorrow, but notwithstanding the gloom which the intelligence had cast over the place, the foreigners, for whose entertainment the hula had been planned, determined not to be disappointed in witnessing a heathen sport—and though the Kin was disinclined to be present out of regard to the memory of Kalaimoku & a wish to stay at home and indulge in grief, the English counsel insisted on his going."[205] Kaahumanu and Keliiahonui went to Hawai'i island on February 13, 1827, aboard the *Waverly*.

3

Undertakers

Starting as early as the obsequies in 1848 for William Pitt Leleiohoku, Moses Kekūāiwa, and Kaʻiminaʻauao, most processions prominently featured an undertaker. The identity of the undertaker, however, is less clear. Robert C. Schmitt, writing for the Hawaiian Historical Society, identified the first undertaker in the Kingdom of Hawaiʻi as C.E. (Charles E.) Williams, "who, in 1859, opened his furniture and mortuary business on Fort Street."[1] C.E. Williams had arrived in Honolulu in 1851. He was subsequently issued a customs permit, signed May 7, 1853, allowing him to depart on the *Sarrita*. Then, four years later, C. E. Williams, his wife and two children arrived from Melbourne, Australia, on the *Vaquero* in June 1857.[2] His youngest son, Henry H. Williams, age 1 when he arrived, was born on May 9, 1856, at Castlemain, Australia.[3] Despite the claim by Schmitt, an early advertisement of C.E. Williams, in August 1859, does not refer to him as an undertaker, instead calling his business "Cabinet Maker and Turner"; it does, nevertheless, mention the availability of "Polished Coffins on hand and made to order."[4] The *Pacific Commercial Advertiser* reported on April 17, 1910, that when Williams returned to Honolulu he founded the first "*furniture* business" (*italics* mine).

The claim for first undertaker, though, may actually go to another individual. An advertisement that appeared in the *Pacific Commercial Advertiser* on October 2, 1858, explicitly referred to the owner, E.J. Smith, as "Undertaker" and offered to "superintend funerals." It read:

E.J. Smith
  Undertaker and Cabinet Maker,
  Begs leave to notify the public that he is now prepared to furnish all kinds of Coffins, and superintend Funerals, at the shortest of notice. From the long experience he has had in the business, he trusts that he may give satisfaction to those who favor him with a call. Ready made pine coffins always on hand, from $4 to $10; Cherry and koa do., varnished, $10 and $25; koa do, polished, $25 and $40.[5]

The business must have changed hands in short order, because a Hawaiian language version of the same advertisement, but signed by H.F. Long, appeared on January 26, 1859, edition of *Ka Hae*:

OLELO HOOLAHA.
KE HAI AKU NEI KA MEA NONA KA inoa malalo, ua makaukau e hana i na pahu kupapau, o kela ano keia ano, me ka hikiwawe, a hooponopono hoi i na hoolewa kupapau, a no kona maa loihi i keia hana, ua lana kona manao e lawa ka makemake o ka poe hele aku ia ia. No na pahu paina, $2.00 a hiki i ka $10.00 ke kumu kuai ; no na pahu koa, a laau haole paha, i waniki ia he $10, a hiki i ka $25. ke kumu kuai; No na pahu koa i hoohinuhinu ia, he $25, a hiki i ke $40, ke kumu kuai. E loaa mau na papa koa kuai ma kona hale hana, ma ke Alanui Alii, e pili la i Polelewa.
Malaila e hana ai, a e hoomaikai hou, a e waniki paha i na noho, moe, pakaukau, a me na mea ano like ae.
27-tf H. F. LONG.

A passenger manifest has H.F. Long, age 38, arriving in Honolulu from San Francisco the *Yankee* on September 1, 1858. An English language version was in placed in the *Pacific Commercial Advertiser* on May 12, 1859.

Other undertakers, however, may have preceded Smith, Long and Williams. The 1848 Order of Procession for William Pitt Leleiohoku, Kaʻiminaʻauao and Moses Kekuaiwa, includes "Undertakers." The procession for Kealiiahonui in 1849 also included "Undertakers." "Undertakers" is again listed in the funeral procession of Kekauʻōnohi in 1851. The orders that follow uniformly list "Undertaker" rather than "Undertakers."

The title is listed as "Undertaker to the late King" in 1864 Order of Procession for Kamehameha IV. The Order of Procession for his advisor, Robert Crichton Wyllie, in 1865 once again referred to just "Undertaker."

The Order of Procession for Victoria Kamāmalu includes "Undertaker." Although no specific undertaker is named, the papers of C.E. Williams that Henry H. Williams donated to the Hawaii State Archives included an Order of Procession from her obsequies. "Undertaker" Kapaʻakea in 1866. "Undertaker" Kekūanāoʻa in 1868.

The entry for C.E Williams in the 1869 *Honolulu Directory, and Historical Sketch of the Hawaiian Or Sandwich Islands* made no mention of "undertaker," calling him only a "furniture dealer."[6] A display advertisement in the directory, too, referred to Williams as an "Importer, Manufacturer, Upholster and dealer in all kinds of furniture."[7] C.E. Williams was Fire Chief from July 1, 1867 to June 30, 1870.

The "Undertaker" is listed in the Order of Procession for Kalama. While no mention of the name of the "Undertaker" for Kamehameha V is given, his son Henry H. Williams donated an Order of Procession for Kamehameha V dated December 31, 1872. "Undertaker" is again used in the Order of Procession for King William Charles Lunalilo, and for his father, Charles Kanaina. "Undertaker of His Late Royal Highness" is used in the Order of Procession for William Pitt Leleiohoku Kalahoolewa in 1877. "Undertaker" appears for Fanny Kekelaokalani 1880 and Keʻelikolani Ruth 1883.

The 1884 *Directory and Hand-book of the Kingdom of Hawaii* featured advertisements for "C.E. Williams Undertaker" at the top edge of periodic pages.[8] While the Order of Procession only lists "Undertaker" for the obsequies for Queen Emma in 1885, the name of the coffin maker, Manuel Silva, was recounted after he died in 1906:

> Mr. Silva [...] arrived in Honolulu in 1862.
> He entered the employ of C.E. Williams, the undertaker, as coffin and cabinet maker, working in that capacity for over 29 years.
> While in the employ of Mr. Williams it will be remembered that Silva's skill as a coffin maker was little short of marvelous.
> Hawaii owes him a mention in its history, for it was he that made the coffins in which most of the kings and queens were buried. Chief among them was the Queen Emma coffin, of which he made a model to remind him of old days.[9]

Only "Undertaker" is listed in the Order of Procession for Kekaulike in 1884 and for Bernice Pauahi Bishop 1885.

The Order of Procession for Likelike was the first to explicitly name the undertaker: "Undertaker—Mr. C.E. Williams." He submitted his bill to the Interior Department on February 28, 1887. The *Pacific Commercial Advertiser* included an extended account of the undertaker for the funeral of Likelike: " The necessary preparations for the funeral were entrusted to Mr. C.E. Williams, undertaker. A hearse was sent out to Waikiki last night at a late hour to bring in the body of Her late Royal Highness."[10] Williams was also praised for the coffin of Likelike: "The coffin of Her Royal highness is a fine piece of workmanship. The body is of koa, and the trimming of kou. No less than 446 pieces of wood were used in its construction. The whole is highly polished and reflects much credit on Mr. C.E. Williams, at whose establishment it was made."[11]

The Order of Procession once again reverted to simply listing "Undertaker" for Edward Abel Keliiahonui in 1887. Although no undertaker is listed, his probate includes a voucher, numbered 1, for $506 paid to C.E. Williams.[12]

No undertaker appeared in the Order of Procession for John Dominis. The death of King Kalākaua in San Francisco meant that a mainland undertaker made the initial arrangements. A memorial took place at Trinity Church before he was returned to Hawaiʻi. In Hawaiʻi, the *Pacific*

Commercial Advertiser reported that H.H. Williams was "busy at work making a coffin for the remains of the late King [Kalākaua]. Made of koa and kou wood of about six hundred pieces."[13]

When C.E. Williams sold his company in June 1895 to the wife of the eldest son, E.A. Williams, and his second son continued in the business under his own name, Honolulu had two furniture shops and undertakers using the Williams name. An advertisement titled "There Is No Mistake" attempted to clarify the situation. It explained that Henry H. Williams, second son of C.E. Williams, "entered the employ of his father about twenty-five years ago, since which time he has made a continuous study of the Furniture and Undertaking Business. He graduated from Dr. S. Rodgers' Perfect Embalming School in 1890, since which time he has made a success of that branch of the business."[14]

The rival company, C.E. Williams & Son, too, advertised its credentials:

Embalming under the personal supervision of Mr. Ed. A. Williams, a graduate from the Clark [*sic* should be Clarke] School of Embalming [of Cincinnati, Ohio] in 1894.

Mr. Williams employs the latest and best method known to science, no mutilation of the body (no partial embalming).[15]

The presence of two Williams firms, nevertheless, led to some confusion following the death of Joseph Nawahi. When the Hawaiian patriot died in San Francisco, the family arranged for H.H. Williams to make arrangements when the body of Nawahi arrived in Honolulu. Not knowing which Williams undertaker was responsible for the body, local family members called for a hearse from E.A. Williams.[16]

Although a newspaper account of the obsequies for Princess Virginia Kapooloku Poʻomaikelani in 1895 report that she was embalmed at Honuakaha, the residence of Queen Kapiʻolani, it does not name the undertaker responsible.

At the 1908 funeral of Prince David Kawānanakoa, the identity of the undertaker is much more apparent. The *Pacific Commercial Advertiser* reported: "Undertaker H.H. Williams rode a charger wearing a blue and gold saddle cloth which is only used at the obsequies of royalty."[17]

Henry H. Williams is prominently listed, as a "Mortician," in the 1925 *Story of Hawaii and Its Builders*. His biographical entry omits the family squabble at the start of his company: "Henry H. Williams entered his father's business after graduating from Punahou School. He eventually acquired ownership and disposed of the furniture part of the business in 1900. He has followed the undertaking business exclusively since."[18]

The Order of Procession for the funeral of Queen Liliʻuokalani explicitly lists H.H. Williams as the undertaker.

H.H.Williams also played a role involving ancient remains. It was H.H. Williams who on March 15, 1918, "removed to his premises the 'small koa coffin' on I'aukea's orders." The casket containing the *kāʻai* from Mauna ʻAla, was transported to Bernice Pauahi Bishop Museum. Albert Francis Judd, a missionary descendant and Supreme Court justice, recounting the transfer, spoke of his conversation with Prince Jonah Kūhiō Kalanianaʻole: "The Prince [...] wished to place these relics with the Museum because he knew that they would be properly taken care of and not given a fictitious value which could not be substantiated historically."[19] The contents of the coffin were described in an inventory:

> 1 Bundle White Tapa enclosed in a braided and woven casket of cocoanut fiber in the form of a limbless human figure, said to contain the bones of Liloa. A circular piece of pearl shell is sewed to the front of the torso.
>
> 1 Bundle, similar throughout to the last mentioned, except that it is said to contain the bones of Umi. The left eye is represented by pearl shell. The right eye socket and mouth have indications that certain pieces, formerly filling these cavities, have gone.
>
> Col. Iaukea explained that the name of Umi was attributed to this specimen only because of Umi and Liloa had always been so closely associated.[20]

Roger G. Rose, in *Reconciling the Past: Two Basketry Kāʻai and the Legendary Līloa and Lonoikamakahiki*, reported the disposition of other items: "In addition to the so-called bones of Kamehameha, a silver plaque inscribed 'Liloa Lonoikamakahiki' was removed from the coffin."[21] The *kāʻai*, identified by Prince Jonah Kuhio Kalanianaole as Līloa and Lonoikamakahiki, went missing from the Bernice Pauahi Bishop Museum in February 1994.

H.H. Williams Mortuary did not pass out of existence. It was sold to Eugene Schamber in 1929; then in 1934 Joseph T. Boyd bought it. After the latter's death his estate ran the mortuary until 1952 when Thelma Akana bought the controlling interest. In 1955 Akana sold the mortuary to Clarence S. Gray and Frank Cuelho.[22] In January 1981 Francis K. and Anna Ordenstein, owners of Hawaiian Memorial Park Mortuary, bought Williams Mortuary, Ltd.,[23] selling it in 1997 to the Loewen Group, a Canadian company.[24] RightStar bought the Hawaiʻi assets of the bankrupt Loewen Group in November 2001. RightStar was later acquired by Vestin Mortgage, a Nevada company. In 2011, NorthStar Hawaii LLC, part of Houston-based NorthStar Memorial Group, purchased the RightStar assets from Vestin Mortgage, included Diamond Head Mortuary, Honolulu; Hawaiian Memorial Park Mortuary, Kaneohe; Homelani Memorial Park and Crematory, Hilo; Kona Memorial Park, Holualoa; Maui Memorial Park, Wailuku; Nakamura Mortuary, Wailuku; and Valley of the Temples, Kaneohe. H.H. Williams, undertaker to kings and queens, survives as Williams Funeral Services.

Conclusion

Na waimaka of ka lani.
The tears of heaven.[1]
—Hawaiian proverb

Despite the dominance of Western forms of funerals, the royal Hawaiian way of death maintained ancient indigenous elements through the obsequies of the twentieth century. Even the staunchest of Christian converts, Keōpūolani, the sacred wife of Kamehameha the Great, allowed wailing—an indigenous expression of grief—to continue, though she commanded an end to more severe practices. Yet even those closest to her continued some practices, as Kamāmalu and other chiefs did when they tattooed their tongues.

While the dissection of the body was replaced with Western embalming, the respectful, round the clock vigil over the body remained. The traditional signs of respect—the *kāhili*—continued to be waved over the deceased.

The *Saturday Press* in 1882 made the oft repeated comparison of traditions at the funeral of William Pitt Leleiohoku, Ka'imina'auao and Moses Kekūāiwa on December 30, 1848: "As usual in those days, great ceremony and form was observed, a mixture of the modern civilized state and recent barbaric customs."[2]

Some customs experienced subtle changes, integrating Western and traditional funerary customs. The funeral dirge composed by Lili'uokalani for her *hānai* sister, Bernice Pauahi Bishop, may have been a translation of a Western hymn, but continued the indigenous tradition of the *kanikau*.

The obsequies became in some instances a location for dispute between Western and indigenous forms. The secreting of the body of Ke'eaumoku took on a symbolic challenge to Western obsequies. So, too, the location of the funeral of Kamehameha III took the services out of the stone church and returned them to the sacred enclosure of the *kauhale* or residential compound of the *ali'i*.

Even Mauna 'Ala, dating from the mid-nineteenth century, maintains an element of ancient practice. Although the burial site is in a known place, both the Kamehameha dynasty and Kalākaua dynasty crypts chose underground vaults, reminiscent, perhaps even symbolic, of the burial caves. The burial at sea of Kealiiahonui, son of the last king of Kaua'i, and Kekāuluohi, the mother of the last king of the Kamehameha dynasty, also reflect traditional indigenous practices. The proposal by Abigail Kekaulike Kawānanakoa for a new tomb at Mauna 'Ala, too, saw discussions regarding by a *kahu* regarding *mana* and the ranking of chiefs, on the one hand, and administrative rules of a state department, on the other hand.

The heavens, too, have provided a continued backdrop to the traditional indigenous aspects of the royal Hawaiian way of death, still weeping at the deaths of *ali'i*.

Glossary

ahuʻula: feathered cloak[1]
ai kapu: restriction prohibiting men and women from eating together.
aliʻi: chief, king[2]
hānai: adopt[3]
haole: white, foreign[4]
kāʻai: basketwork that stored the bones of ancient chiefs
kāhili: royal standard[5]
kahuna: expert practitioner, sorcerer[6]
kanikau: a dirge[7]
kauhale: residential compound
makai: toward the ocean
mauka: inland
pāʻū: woman's skirt[8]
waena: middle

Chapter Notes

1. David E. Stannard, *Puritan Way of Death* (Oxford: Oxford University Press, 1977) 192.

Introduction

1. Mary Kawena Pukui, *Olelo Noeau* (Honolulu: Bishop Museum Press, 1983) 52.
2. *A Preliminary Catalogue of the Bernice Pauahi Bishop Museum of Polynesian Ethnology and Natural History*, 106.
3. Ross H. Gast and Agnes Conrad, *Don Francisco de Paula Marin* (Honolulu: University of Hawaii Press for Hawaiian Historical Society, 1973) 200.
4. Mary Kawena Pukui, *Nā Mele Welo* (Honolulu: Bishop Museum Press, 1995) 63.
5. Malo, *Ruling Chiefs of Hawaii* (Honolulu: Kamehameha Schools Press, 1961) 207.
6. "Extract from the Diary of Ebenezer Townsend, Jr.," Hawaiian Historical Society, Reprints (1787, 1788 and 1789) (Honolulu: Paradise of the Pacific Press, 1926) 8.
7. "Missionary Letters to the American Board of Commissioners for Foreign Missions (A. B. C. F. M.)—Volume 3—1824–1830," HMCS.
8. Hiram Bingham, *A Residence of Twenty-one Years in the Sandwich Islands* (Hartford, Connecticut: Hezekiah Huntington, 1849) 128.
9. Hiram Bingham, *A Residence of Twenty-one Years in the Sandwich Islands* (Hartford, Connecticut: Hezekiah Huntington, 1849) 128.
10. Hiram Bingham, *A Residence of Twenty-one Years in the Sandwich Islands* (Hartford, Connecticut: Hezekiah Huntington, 1849) 128.
11. Missionary Letters to the American Board of Commissioners for Foreign Missions (A. B. C. F. M.)—Volume 3—1824–1830," HMCS.
12. *Loomis Journal*, May 27, 1821–Feb. 6, 1824, Hawaiian Mission Children's Society Library, 61.
13. *Loomis Journal*, May 27, 1821–Feb. 6, 1824, Hawaiian Mission Children's Society Library, 61.
14. *Sandwich Islands Mission Journal*, Feb. 2, 1822, 269.
15. *Missionary Herald at Home and Abroad*, vol. 19, no. 10 (Oct. 1823) Boston: Crocker and Brewster, 318.
16. *Missionary Herald at Home and Abroad*, vol. 19, no. 10 (Oct. 1823) Boston: Crocker and Brewster, 318.
17. 1819–1827 Journal Fragments, Elizabeth Edwards Bishop, Nov. 21, 1823, Hawaiian Mission Children's Society.
18. Missionary Letters to the American Board of Commissioners for Foreign Missions, vol. 3, 892, HMCS.
19. Lucy G. Thurston, *Life and Times of Mrs. Lucy G. Thurston* (Ann Arbor, Michigan: S.C. Andrews, 1882) 93–94.
20. Lucy G. Thurston, *Life and Times of Mrs. Lucy G. Thurston* (Ann Arbor, Michigan: S.C. Andrews, 1882) 93–94.
21. Mary Kawena Pukui, *Olelo Noeau*, 133.
22. *Senate Journal*, 1901, 26.

Chapter 1

1. Mary Kawena Pukui, *Olelo Noeau* (Honolulu: Bishop Museum Press, 1983) 213.
2. Mark Twain, *Roughing It* (New York: Harper and Brothers, 1918) 224.
3. Samuel M. Kamakau, *Ruling Chiefs of Hawaii* (Honolulu: The Kamehameha Schools Press, 1961) 213.
4. Kamakau, 214.
5. Kamakau, 213.
6. Kamakau, 215.
7. Kamakau, 215.
8. David Malo, Malcolm Chun, trans., Ka Moolelo Hawaii, Hawaiian Traditions, A New Translation (Honolulu: FirstPeople's Productions, 1996) 206.

9. Samuel M. Kamakau, *Ruling Chiefs of Hawaii* (Honolulu: Kamehameha Schools Press, 1992) 208.
10. *Missionary Herald*, vol. 19, 319.
11. *Missionary Herald*, vol. 19, 319.
12. *Euanelio A Mataio: Oia Ka Moo Olele Hemolele No Kakou Haku E Ola'i, No Iesu Kristo, I Olelo Hawaii* (Rochester, New York: Paiia Ma Ka Mea Ai Palapala a Lumiki, 1828) 69.
13. *Bible*, Authorized (King James) Version.
14. *Missionary Herald*, vol. 19, 319.
15. *Missionary Herald*, vol. 19, 319.
16. Gast and Conrad, 274.
17. Gast and Conrad, 278.
18. Stewart, 166.
19. Letter from Jeremiah Evarts, et al. to ABCFM dated October 23, 1823, Joint Letters 1820–1823, Hawaiian Mission Children's Society Library. See also similar quote in Howard M Ballou and George R. Carter, "The History of the Hawaiian Mission Press, with Bibliography of Earlier Publications," *Papers of the Hawaiian Historical Society*, Issue 14 (1908) (Honolulu: Paradise of the Pacific Press, 13.
20. Charles S. Stewart, *Journal of a Residence in the Sandwich Islands*, New York: John P. Haven, 1828, 164.
21. Kamakau, 255.
22. William Ellis, *Polynesian Researches*, vol. 4, 136.
23. William Ellis, Polynesian *Researches*, vol. 4, 137.
24. Kamakau, 387.
25. William Richards, *Memoir of Keopuolani*, Boston: Crocker & Brewster, 1825, 40.
26. William Richards, *Memoir of Keopuolani*, Boston: Crocker & Brewster, 1825, 40.
27. William Richards, *Memoir of Keopuolani*, Boston: Crocker & Brewster, 1825, 40.
28. William Ellis, *Polynesian Researches*, vol. 4, 135.
29. William Ellis, *Polynesian Researches*, vol. 4, 135.
30. William Ellis, *Polynesian Researches*, vol. 4, 135.
31. *Ruling Chiefs of Hawaii*, 254.
32. "Sandwich Islands Mission, Journal at Honoruru," *The Missionary Herald for the Year 1825*, vol. 21 (Boston: Crocker and Brewster, 1825) 174.
33. "Sandwich Islands Mission, Journal at Honoruru," *The Missionary Herald for the Year 1825*, vol. 21 (Boston: Crocker and Brewster, 1825) 174.
34. "Sandwich Islands Mission, Journal at Honoruru," *The Missionary Herald for the Year 1825*, vol. 21 (Boston: Crocker and Brewster, 1825) 174.
35. Charles S. Stewart, *Journal of a Residence in the Sandwich Islands*, New York: John P. Haven, 1828, 203.
36. Missionary Letters to the ABCFM, vol. 3, 893–894, HMCS.
37. Stewart, 290–291.
38. Stewart, 290.
39. Stewart, 215.
40. *Bible*, Authorized (King James) Version.
41. David Forbes, *Hawaiian National Bibliography*, vol. 1 (Honolulu: University of Hawaii Press, 1999) 396.
42. *Bible*, Authorized (King James) Version.
43. *A collection of hymns for the use of the tabernacles in Scotland*, 159.
44. *Missionary Records, Sandwich Islands*, 257.
45. William Ellis qtd in Stewart, 223.
46. Ellis, qtd in Stewart. 223.
47. Letter from George Burder to Jeremiah Evarts, July 31, 1824, ABCFM-HEA, HMCS.
48. Norris Whitfield Potter, *History of the Hawaiian Kingdom*, 50.
49. George Anson Byron and Richard Roland Bloxam, *Voyage of H.M.S. Blonde to the Sandwich Islands, in the Years 1824–1825* (London: John Murray, 1826) 79.
50. Byron, 71.
51. Ephriam Eveleth, *History of the Sandwich Islands: With an Account of the American Mission*, 163.
52. Byron, 71.
53. S.M. Kamakau, *Ruling Chiefs of Hawaii*, 1992, 258.
54. Eveleth, 162–163.
55. Charles S. Stewart, *Journal of a Residence in the Sandwich Islands*, New York: John P. Haven, 1828, 276.
56. Eveleth, 163.
57. Eveleth, 163.
58. *Au Okoa*, Nov. 6, 1865, 2.
59. "Missionary Letters to the American Board of Commissioners for Foreign Missions (A. B. C. F. M.)—Volume 03—1824–1830," HMCS.
60. "Brief Extracts from Mr. Bishop's Journal," *The Missionary Herald at Home and Abroad*, Volume 21, 140–141.
61. *Alemanaka Hawaii*, Kahn Collection, Hawaii State Achives.
62. Kamakau, 278.
63. *Ruling Chiefs of Hawaii*, 318.
64. Levi Chamberlain, *Journal*, vol. 13, 10–13.
65. Hiram Bingham, *A Residence of Twenty-one Years in the Sandwich Islands*, Canadaigua, New York: H.D. Goodwin, 1855, 349.
66. Levi Chamberlain, *Journal*, vol. 13, 10–13.
67. Hiram Bingham, *A Residence of Twenty-one Years in the Sandwich Islands*, Canadaigua, New York: H.D. Goodwin, 1855, 349.

68. *Levi Chamberlain's Journal*, vol. 13, 10–13, Hawaiian Mission Children's Society.
69. Kamakau, 339.
70. *Au Okoa*, Nov. 6, 1865, 2.
71. Kamakau, 342.
72. P. Christiaan Klieger, *Moku'ula: Maui's Sacred Isle* (Honolulu: Bishop Museum Press, 1998) 82.
73. Klieger, 95.
74. Sereno Edwards Bishop, *Reminiscences of Old Hawaii* (Honolulu: Hawaiian Gazette, 1916) 36.
75. James Oliver and William Giles Dix, *Wreck of the Glide*, New York: Wiley & Putnam, 1848, 180.
76. James Oliver and William Giles Dix, *Wreck of the Glide*, New York: Wiley & Putnam, 1848, 180.
77. James Oliver and William Giles Dix, *Wreck of the Glide*, New York: Wiley & Putnam, 1848, 180.
78. James Oliver and William Giles Dix, *Wreck of the Glide*, New York: Wiley & Putnam, 1848, 180–181.
79. James Oliver and William Giles Dix, *Wreck of the Glide*, New York: Wiley & Putnam, 1848, 180–181.
80. *Au Okoa*, Nov. 6, 1865, 2.
81. "Make," *Kumu Hawaii*, Dec. 23, 1835, 207.
82. *Au Okoa*, Nov. 6, 1865, 2.
83. "Make," *Kumu Hawaii*, Dec. 23, 1835, 207.
84. Levi Chamberlain, *Journal*, vol. 20, 7.
85. Levi Chamberlain, Journal, vol. 20, 7.
86. *Sandwich Islands Gazette*, Apr. 15, 1837.
87. *Kumu Hawaii*, Feb. 15, 1837, 74.
88. *Native Testimony*, Hawaii State Archives, vol. 2, 246.
89. *Native Testimony*, Hawaii State Archives, vol. 1, 24.
90. *Native Testimony*, Hawaii State Archives, vol. 2, 246.
91. Award 10; R.P. 9; Alakea St. Honolulu; 1 ap.; 1.02 Acs, Waihona 'Aina.
92. Table of consular grievances, 1843–1846, Hawaii State Archives.
93. "Sketches of Lahaina," *Friend*, Dec. 1922, 283.
94. Andelucia Lee Conde, Conde Family Journals, HMCS, 1837–1849.
95. Items of cost in re casket of Kaahumanu II, April 9, 1839, Series 402, Box 5, Folder 99, Chronological File, 1790–1849, 1839: Apr 5, 9, 30, May 1.
96. *Au Okoa*, Nov. 6, 1865, 2.
97. Sir Edward Belcher, *Voyage Round the World*, qtd. in *Colburn's New Monthly Magazine and Humorist*, Vol. 67 (1843), 422.
98. Kamakau, 351.
99. Kamakau, 351–352.
100. Kamakau, 352.
101. Kamakau, 352.
102. Kamakau, 356.
103. Kamakau, 385.
104. *Polynesian*, May 8, 1841, 3.
105. Mary Atherton Richards, *The Chiefs' Children's School* (Honolulu: Honolulu Star-Bulletin, 1937) 126.
106. P. Christiaan Klieger, Moku'ula: Maui's Sacred Isle (Honolulu: Bishop Museum Press, 1998) 82.
107. Kamakau, 385.
108. "Post Mortem Examination," *Polynesian*, Mar. 29, 1845, 183.
109. "Burial of Haalilio," *Polynesian*, Mar. 29, 1845, Page 184.
110. "Burial of Haalilio," *Polynesian*, Mar. 29, 1845, Page 184.
111. "Burial of Haalilio," *Polynesian*, Mar. 29, 1845, Page 184.
112. Thomas G. Thrum, ed., *Hawaiian Almanac and Annual for 1890* (Honolulu: Press Publishing Co., 1890) 74.
113. "Burial of Haalilio," *Polynesian*, Mar. 29, 1845, Page 184.
114. *Polynesian*, June 21, 1845.
115. Letter from Robert Wyllie to Lieutenant Hunt, June 16, 1845, Foreign Office Letter Book, vol. 5, Series 410, Box 2, Hawaii State Archives.
116. Outrigger Canoe Club *Forecast*, Sept 6, 1953.
117. Published by Authority, *Polynesian*, Nov. 25, 1848, 111.
118. *Polynesian*, Nov. 25, 1848, 127.
119. "Reminiscences of Honolulu.—No 19," *Saturday Press*, Jan. 14, 1882, 1.
120. "Order of Procession for the Funeral of the Late William Pitt Leleiohoku"—Chamberlain's Office, December 22, 1848, Broadsides, Foreign Office and Executive, Hawaii State Archives.
121. Order of Procession, Foreign Office and Executive, Broadside, Dec. 22, 1848, Hawaii State Archives.
122. *Polynesian*, Jan. 6, 1849, 134.
123. *Au Okoa*, Nov. 6, 1865, 2.
124. *Au Okoa*, Nov. 6, 1865, 2.
125. Roster, *Legislatures of Hawaii*.
126. "Order of Procession For the Funeral of the Late Chief, Kealiiahonui, Son of Kaumualii, the late King of Kauai"—Chamberlain's Office, June 26, 1849, Broadsides, Foreign Office and Executive, Hawaii State Archives.
127. "Order of Procession For the Funeral of the Late Chief, Kealiiahonui, Son of Kaumualii, the late King of Kauai"—Chamberlain's Office, June 26, 1849, Broadsides, Foreign Office and Executive, Hawaii State Archives.
128. W.D. Alexander,"The Funeral Rites of Kealiiahonui," Hawaiian Historical Society, Annual Reports, 1903, 27–28.

129. *Polynesian,* June 7, 1851, 2.
130. Chamberlain's Notice, *Polynesian,* June 28, 1851, 3.
131. Order of Procession for the Funeral of the Late Lady Chief Kekauonohi, Order of Procession, Foreign Office and Executive, Broadside, June 21, 1851.
132. "Obituary," *Polynesian,* Oct. 4, 1851, 82.
133. First Circuit Court Probate 1760, Hawaii State Archives.
134. Letter from R.C. Wyllie to Foreign Ministers, Oct. 2, 1851, Series 410, Foreign Office Letterbook, v. 13A, Foreign Office and Executive, Hawaii State Archives, 1400.
135. "Obituary," *Polynesian,* Oct. 4, 1851, 82.
136. Died. *Polynesian,* May 8, 1852, 207.
137. Died. *Friend,* Jun. 2, 1853, 48.
138. Died. *Friend,* Jun. 2, 1853, 48.
139. "Letters from Polynesia," *The Sailors' Magazine and Naval Journal,* vol. 27, no. 3 (Apr. 1855), New York: American Seamen's Friend Society, 233.
140. "Letters from Polynesia," *The Sailors' Magazine and Naval Journal,* vol. 27, no. 3 (Apr. 1855), New York: American Seamen's Friend Society, 250.
141. "Funeral of his late Majesty, Kamehameha III," Polynesian, Jan. 13, 1855, 142.
142. Stanley C. Ball, Bishop Museum Handbook, Part II (Honolulu: Bernice Pauahi Bishop Museum, 1929) 12.
143. Payments to Lafrenz & Fischer, Dec. 16, 1854 to Jan. 20, 1855, Foreign Office and Executive, Series 402, Box 9, Kamehameha III, Funeral Expenses, Hawaii State Archives.
144. Privy Council Minutes, Jan. 16, 1855, Series 421, vol. 9, Foreign Office and Executive, Hawaii State Archives, 49.
145. Privy Council Minutes, Jan. 16, 1855, Series 421, vol. 9, Foreign Office and Executive, Hawaii State Archives, 49.
146. Elisha H. Allen, Supplemental Report of the Minister of Finance, April 24, 1855, 31.
147. Payments to Lafrenz & Fischer, Dec. 16, 1854 to Jan. 20, 1855, Foreign Office and Executive, Series 402, Box 9, Kamehameha III, Funeral Expenses, Hawaii State Archives. Report to Kamehameha IV, Jan. 15, 1855, Foreign Office and Executive, Series 402, Box 9, Kamehameha III, Funeral Expenses, Hawaii State Archives.
148. "Letters from Polynesia," *The Sailors' Magazine and Naval Journal,* vol. 27, no. 3 (Apr. 1855), New York: American Seamen's Friend Society, 249.
149. "Funeral of Kamehameha III," *Hawaiian Annual,* 1915, 59.
150. *Friend,* January 1855, 4.
151. Paul Emmert, Funeral of His Late Majesty Kamehameha III. Jan. 10, 1855, The Hawaiian Collection of Paul Markham Kahn, vol. 2, 37/13, Hawaii State Archives.
152. Reminiscences of Mrs. William Hyde Rice as told to Miss Katherine McInyre, Hawaiian Mission Children's Society Library, 17.
153. M-168, Hawaii State Archives.
154. "Funeral of his late Majesty, Kamehameha III," *Polynesian,* Jan. 13, 1855, 142.
155. "Death of Paki," *Friend,* Jun. 15, 1855, 45.
156. *Privy Council Minutes,* vol. 9, 155.
157. *Privy Council Minutes,* vol. 9, 159.
158. *Au Okoa,* Nov. 6, 1865, 2.
159. Chamberlain Journal, HMCS.
160. *Rosters, Legislatures of Hawaii,* Hawaii State Archives.
161. Circular notifying the death of Konia and John Young, July 21, 1857, Foreign Office & Executive, Hawaii State Archives.
162. "The Funeral of Konia," *Polynesian,* Aug. 8, 1857, 108.
163. *Au Okoa,* Nov. 6, 1865, 2.
164. *Pacific Commercial Advertiser,* Sept. 3, 1857, 2.
165. Circular announcing the funeral of His Excellency John Young, dated Aug. 25, 1857, Foreign Office and Executive, Broadsides, Hawaii State Archives.
166. *Polynesian,* Aug. 29. 1857, 133.
167. *Pacific Commercial Advertiser,* Sept. 3, 1857, 2.
168. *Au Okoa,* Nov. 6, 1865, 2.
169. First Circuit Court, Probate 1364, Hawaii State Archives.
170. First Circuit Court, Probate 1364, Hawaii State Archives.
171. *Polynesian,* July 1, 1858, 3.
172. *Friend,* Jul. 26, 1858.
173. Order of procession for the funeral of the Honorable Thos. Chas. Byde Rooke, F.R.C.S., Member of his Majesty's Privy Council of State, and Physician to the King and Royal Family. Chamberlain's Office, December 15, 1858.
174. "Mechanics' Benefit Union," *Friend,* vol. X, no. 1 (Oct. 1, 1853), 69.
175. *Au Okoa,* Nov. 6, 1865, 2.
176. Notes of the Week, *Pacific Commercial Advertiser,* Sep. 17, 1859, 2.
177. Notes of the Week, *Pacific Commercial Advertiser,* Sep. 17, 1859, 2.
178. William F. Wilson, "Professor John Henry Anderson "The Wizard of the North" at Honolulu in 1859," *Forty-Seventh Annual Report for the Year 1938,* Hawaiian Historical Society (Honolulu: Pacific Herald Publishing Company, 1939).
179. Notes of the Week, *Pacific Commercial Advertiser,* Dec. 29, 1859, 2.
180. Notes of the Week, *Pacific Commercial Advertiser,* Dec. 29, 1859, 2.

181. "Death of the Hon. B. Namakeha," *Polynesian*, December 29, 1860, 3.
182. "Death of the Hon. B. Namakeha," *Pacific Commercial Advertiser*, Jan. 3, 1861, 2.
183. *Au Okoa*, Nov. 6, 1865, 2.
184. *Prince Lot Kapuāiwa Chiefs' Children's School Journal, 1844–1845*, Hawaii State Archives, 95.
185. *Translation of the Constitution and Laws of the Hawaiian Islands, Established in the Reign of Kamehameha III*, Lahainaluna, 1842.
186. Mary Atherton Richards, 280.
187. "Act to Allow Certain Divorced Persons to Marry Again," *Laws of His Majesty Kamehameha IV, King of the Hawaiian Islands, Passed by the Nobles and Representatives, At Their Session, 1856*, Honolulu, 1856, 15.
188. *Ka Hae Hawaii*, Feb. 13, 1861, 189.
189. "Died," *Polynesian.*, Jan. 18, 1862, 2.
190. *Au Okoa*, Nov. 6, 1865, 2.
191. "Death of His Royal Highness Prince of Hawaii," *Pacific Commercial Advertiser*, Aug. 28, 1862, 2.
192. "Death of His Royal Highness Prince of Hawaii," *Pacific Commercial Advertiser*, Aug. 28, 1862, 2.
193. Court Circular, *Polynesian*, Aug. 30, 1862, 2.
194. Notes of the Week, *Pacific Commercial Advertiser*, Sept. 11, 1862, 2.
195. Notes of the Week, *Pacific Commercial Advertiser*, Sept. 11, 1862, 2.
196. *Privy Council Minutes*, vol. 11, 91.
197. *Pacific Commercial Advertiser*, Nov. 4, 1865, 2.
198. *Au Okoa*, Nov. 6, 1865, 2.
199. H.P. Baldwin, et al, "Report of the Finance Committee on the State Funeral of Her late Royal Highness Princess Likelike," Legislative Publications, Hawaii State Archives, 1888, 5.
200. *Au Okoa*, Nov. 6, 1865, 2.
201. "Funeral of the Late King," *Pacific Commercial Advertiser*, Feb. 4, 1864, 4.
202. "Funeral of the Late King," *Pacific Commercial Advertiser*, Feb. 4, 1864, 4.
203. *Au Okoa*, Nov. 6, 1865, 2.
204. "Funeral of the Late King," *Pacific Commercial Advertiser*, Feb. 4, 1864, 4.
205. "Episcopacy at the Sandwich Islands," *Missionary Herald*, vol. 60 (1864), 155.
206. *Privy Council Minutes*, Dec. 3, 1863, vol. 11, 123.
207. *Privy Council Minutes*, vol. 11, 148–149.
208. "Episcopacy at the Sandwich Islands," *Missionary Herald*, vol. 60 (1864), 155.
209. H.P. Baldwin, et al, "Report of the Finance Committee on the State Funeral of Her late Royal Highness Princess Likelike," Legislative Publications, Hawaii State Archives, 1888, 5.
210. Foreign Office and Executive, Broadsides, 1864, Hawaii State Archives.
211. *Pacific Commercial Advertiser*, Mar. 26, 1860, #.
212. "Funeral of the Late King," *Pacific Commercial Advertiser*, Feb. 4, 1864, 4.
213. "Episcopacy at the Sandwich Islands, *Missionary Herald*, vol. 60 (1864), 155.
214. "Funeral of the Late King," *Pacific Commercial Advertiser*, Feb. 4, 1864, 4.
215. Foreign Office & Executive, Broadside, October 19, 1865, Hawaii State Archives.
216. *Pacific Commercial Advertiser*, Oct. 28, 1865, 2.
217. Mark Twain, *Letters from the Sandwich Islands*, 122.
218. "Funeral of the Princess Victoria," *Pacific Commercial Advertiser*, July 7, 1866, 3.
219. *Pacific Commercial Advertiser*, Jun. 30, 1866, 2.
220. H.P. Baldwin, et al, "Report of the Finance Committee on the State Funeral of Her late Royal Highness Princess Likelike," Legislative Publications, Hawaii State Archives, 1888, 5.
221. *Pacific Commercial Advertiser*, Jul. 7, 1866, 2.
222. "Funeral," PCA, Aug. 18, 1866, 3.
223. Foreign Office and Executive, Broadsides, 1866, Hawaii State Archives.
224. *Burlington Weekly Free Press*, Aug. 10, 1866, 3.
225. "The Queen of the Sandwich Islands," Richmond Dispatch, Aug. 11, 1866, 2.
226. *National Republican*, Oct. 26, 1866, 2.
227. "Demise of the Mother of a Queen," Evening Telegraph (Philadelphia), Sep. 1, 1866, 5.
228. *New York Herald*, Sep. 26, 1866, 6.
229. "From the Pacific Coast," *Charleston Daily News*, Nov. 23, 1866, 1.
230. Letter from Emma Kaleleonalani to Kamehameha V, October 29, 1866, Emma Collection, M-45, NA-3, Hawaii State Archives.
231. *Hawaiian Gazette*, Dec. 8, 1866, 3.
232. "Another Chief Gone," *Pacific Commercial Advertiser*, Nov. 17, 1866, 3.
233. *Hawaiian Gazette*, Dec. 1, 1875, 3.
234. "Death of His Highness Mataio Kekuanaoa," *Pacific Commercial Advertiser*, November 28, 1868, 2.
235. By Authority, *Hawaiian Gazette*, Dec. 2, 1868, 2.
236. *Friend*, Dec. 1868, 107.
237. *Pacific Commercial Advertiser*, Dec. 19, 1868, 2.
238. Broadsides, Scrap Book, Hawaiian Historical Society, 19.
239. Equity, 220, Hawaii State Archives.
240. Notes of the Week, *Pacific Commercial Advertiser*, Apr. 10, 1869, 3.

241. "Funeral of the Late Hon. Mrs. A.K. Kapaakea," *Hawaiian Gazette*, April 21, 1869, 3.
242. "Funeral of the Late Hon. Mrs. A.K. Kapaakea," *Hawaiian Gazette*, April 21, 1869, 3.
243. "Death of Her Majesty Queen Kalama," *Hawaiian Gazette*, Sep. 21, 1870, 2.
244. *Hawaiian Times*, Oct. 7, 1870, 2.
245. "The Funeral Procession," *Pacific Commercial Advertiser*, Oct. 8, 1870, 3.
246. By Authority, *Hawaiian Gazette*, Oct. 12, 1870, 2.
247. "Funeral of Queen Kalama," *Hawaiian Times*, Oct. 11, 1870, 2.
248. "A Grand Funeral," *Daily Southern Cross* (Aukland), Nov. 17, 1870, 2.
249. Robert Wilson Andrews; Journal, January 1–December 26, 1870, G. W. Blunt White Library, Log 232, 34.
250. *Foreign Relations of the United States, 1894: Affairs in Hawaii*, [Elihu Root collection of United States documents: Ser. A.-F.], Volume 1], Washington, D.C.: Government Printing Office, 1895, 1346.
251. Ulysses Simpson Grant, *The Papers of Ulysses S. Grant, vol. 20, November 1, 1869–October 31, 1870*, Carbondale, Illinois: Southern Illinois University Press, 1995, 88.
252. *Hawaiian Gazette*, Oct. 5, 1870, 3.
253. *Pacific Commercial Advertiser*, Oct. 8, 1870, 3.
254. *Hawaiian Gazette*, Oct. 12, 1870, 2.
255. *Hawaiian Times*, Oct. 7, 1870, 2.
256. *Hawaiian Times*, Oct. 7, 1870, 2.
257. "Funeral of Her late Majesty Queen Dowager Kalama, and its Suggestions," *Pacific Commercial Advertiser*, Oct. 15, 1870, 3.
258. "Funeral of Her late Majesty Queen Dowager Kalama, and its Suggestions," *Pacific Commercial Advertiser*, Oct. 15, 1870, 3.
259. Invitations, Menus, Etc., M-485, Invitations-Royalty-Funerals, Etc., Hawaii State Archives.
260. H.P. Baldwin, et al, "Report of the Finance Committee on the State Funeral of Her late Royal Highness Princess Likelike," Legislative Publications, Hawaii State Archives, 1888, 5.
261. "Death of a Chiefess," *Pacific Commercial Advertiser*, Aug. 2, 1873, 3.
262. "Mare," *Ka Nupepa Kuokoa*, Dec. 20, 1862, 3.
263. S.L. Kaelemakule, "He Moolelo No Jane Loeau," *Ko Hawaii Ponoi*, 13 Aug. 13, 1873.
264. *Ka Nupepa Kuokoa*, Aug. 2, 1873, 2.
265. Alfons Korn, *News from Molokai: Letters Between Peter Kaeao & Queen Emma 1873–1876* (Honolulu: University of Hawaii Press, 1976) 45.
266. "Funeral of King Lunalilo," *Hawaiian Gazette*, Mar. 4, 1874, 2.

267. "The Funeral of Lunalilo," *Pacific Commercial Advertiser*, Mar. 7, 1874, 4.
268. Foreign Office and Executive, Broadsides, 1874, Hawaii State Archives.
269. Foreign Office and Executive, Broadsides, 1874, Hawaii State Archives.
270. "Funeral of King Lunalilo," *Hawaiian Gazette*, Mar. 4, 1874, 2.
271. "Funeral sermon preached by Rev. H.H. Parker at the burial Lunalilo the first—king of the Hawaiian Islands, Feb. 20th 1874," M-118, Hawaii State Archives.
272. Isabella Lucy Bird, The Hawaiian Archipelago (London: John Murry, 1875) 468–469.
273. "Funeral of King Lunalilo," *Hawaiian Gazette*, Mar. 4, 1874, 2.
274. "Funeral of King Lunalilo," *Hawaiian Gazette*, Mar. 4, 1874, 2.
275. H.P. Baldwin, et al, "Report of the Finance Committee on the State Funeral of Her late Royal Highness Princess Likelike," Legislative Publications, Hawaii State Archives, 1888, 5.
276. Notes of the Week, *Pacific Commercial Advertiser*, Nov. 27, 1875, 3.
277. Mary Kawena Pukui, *Olelo Noeau* (Honolulu: Bishop Museum Press, 1983) 205.
278. *Pacific Commercial Advertiser*, Mar. 24, 1877, 2.
279. Jane E. James, "Things Hawaiian," *Paradise of the Pacific*, Aug. 1932, 4.
280. "Palace Grounds," *Pacific Commercial Advertiser*, Jan. 30, 1875, 3.
281. "Death of His Royal Highness William Pitt Leleiohoku," *Hawaiian Gazette*, April 11, 1877.
282. "He Kanikau No Leleiohoku," *Hawaiian Songs with Words and Music, Translated, Composed, or Arranged by Liliuokalani of Hawaii* (Washington, D.C., 1897) 24.
283. "Funeral of the late Prince William Pitt Leleiohoku," *Hawaiian Gazette*, May 2, 1877, 2.
284. "Funeral of the late Prince William Pitt Leleiohoku," *Hawaiian Gazette*, May 2, 1877, 2.
285. Invitations, Menus, Etc., M-485, Invitations-Royalty-Funerals, Etc., Hawaii State Archives.
286. Invitations, Menus, Etc., M-485, Invitations-Royalty-Funerals, Etc., Hawaii State Archives.
287. "Funeral of the late Prince William Pitt Leleiohoku," *Hawaiian Gazette*, May 2, 1877, 2.
288. *Pacific Commercial Advertiser*, Apr. 21, 1877, 2.
289. "Funeral of the late Prince William Pitt Leleiohoku," *Hawaiian Gazette*, May 2, 1877, 2.

290. H.P. Baldwin, et al, "Report of the Finance Committee on the State Funeral of Her late Royal Highness Princess Likelike," Legislative Publications, Hawaii State Archives, 1888, 5.
291. *Pacific Commercial Advertiser*, Oct. 2, 1880, 3.
292. Manuscript Collection, M-186, Hawaii State Archives.
293. *Pacific Commercial Advertiser*, Oct. 2, 1880, 3.
294. *Hawaiian Gazette*, Dec. 1, 1880, 3.
295. *Pacific Commercial Advertiser*, Nov. 27, 1880, 2.
296. *Hawaiian Gazette*, Dec. 1, 1880, 3.
297. *Hawaiian Gazette*, Dec. 1, 1880, 3.
298. *Saturday Press*, Dec. 4, 1880, 3.
299. *Saturday Press*, Dec. 4, 1880, 3.
300. *Saturday Press*, Dec. 4, 1880, 3.
301. Notes of the Week, *Saturday Press*, November 20, 1880, 3.
302. *Saturday Press*, Dec. 4, 1880, 3.
303. "Death of Her Highness Princess Ruth Keelikolani," *Daily Bulletin*, May 28, 1883, 2.
304. "By Authority," *Daily Bulletin*, Jun. 19, 1883, 2.
305. "Death of Princess Ruth," *Pacific Commercial Advertiser*, Jun. 2, 1883, 2.
306. "Death of Princess Ruth," *Pacific Commercial Advertiser*, Jun. 2, 1883, 2.
307. "By Authority," *Daily Bulletin*, Jun. 19, 1883, 2.
308. Local and General News. *Daily Bulletin*, Jun. 18, 1883, 2.
309. *Friend*, April 1920, 86.
310. "H.H. Ruth," *Daily Bulletin*, Jun. 20, 1883, 2.
311. *Pacific Commercial Advertiser*, Jun. 16, 1883, 2.
312. "Princess Ruth's Funeral." *Hawaiian Gazette*, June 20, 1883, 2.
313. Military and Navy Finding Aid, Hawaii State Archives.
314. "H.H. Ruth," *Daily Bulletin*, Jun. 20, 1883, 2.
315. "H.H. Ruth," *Daily Bulletin*, Jun. 20, 1883, 2.
316. "Local & General," Pacific Commercial Advertiser, Jan. 12, 1884, 5.
317. H.P. Baldwin, et al, "Report of the Finance Committee on the State Funeral of Her late Royal Highness Princess Likelike," Legislative Publications, Hawaii State Archives, 1888, 5.
318. Invitations, Menus, Etc., M-485, Invitations-Royalty-Funerals, Etc., Hawaii State Archives.
319. *He Buke Mele Hawaii, I Haku Ponoi, Hoonohonoho, a mahele ia, e, Liliuokalani o Hawaii, He mea hoonanea, No ka la Walea*, Wakinekona, Mokuaina o Kolumepia, 1897 [*Hawaiian Songs with Words and Music, Translated, Composed, or Arranged, by, Liliuokalani of Hawaii*, Washington D.C., 1897], 22–23.
320. Henry Ward Beecher and Charles Beecher, *Plymouth Collection of Hymns and Tunes; for the Use of Christian Congregations*, New York: Barnes, 1855, 357.
321. Henry Ward Beecher and Charles Beecher, *Plymouth Collection of Hymns and Tunes; for the Use of Christian Congregations*, New York: Barnes, 1855, 356.
322. *Hawaiian Gazette*, Oct. 29, 1884, 2.
323. "Bernice Pauahi Bishop," *Saturday Press*, Nov. 8, 1884, 3.
324. "Bernice Pauahi Bishop," *Saturday Press*, Nov. 8, 1884, 3.
325. "Bernice Pauahi Bishop," *Saturday Press*, Nov. 8, 1884, 3.
326. "Bernice Pauahi Bishop," *Saturday Press*, Nov. 8, 1884, 3.
327. "Bernice Pauahi Bishop," *Saturday Press*, Nov. 8, 1884, 3.
328. "The Dead Queen," Saturday Press, May 16, 1885, 2.
329. "The Dead Queen," Saturday Press, May 16, 1885, 2.
330. "The Dead Queen," Saturday Press, May 16, 1885, 2.
331. "The Dead Queen," Saturday Press, May 16, 1885, 2.
332. *Funeral Obsequies of the late Queen Dowager Emma Kaleleonalani, Relict of the late Kamehameha* (Honolulu: J.M. Oat Jr. & Co., 1885) 24.
333. *Funeral Obsequies of the late Queen Dowager Emma Kaleleonalani, Relict of the late Kamehameha* (Honolulu: J.M. Oat Jr. & Co., 1885) 29–30.
334. "The Queen Dowager Emma Kaleleonalani, Laid to Rest," Daily Bulletin, May 18, 1885, 6.
335. *Constitution, By-laws and Rules of Order, Sciota Tribe, No. 214, Improved Order of Red Men, of Pennsylvania. Frankford Avenue and Aramingo Street* (Philadelphia, Pennsylvania: Shaw Brothers, Printers, 1886).
336. M-186, Hawaii State Archives.
337. http://www.pythias.org/.
338. Letter from Samuel G. Wilder to Capt. K. de Livron, March 31, 1879, Interior Department, Letterbook, Hawaii State Archives, 109.
339. "The Dead Queen," Saturday Press, May 23, 1885, 2.
340. *Funeral Obsequies of the late Queen Dowager Emma Kaleleonalani, Relict of the late Kamehameha* (Honolulu: J.M. Oat Jr. & Co., 1885) 31.
341. Correspondence, 1885, Queen Emma's Funeral Expenses, Minister of Finance 2–14, Hawaii State Archives.
342. *Funeral Obsequies of the late Queen*

Dowager Emma Kaleleonalani, Relict of the late Kamehameha (Honolulu: J.M. Oat Jr. & Co., 1885).

343. Invitations, Menus, Etc., M-485, Invitations-Royalty-Funerals, Etc., Hawaii State Archives.

344. "Funeral of the late Princess Likelike," *Pacific Commercial Advertiser*, Feb. 28, 1887, 2.

345. *Na Himeni Haipule Hawaii* (Honolulu, 1972) 64.

346. "Funeral of the late Princess Likelike," *Pacific Commercial Advertiser*, Feb. 28, 1887, 2.

347. Nicholas Brady and Nahum Tate, *A New Version of the Psalms of David: Fitted to the Tunes Used in Churches*, (Oxford: Clarenden Press, 1818).

348. *Pacific Commercial Advertiser*, Feb. 28, 1887, 2.

349. "Funeral of the late Princess Likelike," *Pacific Commercial Advertiser*, Feb. 28, 1887, 2.

350. "Funeral of the late Princess Likelike" *Pacific Commercial Advertiser*, Feb. 28, 1887, 2.

351. "Funeral of the late Princess Likelike," *Pacific Commercial Advertiser*, Feb. 28, 1887, 2.

352. Broadside, March 7, 1887, Foreign Office and Executive, Hawaii State Archives.

353. Broadside, March 14, 1887, Foreign Office and Executive, Hawaii State Archives.

354. H.P. Baldwin, et al, "Report of the Finance Committee on the State Funeral of Her late Royal Highness Princess Likelike," Legislative Publications, Hawaii State Archives, 1888, 3.

355. H.P. Baldwin, et al, "Report of the Finance Committee on the State Funeral of Her late Royal Highness Princess Likelike," Legislative Publications, Hawaii State Archives, 1888, 3–4.

356. Correspondence, 1885, Queen Emma's Funeral Expenses, Minister of Finance 2–14, Hawaii State Archives.

357. H.P. Baldwin, et al, "Report of the Finance Committee on the State Funeral of Her late Royal Highness Princess Likelike," Legislative Publications, Hawaii State Archives, 1888, 5–6.

358. H.P. Baldwin, et al, "Report of the Finance Committee on the State Funeral of Her late Royal Highness Princess Likelike," Legislative Publications, Hawaii State Archives, 1888, 6.

359. H.P. Baldwin, et al, "Report of the Finance Committee on the State Funeral of Her late Royal Highness Princess Likelike," Legislative Publications, Hawaii State Archives, 1888, 6–7.

360. H.P. Baldwin, et al, "Report of the Finance Committee on the State Funeral of Her late Royal Highness Princess Likelike," Legislative Publications, Hawaii State Archives, 1888, 8.

361. Broadside, FO&Ex, Notice of Godfrey Brown, Department of Foreign Affairs, dated Sept. 22, 1887, Re: the death of Prince Edward Keliiahonui, Hawaii State Archives.

362. "Prince Keliihonui," *Pacific Commercial Advertiser*, Sep. 22, 1887, 3.

363. Broadside, FO&Ex, Notice of Godfrey Brown, Department of Foreign Affairs, dated Sept. 22, 1887, Re: the death of Prince Edward Keliiahonui, Hawaii State Archives.

364. "Funeral Obsequies," *PCA* Sep. 26, 1887, 3.

365. Antone Rosa, Annual Address, November 26, 1887, Hale Naua, M-469, Hale Naua, Records of Society Activities, Addresses and Speeches, Hawaii State Archives.

366. "Funeral Obsequies," *PCA* Sep. 26, 1887, 3.

367. "Funeral Obsequies," *PCA* Sep. 26, 1887, 3.

368. "The Dead Monarch," *Daily Alta California*, Jan. 22, 1891, 8.

369. "The Dead Monarch," *Daily Alta California*, Jan. 22, 1891, 8.

370. "The Dead Monarch," *Daily Alta California*, Jan. 22, 1891, 8.

371. "The Dead Monarch," *Daily Alta California*, Jan. 22, 1891, 8.

372. "The Dead Monarch," *Daily Alta California*, Jan. 22, 1891, 8.

373. "The Dead Monarch," *Daily Alta California*, Jan. 22, 1891, 8.

374. "The Dead Monarch," *Daily Alta California*, Jan. 22, 1891, 8.

375. "The Dead Monarch," *Daily Alta California*, Jan. 22, 1891, 8.

376. Historical and Misc. Manuscripts Dated 1890–1893, M-418, Hawaii State Archives.

377. "The Dead Monarch," *Daily Alta California*, Jan. 22, 1891, 8.

378. "The Dead Monarch," *Daily Alta California*, Jan. 22, 1891, 8.

379. "America's Tribute," *Daily Alta California*, Jan. 23, 1891, 8.

380. "King Kalakaua Dead," *Pacific Commercial Advertiser*, Jan. 30, 1891, 2.

381. Letter from Ida Pope to My Dear Popes, Pope, Ida, Kamehameha School for Girls, Corres & Biographical items, copies 1910–1919, Hawaiian Historical Society Uncataloged Manuscripts.

382. Mary Krout, *Reminiscences of Mrs. Mary S. Rice* (Honolulu: Hawaiian Gazette, 1908) 112.

383. Mary Krout, *Reminiscences of Mrs. Mary S. Rice* (Honolulu: Hawaiian Gazette, 1908) 112.

384. Mary Krout, *Reminiscences of Mrs. Mary S. Rice* (Honolulu: Hawaiian Gazette, 1908) 112.

385. Invitations, Menus, Etc., M-485, Invitations-Royalty-Funerals, Etc., Hawaii State Archives.
386. *Constitution and By-laws of the Hale Naua or Temple of Science*, San Francisco: Bancroft Company, 1890, 27. [M-469]
387. "King Kalakaua Dead," *Pacific Commercial Advertiser*, Jan. 30, 1891, 2.
388. Godfrey Thring, *A Church of England Hymn Book* (London: W. Skeffington, 1880).
389. "King Kalakaua Dead," *Pacific Commercial Advertiser*, Jan. 30, 1891, 2.
390. "King Kalakaua Dead," *Pacific Commercial Advertiser*, Jan. 30, 1891, 2.
391. "By Authority," *Pacific Commercial Advertiser*, Jan. 30, 1891, 2.
392. Correspondence, January 1891, Minister of Finance, Hawaii State Archives.
393. Correspondence, February 1891, Funeral Expenses of King Kalakaua, Hawaii State Archives.
394. "A Second Sorrow," *Daily Bulletin*, Aug. 28, 1891, 3.
395. "A Second Sorrow," *Daily Bulletin*, Aug. 28, 1891, 3.
396. "A Second Sorrow," *Daily Bulletin*, Aug. 28, 1891, 3.
397. Broadsides, FO&Ex, Order of Procession for the Funeral of His Late Royal Highness Prince John Owen Dominis, dated Sept. 4, 1891, Hawaii State Archives.
398. "At Rest," *Pacific Commercial Advertiser*, Sep. 7, 1891, 2.
399. Mary Kawena Pukui, *Olelo Noeau* (Honolulu: Bishop Museum Press, 1983) 150.
400. "Sudden Death," *Pacific Commercial Advertiser*, Oct. 2, 1895, 1.
401. "Death of an Alii," *Independent*, Oct. 3, 1895, 3.
402. "Laid to Test," *Pacific Commercial Advertiser*, Oct. 4, 1895, 6.
403. "Laid to Test," *Pacific Commercial Advertiser*, Oct. 4, 1895, 6.
404. "Laid to Test," *Pacific Commercial Advertiser*, Oct. 4, 1895, 6.
405. "Laid to Test," *Pacific Commercial Advertiser*, Oct. 4, 1895, 6.
406. "Laid to Test," *Pacific Commercial Advertiser*, Oct. 4, 1895, 6.
407. Interior Department Book, Oct. 3, 1895, vol. 74, 113, Hawaii State Archives.
408. Broadsides, FO&Ex, Oct 21, 1899, Hawaii State Archives.
409. Broadsides, FO&Ex, 1899, Hawaii State Archives.
410. Broadsides, FO&Ex, 1899, Invitation of the Religious Services on the Occasion of the Funeral of the late Queen Dowager Kapiolani, unsigned, dated June 29, 1899. Sent to Foreign Consuls, Council of State, Judges Supreme Court and others, Hawaii State Archives.
411. "By Authority," *Evening Bulletin*, Jun. 30, 1899, 1.
412. Invitations, Menus, Etc., M-485, Invitations-Royalty-Funerals, Etc., Hawaii State Archives.
413. Mary Kawena Pukui, *Olelo Noeau* (Honolulu: Bishop Museum Press, 1983) 291.
414. "Poolas Will Draw the Catafalque of the Prince," *Pacific Commercial Advertiser*, Mar. 13, 1903, 1.
415. *House Journal*, Territory of Hawaii, 1903, 189.
416. *House Journal*, Territory of Hawaii, 1903, 189.
417. *Pacific Commercial Advertiser*, Mar. 15, 1903, 1.
418. "Afternoon Dispatches from the Associated Press," *Hawaiian Gazette*, Mar. 24, 1903, 1.
419. Funeral Notice and Order of Procession, GOV1-3 Dole Miscellaneous, I-L, AH.
420. "Poolas Will Draw the Catafalque of the Prince," *Pacific Commercial Advertiser*, Mar. 13, 1903, 1.
421. "Last Prince of the Kamehamehas," *Pacific Commercial Advertiser*, Mar. 16, 1903, 3.
422. "Time's Changes," *Independent*, Mar. 16, 1903, 3.
423. "Robert Wilcox at Rest: Large Funeral for Late Native Chieftain," *Hawaiian Gazette*, Nov. 10, 1903, 5.
424. "Robert Wilcox at Rest: Large Funeral for Late Native Chieftain," *Hawaiian Gazette*, Nov. 10, 1903, 5.
425. "Robert Wilcox at Rest: Large Funeral for Late Native Chieftain," *Hawaiian Gazette*, Nov. 10, 1903, 5.
426. "Attentions Beyond Reason," *Independent*, Apr. 14, 1904, 4.
427. "Attentions Beyond Reason," *Independent*, Apr. 14, 1904, 4.
428. "Attentions Beyond Reason," *Independent*, Apr. 14, 1904, 4.
429. *Ke Aloha Aina*, Apr. 9, 1904, 5.
430. "Dived into Sea to Her Death," *Pacific Commercial Advertiser*, Apr. 7, 1904, 9.
431. Local Brevities, *Pacific Commercial Advertiser*, Apr. 8, 1904, 9.
432. "The Kunuiakea Funeral," *Hawaiian Star*, Apr. 7, 1904, 5.
433. *Ke Aloha Aina*, Apr. 9, 1904, 5.
434. "Alii Laid to Rest with Imposing Ceremonies," *Hawaiian Gazette*, June 23, 1908, 3.
435. "Alii Laid to Rest with Imposing Ceremonies," *Hawaiian Gazette*, June 23, 1908, 3.
436. Letter from A.S. Cleghorn to D.L. Conkling, June 22, 1908, Gov. Frear, GOV 3-10, David Kawananakoa Funeral, Hawaii State Archives.
437. Letter from Theresa Wilcox to D.L. Conkling, June 18, 1908, Gov. Frear, GOV 3–

10, Frear—Miscellaneous, David Kawananakoa—Funeral, Hawaii State Archives.

438. Letter D.L. Conkling to Theresa Wilcox, June 18, 1908, Gov. Frear, GOV 3–10, Frear—Miscellaneous, David Kawananakoa—Funeral, Hawaii State Archives.

439. Letter from Theresa Wilcox to D.L. Conkling, June 18, 1908, Gov. Frear, GOV 3–10, Frear—Miscellaneous, David Kawananakoa—Funeral, Hawaii State Archives.

440. "Why Theresa Was Absent," *Hawaiian Gazette,* June 23, 1908, 8.

441. "Some Rival Claimants," *Hawaiian Star,* January 27, 1899, 3.

442. *Pacific Commercial Advertiser,* June 20, 1908.

443. *Hawaiian Star,* Jun. 3, 1908, 7.

444. [Newspaper Clipping] *Pacific Commercial Advertiser,* n.d., n.p., David Kawananakoa Funeral, GOV3–10, Hawaii State Archives.

445. [Newspaper Clipping] *Pacific Commercial Advertiser,* n.d., n.p., David Kawananakoa Funeral, GOV3–10, Hawaii State Archives.

446. [Newspaper Clipping] *Pacific Commercial Advertiser,* n.d., n.p., David Kawananakoa Funeral, GOV3–10, Hawaii State Archives.

447. "Honors Paid the Late Gov. Cleghorn," *Hawaiian Star,* Nov. 2, 1910, 1.

448. Order of Procession, n.d., Frear Miscellaneous (By Name) A-C, Walter Fransic Frear, Governor of Hawaii GOV3–11, Hawaii State Archives.

449. Order of Procession, n.d., Frear Miscellaneous (By Name) A-C, Walter Fransic Frear, Governor of Hawaii GOV3–11, Hawaii State Archives.

450. "Military Honor at Cleghorn Funeral," *Evening Bulletin,* Nov. 5, 1910, 1.

451. "Pay Respects to Late C.R. Bishop," *Honolulu Star-Bulletin,* June 23, 1915, 1.

452. "Pay Respects to Late C.R. Bishop," *Honolulu Star-Bulletin,* June 23, 1915, 1.

453. GOV4 Pinkham Miscellaneous, Proclamations, Executive Orders, Hawaii State Archives.

454. "Liliuokalani is Laid to Final Rest," *Hawaiian Gazette,* November 20, 1917, 1.

455. "Liliuokalani is Laid to Final Rest," *Hawaiian Gazette,* Nov. 20, 1917, 3.

456. Letter from Lorrin Andrews to Curtis P. Iuakea, W.O. Smith, S.M. Damon, and J.K. Kalanianaole, Nov. 9, 1917, Liliuokalani Death (1917), Liliuokalani Trust, M-397, Hawaii State Archives.

457. *Hawaiian Gazette,* Nov. 16, 1917, 1.

458. "Dead Queen Rests Amid Setting of Somber Splendor," *Hawaiian Gazette,* Nov. 16, 1918, 1.

459. "Dead Queen Rests Amid Setting of Somber Splendor," *Hawaiian Gazette,* Nov. 16, 1918, 1.

460. "Dead Queen Rests Amid Setting of Somber Splendor," *Hawaiian Gazette,* Nov. 16, 1918, 1.

461. "Order of Service for the Funeral of Her Late Majesty Liliuokalani," Nov. 18, 1917, Invitations, Menus, Etc., M-485, Invitations-Royalty-Funerals, Etc., Hawaii State Archives.

462. "Order of Service for the Funeral of Her Late Majesty Liliuokalani," Nov. 18, 1917, Invitations, Menus, Etc., M-485, Invitations-Royalty-Funerals, Etc., Hawaii State Archives.

463. "Royal Honors Paid to Queen in Throne Room," *Hawaiian Gazette,* Nov. 20, 1917, 2.

464. *Baibala Hemolele,* 1868.

465. Gordon to Curtis P. Iaukea, Nov. 14, 1917, Liliuokalani Death (1917), Liliuokalani Trust, M-397, Hawaii State Archives.

466. Gordon to Curtis P. Iaukea, Nov. 16, 1917, Liliuokalani Death (1917), Box 2, Folder 12, Liliuokalani Trust, M-397, Hawaii State Archives.

467. "To Shape Details of Funeral Today," *Hawaiian Gazette,* Nov. 16, 1917, 3.

468. Letter from John F. Colburn to J.K. Kalanianaole and Curtis P. Iuakea, Nov. 14, 1917, Liliuokalani Death (1917), Liliuokalani Trust, M-397, Hawaii State Archives.

469. "Royal Honors Paid to Queen in Throne Room," *Hawaiian Gazette,* Nov. 20, 1917, 3.

470. "Queen's Funeral Cortege to be Great Spectacle," *Pacific Commercial Advertiser,* Nov. 17, 1917, 1.

471. Thomas G. Thrum, ed., "Death, Lying in State and Obsequies of Queen Liliuokalani," *Hawaiian Almanac and Annual for 1918,* Honolulu, 1917, 109.

472. "Order of Service for the Funeral of Her Late Majesty Liliuokalani," Nov. 18, 1917, Invitations, Menus, Etc., M-485, Invitations-Royalty-Funerals, Etc., Hawaii State Archives.

473. Agreement dated 14 Jan, 1918,, Liliuokalani Funeral Expense, Box 2, Folder 13, Liliuokalani Trust, M-397, Hawaii State Archives.

474. Queen Liliuokalani Funeral Expenses, Liliuokalani Funeral Expenses, May 1, 1918, Liliuokalani Trust, M-397, Hawaii State Archives.

475. Letter from W.O. Smith to A.P. Taylor, Nov. 15, 1917, Liliuokalani Death (1917), Liliuokalani Trust, M-397, Hawaii State Archives.

476. *Senate Journal,* Special Session of 1918, 177.

477. *Senate Journal,* Special Session, 1918, 27.

478. Memorial Services of the Legislature of Hawaii, Special Session of 1918, Hawaii State Archives.

479. "Thousands See Prince's Face for Last Time," *Honolulu Star-Bulletin,* Jan. 14, 1922, 1.

480. "Thousands See Prince's Face for Last Time," *Honolulu Star-Bulletin*, Jan. 14, 1922, 1.
481. "Monarchy Sentiment Of Hawaiians Last At Prince's Funeral, *Honolulu Advertiser*, Jan. 15, 1922, 2.
482. Kalanianaole, Honorable J.K.—State Funeral, GOV6-21, Hawaii State Archives.
483. "Kuhio's Tomb in Mausoleum Now Sealed," *Honolulu Advertiser*, Jan. 17, 1922, 3.
484. "Funeral Pictures and New Organ Features of Liberty's Program," *Honolulu Advertiser*, Jan. 22, 1922, 3.
485. "Will Film Funeral," *Honolulu Star-Bulletin*, Jan. 13, 1922, 2.
486. "Kuhio Came From Long Kingly Line," *Honolulu Advertiser*, Jan.16, 1922, 2.
487. "High Chiefess Pratt Dies at the Age of 94," *Honolulu Star-Bulletin*, December 20, 1928, 1.
488. "Last of Great Aliis Hears Final Call," *Honolulu Advertiser*, Dec. 21, 1928, 1.
489. "Pratt Services Set for Sunday," *Honolulu Star-Bulletin*, Dec. 21, 1928, 1.
490. John C. Reed, "Funeral of Great Alii Closes Cycle," *Honolulu Advertiser*, December 24, 1928, 1.
491. John C. Reed, "Funeral of Great Alii Closes Cycle," *Honolulu Advertiser*, December 24, 1928, 2.
492. John C. Reed, "Funeral of Great Alii Closes Cycle," *Honolulu Advertiser*, December 24, 1928, 2.
493. John C. Reed, "Funeral of Great Alii Closes Cycle," *Honolulu Advertiser*, December 24, 1928, 2.
494. "Services for Mrs. Woods at 3 p.m. Sunday," *Honolulu Star-Bulletin*, Feb. 20, 1932, 1.
495. "All Races Join in Service for Late Princess," *Honolulu Star-Bulletin*, Feb. 22, 1932, 3.
496. "All Races Join in Service for Late Princess," *Honolulu Star-Bulletin*, Feb. 22, 1932, 3.
497. "All Races Join in Service for Late Princess," *Honolulu Star-Bulletin*, Feb. 22, 1932, 3.
498. "Services for Mrs. Woods at 3 p.m. Sunday," Honolulu Star Bulletin, Feb. 20, 1932, 1.
499. "All Races Join in Service for Late Princess," *Honolulu Star-Bulletin*, Feb. 22, 1932, 3.
500. "All Races Join in Service for Late Princess," *Honolulu Star-Bulletin*, Feb. 22, 1932, 3.
501. "Skies Weep As Princess Goes to Rest," Honolulu Advertiser,, Feb. 22, 1932, 3.
502. Proclamation from Ingram M. Stainback, Apr. 13, 1943, GOV9-37, Proclamations, Sept. 1942–May 1948, Hawaii State Archives.
503. *Senate Journal*, 1945, 583
504. *House Journal*, 1945, 1051.
505. "Hawaiian Skies Weep As Last of Alii Rests," *Honolulu Advertiser*, Apr. 16, 1945, 1.
506. "Hawaiian Skies Weep As Last of Alii Rests," *Honolulu Advertiser*, Apr. 16, 1945, 1.
507. "Hawaiian Skies Weep As Last of Alii Rests," *Honolulu Advertiser*, Apr. 16, 1945, 7.
508. "Hawaiian Skies Weep As Last of Alii Rests," *Honolulu Advertiser*, Apr. 16, 1945, 2.
509. "Hawaiian Skies Weep As Last of Alii Rests," *Honolulu Advertiser*, Apr. 16, 1945, 7.
510. "Hawaiian Skies Weep As Last of Alii Rests," *Honolulu Advertiser*, Apr. 16, 1945, 7.
511. "Hawaiian Skies Weep As Last of Alii Rests," *Honolulu Advertiser*, Apr. 16, 1945, 1.
512. "Hawaiian Skies Weep As Last of Alii Rests," *Honolulu Advertiser*, Apr. 16, 1945, 1.
513. "Kawananakoa Succumbs to Heart Attack," *Honolulu Star-Bulletin*, May 20, 1953, 1.
514. "Kawananakoa Succumbs to Heart Attack," *Honolulu Star-Bulletin*, May 20, 1953, 1.
515. "Final Royal Funeral Service Honors Son of Prince David," *Honolulu Star-Bulletin*, May 25, 1953, 6.
516. "Final Royal Funeral Service Honors Son of Prince David," *Honolulu Star-Bulletin*, May 25, 1953, 6.
517. "Final Royal Funeral Service Honors Son of Prince David," *Honolulu Star-Bulletin*, May 25, 1953, 6.
518. "Kawananakoa to Lie in State at Kawaiahao," *Honolulu Star-Bulletin*, May 21, 1953, 1.
519. "Final Royal Funeral Service Honors Son of Prince David," *Honolulu Star-Bulletin*, May 25, 1953, 6.
520. "Final Royal Funeral Service Honors Son of Prince David," *Honolulu Star-Bulletin*, May 25, 1953, 6.
521. "Final Royal Funeral Service Honors Son of Prince David," *Honolulu Star-Bulletin*, May 25, 1953, 6.

Chapter 2

1. Mary Kawena Pukui, *Olelo Noeau* (Honolulu: Bishop Museum Press, 1983) 141.
2. Malcolm Naea Chun, "Mauna Ala—Burial Place of Sovereigns, High Chiefs," *Ka Wai Ola O OHA*, June 1989, 14.
3. Malcolm Naea Chun, "Mauna Ala—Burial Place of Sovereigns, High Chiefs," *Ka Wai Ola O OHA*, June 1989, 14.
4. Levi Chamberlain re reburial of bones of ali'i taken from Hale o Keawe, Honaunau, February 1829. "The above is a copy of a memorandum made by L. Chamberlain, Sen." One page typescript, with handwritten notes. Hawaiian Historical Society, Uncataloged Manuscripts, Vol. 1, Chamberlain, Levi.
5. Malcolm Naea Chun, "Mauna Ala—Burial Place of Sovereigns, High Chiefs," *Ka Wai Ola O OHA*, June 1989, 14.
6. Pat Namaka Bacon, and Nathan Napoka, eds., *Na Mele Welo: Songs of Our Heritage*

(Honolulu: Bishop Museum Press, 1995) 28–29.

7. Lorrin Andrews, *A Dictionary of the Hawaiian Language* (Honolulu: Island Heritage, 2003) 65.

8. "Missionary Letters to the American Board of Commissioners for Foreign Missions (A. B. C. F. M.)—Volume 03—1824–1830," HMCS.

9. S.M. Kamakau, *Ruling Chiefs of Hawaii: Revised Edition* (Honolulu: Kamehameha Schools Press,1992) 322.

10. W.D. Alexander, "The Hale of Keawe at Honaunau, Hawaii," Maile Wreath, Feb. 1, 1890, 6.

11. "The Old Fort," PCA, Jan. 15, 1857, 2.

12. Interior Department, Feb. 16, 1854, Hawaii State Archives.

13. Levi Chamberlain, Journal, vol. 20, 7.

14. Levi Chamberlain, Journal, vol. 20, 7.

15. Privy Council Records, vol. 4, 414.

16. "Reminiscences of Honolulu—No 19," *Saturday Press*, Jan. 14, 1882, 1.

17. Privy Council Records, vol. 3A, 413–414.

18. Privy Council Records, vol. 3B, 446.

19. "Letters from Polynesia," *The Sailors' Magazine and Naval Journal*, vol. 27, no. 3 (Apr. 1855), New York: American Seamen's Friend Society, 250.

20. ["Honolulu," Hours at Home, vol. 1 (July 1865), 249–250]

21. "Appointments," *Pacific Commercial Advertiser*, Dec. 17, 1863, 3.

22. *Hawaiian Gazette*, Jan. 14, 1880, 5.

23. Gorham D. Gilman, "Streets of Honolulu in the Early Forties," *Hawaiian Annual* (Honolulu: Thomas G. Thrum, 1904) 94.

24. "Old Honolulu Days," *Pacific Commercial Advertiser*, May 21, 1909, 4.

25. "Old Honolulu Days," *Pacific Commercial Advertiser*, May 21, 1909, 4.

26. "Old Honolulu Days," *Pacific Commercial Advertiser*, May 21, 1909, 4.

27. "Leaden Coffin Believed That of Princess Kekupuohi, Old Hawaii's Helen, Dug Up in Palace Grounds," Honolulu Advertiser, Jan. 22, 1931, 6.

28. *Kumu Hawaii*, Mar. 16, 1836, 24.

29. "Brief Historical Sketch of Royal Tomb," U-178, 1942, Hawaii State Archives.

30. Henry P. Judd, *Honolulu Advertiser*, Apr. 28, 1946, 10.

31. *Minutes*, Privy Council, vol. 11, 125, Hawaii State Archives.

32. Minutes, Privy Council, vol. 11, 143, Hawaii State Archives.

33. *Minutes*, Privy Council, vol. 11, 125, Hawaii State Archives.

34. *Minutes*, Privy Council, vol. 11, 142–143, Hawaii State Archives.

35. *Minutes*, Privy Council, vol. 11, 142–143, Hawaii State Archives.

36. *Minutes*, Privy Council, vol. 11, 161, Hawaii State Archives.

37. "The Royal Mausoleum," *Hawaiian Gazette*, Mar. 4, 1874, 2.

38. "The Royal Mausoleum," *Hawaiian Gazette*, Mar. 4, 1874, 2.

39. Letter from R.D. King to L.M. Whitehouse, April 9, 1942, Pamphlet file, Hawaii State Library, Hawaii and Pacific Unit.

40. [Brochure] "Mauna Ala: The Royal Mausoleum," Apr. 1997, Honolulu: Charles Reed Bishop Trust. Included as Daniel S. Quinn, "Request for Authorization for the Construction and Use of a Burial Tomb on the Grounds of the Royal Mausoleum State Monument for Abigail K. Kawananakoa and Delegation of Authority to the Chairperson to Issue a Construction Right of Entry for said Tomb at Mauna 'Ala, Kawananakoa, Nu'uanu Valley, O'ahu, TMK: (1) 2-2-021:012 (por.)," Exhibit C, April 26, 2013, 12.

41. [Brochure] "Mauna Ala: The Royal Mausoleum," Apr. 1997, Honolulu: Charles Reed Bishop Trust.

42. [Brochure] "Mauna Ala: The Royal Mausoleum," Apr. 1997, Honolulu: Charles Reed Bishop Trust.

43. "Removal of the Royal Remains," *Pacific Commercial Advertiser*, Nov. 12, 1887, 3.

44. "Removal of the Royal Remains," *Pacific Commercial Advertiser*, Nov. 12, 1887, 3.

45. "Removal of the Royal Remains," *Pacific Commercial Advertiser*, Nov. 12, 1887, 3.

46. [Brochure] "Mauna Ala: The Royal Mausoleum," Apr. 1997, Honolulu: Charles Reed Bishop Trust.

47. "The Royal Mausoleum," *Hawaiian Gazette*, Feb. 17, 1891, 4.

48. [Brochure] "Mauna Ala: The Royal Mausoleum," Apr. 1997, Honolulu: Charles Reed Bishop Trust.

49. "The Royal Mausoleum," *Hawaiian Gazette*, Feb. 17, 1891, 4.

50. [Brochure] "Mauna Ala: The Royal Mausoleum," Apr. 1997, Honolulu: Charles Reed Bishop Trust.

51. "The Royal Dead of Hawaii," PCA, Nov. 4, 1865, 2.

52. [Brochure] "Mauna Ala: The Royal Mausoleum," Apr. 1997, Honolulu: Charles Reed Bishop Trust.

53. "The Royal Mausoleum," *Hawaiian Gazette*, Feb. 17, 1891, 4.

54. [Brochure] "Mauna Ala: The Royal Mausoleum," Apr. 1997, Honolulu: Charles Reed Bishop Trust.

55. "The Royal Mausoleum," *Hawaiian Gazette*, Feb. 17, 1891, 4.

56. [Brochure] "Mauna Ala: The Royal

Mausoleum," Apr. 1997, Honolulu: Charles Reed Bishop Trust.
57. "The Royal Mausoleum," *Hawaiian Gazette*, Feb. 17, 1891, 4.
58. [Brochure] "Mauna Ala: The Royal Mausoleum," Apr. 1997, Honolulu: Charles Reed Bishop Trust.
59. "The Royal Mausoleum," *Hawaiian Gazette*, Feb. 17, 1891, 4.
60. [Brochure] "Mauna Ala: The Royal Mausoleum," Apr. 1997, Honolulu: Charles Reed Bishop Trust.
61. "The Royal Mausoleum," *Hawaiian Gazette*, Feb. 17, 1891, 4.
62. [Brochure] "Mauna Ala: The Royal Mausoleum," Apr. 1997, Honolulu: Charles Reed Bishop Trust.
63. [Brochure] "Mauna Ala: The Royal Mausoleum," Apr. 1997, Honolulu: Charles Reed Bishop Trust.
64. [Brochure] "Mauna Ala: The Royal Mausoleum," Apr. 1997, Honolulu: Charles Reed Bishop Trust.
65. "The Royal Mausoleum," *Hawaiian Gazette*, Feb. 17, 1891, 4.
66. [Brochure] "Mauna Ala: The Royal Mausoleum," Apr. 1997, Honolulu: Charles Reed Bishop Trust.
67. [Brochure] "Mauna Ala: The Royal Mausoleum," Apr. 1997, Honolulu: Charles Reed Bishop Trust.
68. "The Royal Mausoleum," *Hawaiian Gazette*, Feb. 17, 1891, 4.
69. [Brochure] "Mauna Ala: The Royal Mausoleum," Apr. 1997, Honolulu: Charles Reed Bishop Trust.
70. "The Royal Mausoleum," *Hawaiian Gazette*, Feb. 17, 1891, 4.
71. [Brochure] "Mauna Ala: The Royal Mausoleum," Apr. 1997, Honolulu: Charles Reed Bishop Trust.
72. "The Royal Mausoleum," *Hawaiian Gazette*, Feb. 17, 1891, 4.
73. [Brochure] "Mauna Ala: The Royal Mausoleum," Apr. 1997, Honolulu: Charles Reed Bishop Trust.
74. "The Royal Mausoleum," *Hawaiian Gazette*, Feb. 17, 1891, 4.
75. [Brochure] "Mauna Ala: The Royal Mausoleum," Apr. 1997, Honolulu: Charles Reed Bishop Trust.
76. "The Royal Mausoleum," *Hawaiian Gazette*, Feb. 17, 1891, 4.
77. [Brochure] "Mauna Ala: The Royal Mausoleum," Apr. 1997, Honolulu: Charles Reed Bishop Trust.
78. "The Royal Mausoleum," *Hawaiian Gazette*, Feb. 17, 1891, 4.
79. [Brochure] "Mauna Ala: The Royal Mausoleum," Apr. 1997, Honolulu: Charles Reed Bishop Trust.
80. "The Royal Mausoleum," *Hawaiian Gazette*, Feb. 17, 1891, 4.
81. [Brochure] "Mauna Ala: The Royal Mausoleum," Apr. 1997, Honolulu: Charles Reed Bishop Trust.
82. "The Royal Mausoleum," *Hawaiian Gazette*, Feb. 17, 1891, 4.
83. [Brochure] "Mauna Ala: The Royal Mausoleum," Apr. 1997, Honolulu: Charles Reed Bishop Trust.
84. "The Royal Mausoleum," *Hawaiian Gazette*, Feb. 17, 1891, 4.
85. The Royal Dead of Hawaii," *PCA*, Nov. 4, 1865, 2.
86. [Brochure] "Mauna Ala: The Royal Mausoleum," Apr. 1997, Honolulu: Charles Reed Bishop Trust.
87. "The Royal Mausoleum," *Hawaiian Gazette*, Feb. 17, 1891, 4.
88. David Parker, *Crypts of the Ali'i*, http://www.alulike.org/services/talesofourhawaii_vol3.pdf.
89. [Brochure] "Mauna Ala: The Royal Mausoleum," Apr. 1997, Honolulu: Charles Reed Bishop Trust.
90. "Kamehameha Tomb," Hawaiian Annual, 1904, 180.
91. "To dedicate Royal Tombs," *Independent*, June 15, 1904, 3.
92. "Kamehameha Tomb is Consecrated by Church," *Pacific Commercial Advertiser*, Jun. 20, 1904, 1.
93. "Kamehameha Tomb is Consecrated by Church," *Pacific Commercial Advertiser*, Jun. 20, 1904, 2.
94. [Brochure] "Mauna Ala: The Royal Mausoleum," Apr. 1997, Honolulu: Charles Reed Bishop Trust.
95. "To dedicate Royal Tombs," *Independent*, June 15, 1904, 3.
96. [Brochure] "Mauna Ala: The Royal Mausoleum," Apr. 1997, Honolulu: Charles Reed Bishop Trust.
97. "To dedicate Royal Tombs," *Independent*, June 15, 1904, 3.
98. [Brochure] "Mauna Ala: The Royal Mausoleum," Apr. 1997, Honolulu: Charles Reed Bishop Trust.
99. "The Royal Mausoleum," *Hawaiian Gazette*, Feb. 17, 1891, 4.
100. "To dedicate Royal Tombs," *Independent*, June 15, 1904, 3.
101. [Brochure] "Mauna Ala: The Royal Mausoleum," Apr. 1997, Honolulu: Charles Reed Bishop Trust.
102. "The Royal Mausoleum," *Hawaiian Gazette*, Feb. 17, 1891, 4.
103. "To dedicate Royal Tombs," *Independent*, June 15, 1904, 3.
104. [Brochure] "Mauna Ala: The Royal Mausoleum," Apr. 1997, Honolulu: Charles Reed Bishop Trust.

105. "To Dedicate Royal Tombs," *Independent*, June 15, 1904, 3.
106. "The Royal Mausoleum," *Hawaiian Gazette*, Feb. 17, 1891, 4.
107. [Brochure] "Mauna Ala: The Royal Mausoleum," Apr. 1997, Honolulu: Charles Reed Bishop Trust.
108. "The Royal Mausoleum," *Hawaiian Gazette*, Feb. 17, 1891, 4.
109. "To dedicate Royal Tombs," *Independent*, June 15, 1904, 3.
110. [Brochure] "Mauna Ala: The Royal Mausoleum," Apr. 1997, Honolulu: Charles Reed Bishop Trust.
111. "The Royal Mausoleum," *Hawaiian Gazette*, Feb. 17, 1891, 4.
112. "To dedicate Royal Tombs," *Independent*, June 15, 1904, 3.
113. [Brochure] "Mauna Ala: The Royal Mausoleum," Apr. 1997, Honolulu: Charles Reed Bishop Trust.
114. "To dedicate Royal Tombs," *Independent*, June 15, 1904, 3.
115. "The Royal Mausoleum," *Hawaiian Gazette*, Feb. 17, 1891, 4.
116. [Brochure] "Mauna Ala: The Royal Mausoleum," Apr. 1997, Honolulu: Charles Reed Bishop Trust.
117. "To dedicate Royal Tombs," *Independent*, June 15, 1904, 3.
118. *The Fourth Legislature of the Territory of Hawaii, Regular Session, 1907, Journal of the Senate* (Honolulu: Hawaiian Star Print, 1907) 392.
119. *The Fourth Legislature of the Territory of Hawaii, Regular Session, 1907, Journal of the Senate* (Honolulu: Hawaiian Star Print, 1907) 847.
120. *The Fourth Legislature of the Territory of Hawaii, Regular Session, 1907, Journal of the Senate* (Honolulu: Hawaiian Star Print, 1907) 873.
121. *The Fourth Legislature of the Territory of Hawaii, Regular Session, 1907, Journal of the Senate* (Honolulu: Hawaiian Star Print, 1907) 1133.
122. *Laws of the Territory of Hawaii Passed by the Legislature at its Regular Session, 1907* (Honolulu: The Bulletin Publishing Co., 1907) 188.
123. Letter from Marston Campbell to Liliʻuokalani, Feb. 19, 1908, DAGS 7–18, Hawaii State Archives.
124. Letter from Liliʻuokalani to Marston Campbell, June 28, 1909, DAGS 7–18, Hawaii State Archives.
125. Letter from J. Kalanianaole to Marston Campbell, June 30, 1909, DAGS 7–18, Hawaii State Archives.
126. Letter from Marston Campbell the Mayor of the City and County of Honolulu, June 22, 1910, DAGS 7–18, Hawaii State Archives.
127. Letter from Marston Campbell to Liliʻuokalani, Aug. 29, 1910, DAGS 7–18, Hawaii State Archives.
128. Letter from H.E. Hendricks to Marston Campbell, Sept. 29, 1910, DAGS 7–18, Hawaii State Archives.
129. Letter from Marston Campbell to H.E. Hendricks, Feb. 6, 1911, DAGS 7–18, Hawaii State Archives.
130. Letter from Liliʻuokalani to Marston Campbell, July 24, 1912, DAGS 7–18, Hawaii State Archives.
131. [Brochure] "Mauna Ala: The Royal Mausoleum," Apr. 1997, Honolulu: Charles Reed Bishop Trust.
132. "The Royal Mausoleum," *Hawaiian Gazette*, Feb. 17, 1891, 4.
133. Albert Pierce Taylor, "Royal Tombs of Hawaii," *Paradise of the Pacific*, June 1928, 13.
134. [Brochure] "Mauna Ala: The Royal Mausoleum," Apr. 1997, Honolulu: Charles Reed Bishop Trust.
135. Albert Pierce Taylor, "Royal Tombs of Hawaii," *Paradise of the Pacific*, June 1928, 13.
136. [Brochure] "Mauna Ala: The Royal Mausoleum," Apr. 1997, Honolulu: Charles Reed Bishop Trust.
137. Albert Pierce Taylor, "Royal Tombs of Hawaii," *Paradise of the Pacific*, June 1928, 13.
138. [Brochure] "Mauna Ala: The Royal Mausoleum," Apr. 1997, Honolulu: Charles Reed Bishop Trust.
139. Albert Pierce Taylor, "Royal Tombs of Hawaii," *Paradise of the Pacific*, June 1928, 13.
140. [Brochure] "Mauna Ala: The Royal Mausoleum," Apr. 1997, Honolulu: Charles Reed Bishop Trust.
141. "The Royal Mausoleum," *Hawaiian Gazette*, Feb. 17, 1891, 4.
142. Albert Pierce Taylor, "Royal Tombs of Hawaii," *Paradise of the Pacific*, June 1928, 13.
143. [Brochure] "Mauna Ala: The Royal Mausoleum," Apr. 1997, Honolulu: Charles Reed Bishop Trust.
144. Albert Pierce Taylor, "Royal Tombs of Hawaii," *Paradise of the Pacific*, June 1928, 13.
145. [Brochure] "Mauna Ala: The Royal Mausoleum," Apr. 1997, Honolulu: Charles Reed Bishop Trust.
146. Albert Pierce Taylor, "Royal Tombs of Hawaii," *Paradise of the Pacific*, June 1928, 13.
147. [Brochure] "Mauna Ala: The Royal Mausoleum," Apr. 1997, Honolulu: Charles Reed Bishop Trust.
148. [Brochure] "Mauna Ala: The Royal Mausoleum," Apr. 1997, Honolulu: Charles Reed Bishop Trust.
149. "The Royal Mausoleum," *Hawaiian Gazette*, Feb. 17, 1891, 4.

150. [Brochure] "Mauna Ala: The Royal Mausoleum," Apr. 1997, Honolulu: Charles Reed Bishop Trust.
151. "The Royal Mausoleum," *Hawaiian Gazette*, Feb. 17, 1891, 4.
152. [Brochure] "Mauna Ala: The Royal Mausoleum," Apr. 1997, Honolulu: Charles Reed Bishop Trust.
153. "The Royal Mausoleum," *Hawaiian Gazette*, Feb. 17, 1891, 4.
154. [Brochure] "Mauna Ala: The Royal Mausoleum," Apr. 1997, Honolulu: Charles Reed Bishop Trust.
155. [Brochure] "Mauna Ala: The Royal Mausoleum," Apr. 1997, Honolulu: Charles Reed Bishop Trust.
156. [Brochure] "Mauna Ala: The Royal Mausoleum," Apr. 1997, Honolulu: Charles Reed Bishop Trust.
157. "The Royal Mausoleum," *Hawaiian Gazette*, Feb. 17, 1891, 4.
158. Albert Pierce Taylor, "Royal Tombs of Hawaii," *Paradise of the Pacific*, June 1928, 13.
159. [Brochure] "Mauna Ala: The Royal Mausoleum," Apr. 1997, Honolulu: Charles Reed Bishop Trust.
160. Albert Pierce Taylor, "Royal Tombs of Hawaii," *Paradise of the Pacific*, June 1928, 13.
161. [Brochure] "Mauna Ala: The Royal Mausoleum," Apr. 1997, Honolulu: Charles Reed Bishop Trust.
162. Albert Pierce Taylor, "Royal Tombs of Hawaii," *Paradise of the Pacific*, June 1928, 13.
163. [Brochure] "Mauna Ala: The Royal Mausoleum," Apr. 1997, Honolulu: Charles Reed Bishop Trust.
164. "Some Genealogy," *Hawaiian Gazette*, May 27, 1898, 5.
165. [Brochure] "Mauna Ala: The Royal Mausoleum," Apr. 1997, Honolulu: Charles Reed Bishop Trust.
166. 108.
167. [Brochure] "Mauna Ala: The Royal Mausoleum," Apr. 1997, Honolulu: Charles Reed Bishop Trust.
168. Albert Pierce Taylor, "Royal Tombs of Hawaii," *Paradise of the Pacific*, June 1928, 13.
169. [Brochure] "Mauna Ala: The Royal Mausoleum," Apr. 1997, Honolulu: Charles Reed Bishop Trust.
170. "The Royal Mausoleum," *Hawaiian Gazette*, Feb. 17, 1891, 4.
171. Thomas Thrum, *Hawaiian Annual*, 1909, 109.
172. http://www.pacificworlds.com/nuuanu/memories/kaai.cfm.
173. "The Royal Mausoleum," *Hawaiian Gazette*, Feb. 17, 1891, 4.
174. "The Royal Mausoleum," *Hawaiian Gazette*, Feb. 17, 1891, 4.
175. The Royal Dead of Hawaii," *PCA*, Nov. 4, 1865, 2.
176. "The Royal Mausoleum," *Hawaiian Gazette*, Feb. 17, 1891, 4.
177. "Na Alii Hawaii I Mauna Ala," *Ke Hawaii Pae Aina*, Feb 14, 1891.
178. "The Royal Mausoleum," *Hawaiian Gazette*, Feb. 17, 1891, 4.
179. "The Royal Mausoleum," *Hawaiian Gazette*, Feb. 17, 1891, 4.
180. "The Royal Mausoleum," *Hawaiian Gazette*, Feb. 17, 1891, 4.
181. "Na Alii Hawaii I Mauna Ala," *Ko Hawaii Pae Aina*, Feb 14, 1891, 2.
182. Liber 304, 60, Bureau of Conveyances, State of Hawaii.
183. Sarah Zoellick, "Sacred Grounds: Abigail Kawananakoa 'has the genealogy' to be buried at the Royal Mausoleum, but her state-approved request still has been devisive," *Honolulu Star-Advertiser*, June 9, 2013, A-1.
184. Sarah Zoellick, "Sacred Grounds: Abigail Kawananakoa 'has the genealogy' to be buried at the Royal Mausoleum, but her state-approved request still has been devisive," *Honolulu Star-Advertiser*, June 9, 2013, A-6.
185. Lee Cataluna, "Groups share responsibility in perpetuating Mauna Ala," *Honolulu Star-Advertiser*, May 20, 2016.
186. "The Tomb of Lunalilo," *Pacific Commercial Advertiser*, Jul. 10, 1875, 3.
187. [Brochure] "Mauna Ala: The Royal Mausoleum," Apr. 1997, Honolulu: Charles Reed Bishop Trust.
188. [Brochure] "Mauna Ala: The Royal Mausoleum," Apr. 1997, Honolulu: Charles Reed Bishop Trust.
189. "The Royal Mausoleum," *Hawaiian Gazette*, Feb. 17, 1891, 4.
190. "The Royal Mausoleum," *Hawaiian Gazette*, Feb. 17, 1891, 4.
191. Interior Department, Book 15, 229, Aug. 14, 1878, Hawaii State Archives.
192. *Pacific Commercial Advertiser*, Mar. 1, 1879, 4.
193. *Pacific Commercial Advertiser*, Aug. 10, 1878, 3.
194. *Honolulu Advertiser*, Apr. 2, 1941, 2.
195. *Honolulu Star-Bulletin*, Jun. 6, 1967, B2.
196. Pukui, *Hawaiian Dictionary*, 1986.
197. Letter from Bennet Namakeha to Emma Rooke, Oct. 4, 1854, Interior Department, Misc., October 1854, Box 146, Hawaii State Archives.
198. "The Royal Mausoleum," *Hawaiian Gazette*, Feb. 17, 1891, 4.
199. *Polynesian*, May 8, 1852, 207.
200. *Friend*, January 1, 1845, 8.
201. Letter from Davida Malo to Dwight Baldwin, November 4, 1844, Hawaiian Mission Children's Society Archives.

202. Chamberlain Journal, HMCS.
203. Letter from R. Charlton to Joseph Planta, Jr., February 27, 1827, Foreign Office & Executive, Chronological File, 1790–1849, 1827: Jan.–Mar., Series 402, Box 3, Folder 23, Hawaii State Archives.
204. Lorrin Andrews, *A Dictionary of the Hawaiian Language* (Honolulu: Henry M. Whitney, 1865) 557.
205. Levi Chamberlain, Journal, vol. 7, 31, HCMS.

Chapter 3

1. Robert C. Schmitt, "Cemeteries," https://www.hawaiianhistory.org/time-capsules/daily-life/cemeteries/.
2. "Passengers," *Pacific Commercial Advertiser*, June 25, 1857, 2.
3. Name Index, Hawaii State Archives from *Honolulu Advertiser*, May 9, 1930, 5.
4. [Advertisement] "C.E. Williams," *Pacific Commercial Advertiser*, Aug. 18, 1859, 1.
5. [Advertisement] "H.F. Long," *Pacific Commercial Advertiser*, Aug. 18, 1859, 1.
6. Chauncey C. Bennett, *Honolulu Directory, and Historical Sketch of the Hawaiian Or Sandwich Islands* (Honolulu: C.C. Bennett, 1869) 99.
7. Chauncey C. Bennett, *Honolulu Directory, and Historical Sketch of the Hawaiian Or Sandwich Islands* (Honolulu: C.C. Bennett, 1869) 112.
8. Frederick Bagot, ed., *Directory and Hand-book of the Kingdom of Hawaii* (Oakland, California: Pacific Press Pub. Co., 1884) 154.
9. "First Portuguese, Deceased," *Pacific Commercial Advertiser*, Aug. 20, 1906, 8.
10. "Departed," Pacific Commercial Advertiser, Feb. 3, 1887, 2.
11. "Funeral of the late Princess Likelike," *Pacific Commercial Advertiser*, Feb. 28, 1887, 2.
12. First Circuit Court, Probate 2101, Hawaii State Archives.
13. Name Index, Hawaii State Archives.
14. [Advertisement] "There Is No Mistake," *Evening Bulletin*, Aug. 5, 1895, 7.
15. [Advertisement] "To Whom It May Concern," *Pacific Commercial Advertiser*, Aug. 2, 1895, 6.
16. [Letter to the Editor] "A Correction," *Pacific Commercial Advertiser*, Sept. 30, 1896, 6.
17. [Newspaper Clipping] *Pacific Commercial Advertiser*, n.d., n.p., David Kawananakoa Funeral, GOV3–10, Hawaii State Archives.
18. George F. Nellist, ed., *Story of Hawaii and Its Builders* (Honolulu: Honolulu Star-Bulletin, 1925) 876.
19. Quoted in Roger G. Rose, *Reconciling the Past: Two Basketry Kā'ai and the Legendary Līloa and Lonoikamakahiki* (Honolulu: Bishop Museum Press, 1992) 32.
20. Quoted in Roger G. Rose, *Reconciling the Past: Two Basketry Kā'ai and the Legendary Līloa and Lonoikakahiki* (Honolulu: Bishop Museum Press, 1992) 32.
21. Roger G. Rose, *Reconciling the Past: Two Basketry Kā'ai and the Legendary Līloa and Lonoikakahiki* (Honolulu: Bishop Museum Press, 1992) 32–33.
22. "He Made Royal Caskets," *Honolulu Advertiser*, Jun. 23, 1959, 40.
23. "Hawaiian Memorial Buys Williams," *Honolulu Star-Bulletin*, Jan. 5, 1981, A14.
24. Telephone conversation with William Amigone, Diamond Head Mortuary, Sep. 26, 2016.

Conclusion

1. Mary Kawena Pukui, *Olelo Noeau* (Honolulu: Bishop Museum Press, 1983) 251.
2. "Reminiscences of Honolulu.—No 19," *Saturday Press*, Jan. 14, 1882, 1.

Glossary

1. Henry P. Judd, *Handy Hawaiian Dictionary* (Honolulu: Mutual Publishing, 1995).
2. Henry P. Judd, *Handy Hawaiian Dictionary* (Honolulu: Mutual Publishing, 1995).
3. Henry P. Judd, *Handy Hawaiian Dictionary* (Honolulu: Mutual Publishing, 1995).
4. Henry P. Judd, *Handy Hawaiian Dictionary* (Honolulu: Mutual Publishing, 1995).
5. Henry P. Judd, *Handy Hawaiian Dictionary* (Honolulu: Mutual Publishing, 1995).
6. Henry P. Judd, *Handy Hawaiian Dictionary* (Honolulu: Mutual Publishing, 1995).
7. Henry P. Judd, *Handy Hawaiian Dictionary* (Honolulu: Mutual Publishing, 1995).
8. Henry P. Judd, *Handy Hawaiian Dictionary* (Honolulu: Mutual Publishing, 1995).

Bibliography

Books

The Bible. Authorized (King James) Version.
Bingham, Hiram. *A Residence of Twenty-one Years in the Sandwich Islands.* Hartford, Connecticut: Hezekiah Huntington, 1849.
Bishop, Sereno Edwards. *Reminiscences of Old Hawaii.* Honolulu: Hawaiian Gazette, 1916.
Byron, George Anson Byron, and Richard Roland Bloxam. *Voyage of H.M.S. Blonde to the Sandwich Islands, in the Years 1824–1825.* London: John Murray, 1826.
Ellis, William. *Polynesian Researches,* vol. 4.
Euanelio A Mataio: Oia Ka Moo Olele Hemolele No Kakou Haku E Ola'i, No Iesu Kristo, I Laweia I Olelo Hawaii. Rochester, New York: Paiia Ma Ka Mea Ai Palapala a Lumiki, 1828.
Eveleth, Ephriam. *History of the Sandwich Islands: With an Account of the American Mission.*
Forbes, David. *Hawaiian National Bibliography,* vol. 1. Honolulu: University of Hawaii Press, 1999.
Gast, Ross H., and Agnes Conrad, *Don Francisco de Paula Marin.* Honolulu: University of Hawaii Press for Hawaiian Historical Society, 1973.
Grant, Ulysses Simpson. *Papers of Ulysses S. Grant,* vol. 20, November 1, 1869-October 31, 1870. Carbondale, Illinois: Southern Illinois University Press, 1995.
Kamakau, Samuel M. *Ruling Chiefs of Hawaii.* Honolulu: The Kamehameha Schools Press, 1961, 1992.
Klieger, P. Christiaan. *Moku'ula: Maui's Sacred Isle.* Honolulu: Bishop Museum Press, 1998.
Korn, Alfons. *News from Molokai: Letters Between Peter Kaeo & Queen Emma 1873–1876.* Honolulu: University of Hawaii Press, 1976.
Malo, David. *Ruling Chiefs of Hawaii.* Honolulu: Kamehameha Schools Press, 1961.
Malo, David, Malcolm Chun, trans. *Ka Moolelo Hawaii, Hawaiian Traditions: A New Translation.* Honolulu: FirstPeople's Productions, 1996.
Nellist, George F., ed. *Story of Hawaii and Its Builders.* Honolulu: Honolulu Star-Bulletin, 1925.
Oliver, James, and William Giles Dix. *Wreck of the Glide.* New York: Wiley & Putnam, 1848.
Potter, Norris Whitfield. *History of the Hawaiian Kingdom.*
Pukui, Mary Kawena. *Nā Mele Welo.* Honolulu: Bishop Museum Press, 1995.
Pukui, Mary Kawena. *Olelo Noeau.* Honolulu: Bishop Museum Press, 1983.
Richards, Mary Atherton. *The Chiefs' Children's School.* Honolulu: Honolulu Star-Bulletin, 1937.
Richards, William. *Memoir of Keopuolani.* Boston: Crocker & Brewster, 1825.

Rose, Roger G. *Reconciling the Past: Two Basketry Kā'ai and the Legendary Līloa and Lonoika-makahiki*. Honolulu: Bishop Museum Press, 1992.
Stannard, David E. *Puritan Way of Death*. Oxford: Oxford University Press, 1977.
A Preliminary Catalogue of the Bernice Pauahi Bishop Museum of Polynesian Ethnology and Natural History.
Stewart, Charles S. *Journal of a Residence in the Sandwich Islands*. New York: John P. Haven, 1828.
Thurston, Lucy G. *Life and Times of Mrs. Lucy G. Thurston*. Ann Arbor, Michigan: S.C. Andrews, 1882.
Twain, Mark. *Roughing It*. New York: Harper and Brothers, 1918.

Hawaii Newspapers

Au Okoa
Friend
Hawaiian Gazette
Honolulu Advertiser
Honolulu Star-Bulletin

Kumu Hawaii
Pacific Commercial Advertiser
Polynesian
Sandwich Islands Gazette

Mainland Newspapers

Burlington Weekly Free Press
Charleston Daily News
Evening Telegraph (Philadelphia)

National Republican
New York Herald
Richmond Dispatch

Index

Numbers in *bold italics* indicate pages with illustrations

Abigail Kawānanakoa Foundation 204
ahu'ula 29, 129, 161
ai kapu 38
Aila, William J. 199, 202–203
Āinahau 121, 153, 156
Akaka, Daniel K. 203, 204
Akana, Akaiko 167
Alapa'i, Juliana 65, 198
ali'i 1, 3, 4, 7–9. 13, 14, 17, 18, 20–21, 28, 33, 35, 36, 42, 58, 91, 147, 177, 178, 181, 191, 197, 202, 204, 207, 216
American Board of Commissioners for Foreign Missions 8, 13, 35, 76, 178
American Legion of Honor 120, 123, 133, 137
Ana, Keoni 38, 41, 54, 55, 56, 64, *65*, 66, 72, 105, 187, 191, 198
Ancient Order of Foresters 104, 123, 133
Anglican Church 79, 94, 96, 108, 110, 113, 115, 117, 120, 123, 127, 140, 141, 157
Auhea *see* Kekāuluohi
Ault, William 157

Beckley, Frederick William 147
Bernice Pauahi Bishop Estate 204
Bernice Pauahi Bishop Museum 213, 219, *222*, 236
bier 24, 27, 40, 91, 114, 125, 147, 148, 160, 170
Bingham, Hiram 8, *10*, 19, 29, 37, 96, 208
Bingham, Levi Parsons 9–10, *11*, 19
Bingham, Sybil 9, *10*
Bird, Isabel 98
Bishop, Artemas 12, 27
Bishop, Charles Reed 74, 110, 112, 157, 177, 189–190, 198, 201, 204
Bishop, Elizabeth Edwards 8–10
Bishop Memorial 177, 198, 201
Bishop of Arathea 77, 81–82, 87, 94, 96
Bishop of Honolulu 77, 80, 94, 96, 102, 104, 108, 111, 113, 123, 127, 133, 135, 142, 161–162, 169

Bishop of Olba 104, 108, 111–113, 133–134
Bishop of Panapolis 142, 146
Boeynaems, Libert H. 148, 151, 153, 154
Boki 25, 35, 38, *46*, 47, 180, 207
Bray, David 176
broadside 13, 53, 55, 67, 76, 96, 112, 125–126, 137, 141, 168
burial 1, 3, 5, 8–10, 12, 14, 18 20–22, 24–25, 27, 30, 33, 36, 38, 39, 40–41, 43, 46–48, 50–51, 54, 56–57, 61, 66, 68, 70, 73, 75, 82, 84, 87–88, 95, 97, 103, 105, 110, 120–121, 124–125, 127, 135, 137, 139, 150, 156, 157–158, 163, 165, 167, 169, 170–172, 174–178, 180–184, 186, 190, 192–194, 196–204, 206, 208, 216

California 83, 111, 128–130, 157, 175, 198
Campbell, Abigail Wahi'ika'ahu'ula 154, 172–175, 195
caparisoned horse 63, 78
Carter, George Robert 192
casket 27, 43–44, 54, 59, 104, 107, 129, 130, 136, 147–148, 150–151, 161, 165, 167, 171–172, 176, 194–196, 213
catafalque 56, 78, 181, 109, 112, 114, 123–124, 129, 133–134, 142, 144–145, 148–149, 151, 154–155, 164, 169
cavalry 14, 62, 77, 79, 81, 84, 86–87, 89–90, 93, 94, 102, 108–110, 112–114, 117, 123, 139, 164
cenotaph 198, 201
Chamberlain 51–53, 55, 63–65, 67, 76, 78, 85–86, 89, 93, 96, 106, 111–112, 121, 127, 131, 133, 136, 181, 207
Chamberlain, Levi 37–38, 41, 181, 207–208
chant 6, 113, 123, 125, 176, 178
Charles Reed Bishop Trust 204
Chiefs' Children's School 48, 57, 70, 112, 170, 202
Clarke School of Embalming 212
Cleghorn, Archibald Scott 13–14, 96, 102,

237

238 Index

121, 123, 133–134, 139, 142, 145–146, 153–154, 156–157, 192–194, 196
coffin 9, 12, 19, 26, 28, 31–32, 35, 37, 38, 40, 42–43, 45, 49, 52–55, 59–61, 64, 66–70, 72–75, 77, 81, 84, 89–91, 95–96, 98–99, 102, 108, 110, 112, 114–115, 117, 121–123, 125, 129–131, 135, 137–138, 148, 150, 156–158, 163, 167, 176, 182–184, 211–213
Colburn, John F. 160, 164
Committee of Safety 192
Conde, Andelucia Lee 43
Coney, William Hulilauakea 152
Cook, James 3, *4*
Cooke, Amos Starr 48, 71, 94
corpse 3, 12, 18,-19, 25, 27–28, 35, 44, 49, 75, 79, 87, 91, 98, 137
crown lands 77, 81, 94, 96, 123, 146, 149

Daughters and Sons of Hawaiian Warriors 169–170
Davis, Isaac 5–6, 56, 74
Davis, Isaac Young 74, 106, 190
Davis, Sarah 56
death certificate 130
dirges 15, 26, 101, 110, 130, 135, 215
Dr. S. Rodgers' Perfect Embalming School 212
Dole, Sanford Ballard 14, 145–147, 152, 157
Dominis, John Owen 114, 136, 159, 194, 211, 227
Dominis, Mary 136

Edinburgh, Scotland 156
Ellis, William 13, 22, 25, 29–30, 34
embalming 128
Emmert, Paul 20, 59–60, 62
Episcopal Church 167
Executive Order 201

feather capes 131
Frear, Walter F. 157, 171
funeral 1, 3, 6–10, 12–15, 17, 19–21, 24, 26–27, 29, 32–37, 39–41, 43, 45, 49–59, 61–62, 64–65, 67–70, 72–105, 107–115, 117–118, 120–127, 129–134, 136–141, 142–144, 146–158, 160–169, 171–175, 178, 183, 207, 210–213, 215

Glens Falls, New York 158, 198
Good Templars 94, 96, 156
Grand Army of the Republic 117, 120, 123, 133, 137

Haalelea, Levi 55, 180, 197
Haʻalilio 48, *49*, 50, 52, 55, 61, 182, 196–197
Hale Aliʻi 14, 41, 54, 63, 72, 75
Hale Naua 123, 127, 133–134, 137
Hale o Keawe 177–178, *179*
Hale o Līloa 177–178, 207
Hale O Na Alii 176
Hall, Dana Naone 203

hānai 40, 48, 51, 57–58, 63, 66, 70–71, 74–75, 82–83, 88, 96, 100, 103, 106, 108, 112–113, 115, 190–191, 194, 198–199, 215, 217
haole 5, 6, 43, 56, 74, 158, 210, 217
Hawaiian Flag 52–56, 65, 67
Hawaiian Memorial Park Mortuary 213
Hawaiian Mission Academy 175
Hawes, Alexander G. 149
hearse 31, 34, 62, 81, 88, 90, 102–103, 105, 100, 127, 131, 151, 160, 161, 174, 176, 211–212
Henriques, Lucy K. 152
Hikoni 56
Hoapili 18, 24, 35, 43, 46–48, 151, 180, 202
Hoapili Wahine 48
Honolulu 20, 24, 29, 31, 34, 37, 41, 46–48, 54, 56, 57, 59. 64, 69, 71, 73, 76–81, 85–87, 89–91, 93–97, 100, 102, 104, 106, 108, 109, 111–113, 115, 117, 119–121, 123, 127, 130–131, 133, 157, 159, 169, 173–175, 177–178, 181–184, 192, 197–198, 206–207, 209, 211–212
Honolulu Fire Department 81, 86, 93, 96, 102, 108–109, 111, 117, 119, 133, 137
Honolulu Rifles 77–79, 87, 89, 90, 94, 117, 120, 123
Hoʻolulu 202
Hopu, Thomas 12
House of Nobles 53, 56, 63–64, 66, 70, 77, 83–85, 87, 89, 95, 99, 102, 105–106, 110, 119, 127, 139, 158
Houston, Victor S.K. 174
Hubbard, Lela 203
Hui Kaʻahumanu 154, 169, 170
hymns: Aole make e uwe 96; E pili i ou la wau, E kuu Iesu 122; Forever with the Lord 122; IEHOVA e aroha mai 34; Jerusalem, the Golden 130; The Lord Is My Shepherd 125, 166; *Na Himeni Hawaii* 13, 29, 34; Nearer My God to Thee 122; Now the Laborer's Task Is O'er 121, 124, 125, 135, 160, 163, 165; Peace, perfect peace, in this dark world of sin? 165; Rock of Ages 130; Through All the Changing Scenes of Life 123

Iaukea, Curtis Piehu 164, 203, 205, 208, 215–216, 225, 280
interment 12, 19, 20, 22, 27, 30, 51, 56–57, 152, 180
ʻIolani Palace 14, 77, 81–82, 92–93, 97, 100, 121–122, 124, 126, 130, 133, 145, 147, 149, 152–153, 156, 161, 164, 169, 173, 175, 183–184, 199, 204
Iwikauikaua 88, 98, 103, 133, 161, 169, 177

Johnson, Andrew 83
Judd, Albert Francis 139, 213
Judd, Gerrit Parmele 50, 182–184

Kaʻahumanu 5, 6, 23, 25, 28, 30–31, 36–37, 38, *39*, 40, 46, 47, 53, 58, 80, 101, 178–179, 181, 189

Index

kāʻai 33, 177–178, 196, 199, 207, 213, 217, 234, 236
Kaʻawaloa 3, 178–179
Kaeo, Joshua 66, 72, 105
Kaeo, Peter Young 66, 72, 77, 104, 105–106, 191, 198
Kahale, Edward 174–175
Kahanamoku, Duke 174
Kahanawai, Hiram 138
Kahanu, Elizabeth 120, 154, *170*, 171
Kaheiheimālie *see* Hoapili Wahine
kāhili 14–15, 24, 43–44, 52–56, 59, 61–62, 66–67, 77, 79, 81, 84, 87–88, 90, 93–94, 96, 100, 102–105, 107–108, 110, 112–115, 117, 123, 127, 131, 133, 137, 142, 144, 146–148, 154, 156, 158, 164, 166, 169, 171, 174, 176, 193, 215, 217
Kaikioʻewa 8, 25, 207
Kailua 12, 18, 27, 36, 106–107, 184, 207–208
Kaʻiminaʻauao 51, 52, 58, 61, 64, 209–210, 215
Kaʻiulani 13–14, 121, 123, 125, 133–134, 139, *140*, *141*, *142*, 147, 152, 156–157, 194, 196
Kakohe 196–198
Kalahoolewa, William Pitt Leleiohoku 88, *100*, 102, 211
Kalākaua, David 8, 51, 57, 62, 83–84, 87, 90, 94, 100, 103–104, 112, 127, *128*, 130, *131*, *132*, *134*, *135*, 143, 154, 159, 163, 195, 198
Kalākaua Crypt 157, 163, 174, 187, 192, *193*, 194, 196–200, 207
Kalākaua dynasty 98–101, 103, 105, 107, 109, 111, 113, 115, 117, 119, 121, 123, 125, 127, 129, 133, 135, 137, 149, 174, 176, 188, 192, 202, 216
Kalakua *see* Hoapili Wahine
Kalama 38, 43, 48, 50–51, 58, 88, *89*, 90–91, 95, 154, 169, 187–189, 210
Kalanianaʻole, Elizabeth *see* Kahanu, Elizabeth
Kalanianaʻole, Jonah Kūhiō 111, 157–158, 164, 166, *167*, *168*, 171–172, 192–193, 195, 204, 213
Kalanimoku 8, 9, 18, 20–21, 25, 27, 34, 35–36, 51, 106, 189, 207–208
Kalauokalani, David 151–152
Kaleioku 198
Kaleleonalani, Emma 5, 41–42, 58, 66, *67*, 69, 72–75, 77–84, 91, 94, 96, 99–100, 103–106, 108, 110, 115, *116*, 117, *118*, *119*, 120–121, 125, 127, 130, 143, 186, 188, 190–191, 197, 204, 206–207, 211
Kaliokalani 57, 207
Kamakau, Samuel Manaiakalani 19, 21, 24, 26–27, 33, 36, 38, 46–48, 177–178
Kamāmalu 8, *9*, 17, 22, 31, 33–35, 37, 39, 48, 59, 75, 158, 180–181, 184, 186–187, 189, 215
Kamāmalu, Victoria 17, 19, 41, 44, 57, 67 72, *80*, 81–82, 85, 87, 106, 125, 187, 189, 210
Kamanele 18, 186, 196–197, 207
Kameʻeiamoku 4, *5*, 87, 197
Kamehamalu *see* Kamāmalu

Kamehameha, David 40, 41, 187, 189
Kamehameha I 5–6, *7*, 8, 13, 17–19, 25, 28, 31, 36, 38, 40–41, 43, 47–48, 50–51 53, 38, 46, 48, 50, 55, 58–59, 70, 180–182, 184, 186, 188–189, 207
Kamehameha III 13, 24–25, 36–38, 50–52, 56, *58*, 59, *60*, 61, *62*, 63, 65, 72, 74, 88–89, 91, 92, 100, 119, 147–148, 151, 180, 186–189, 191, 197, 201, 215
Kamehameha IV 13, 41, 44, 48, 58, 61, 68–69, 72–74, *75*, 76–80, 82, 85, 92, 100, 103, 106, 108, 115, 120, 130, 186–189, 207, 210
Kamehameha dynasty 50–51, 81, 87, 95, 98, 100, 103, 127, 151, 187–188, 190, 206, 216
Kamehameha School 33, 141, 144, 148, 169, 174, 176
Kamehameha the Great *see* Kamehameha I
Kamehameha Tomb 114, 158, 177, 187, *188*, 190, 197, 199, 201
Kamehameha V 41, 44, 48, 65, 71, 80, 83, 85, 87, *92*, 93, 94, 106, 125, 139, 156, 187, 189, 210
Kanahele, Kamaki 203
Kanaʻina, Charles 38, 50, 94, 96, 98, *99*, 100, 182, 205–206, 211
Kanehoa, James Young 56, 57, 187
Kanekapolei 64, 106, 207
kanikau 6, 26, 36, 39, 77, 78, 92, 101, 113, 145, 215, 217
Kaʻōanaʻeha 55, 65, 82, 103, 187, 191
Kaoleioku 6, 64, 106, 178, 207
Kapaʻakea 77, 82, *84*, 87, 99–100, 121, 127, 159, 194–195, 210
Kapena, John M. 96, 104, 120
Kapiʻolani, Chiefess 25, 47–48, 195, 191, 197
Kapiʻolani, Queen 99, 102, 111, 114, 122, 133, 138, *143*, *144*, *145*, 146–147, 154, 164, 169, 171, 194, 196, 197, 198, 204, 212
Kapule 28, 54
Kauaʻi 10, 12, 17, 28, 30, 36, 43, 51, 53, 55, 70–72, 111, 143, 202, 207, 216
Kaumualiʻi 17, 25, 28–31, 34, 37, 53–54, 111, 143, 180, 202
Kauwai 18, 19, *20*, 21, 50, 180
Kawaiahaʻo 11, 13–14, 37, 40, 49, 50–51, 61, 68, 80–81, 84, 87–88, 93, 95–98, 101, 108, 110, 117–118, 132–133, 140–141, 143–144, 158, 160, 162, 167, 171, 174, 182, 186, 197, 205, 206
Kawaiahaʻo Cemetery 84, 197
Kawaihau Club 108, 122–123, 125
Kawānanakoa, Abigail Campbell *see* Campbell, Abigail Wahiʻikaʻahuʻula
Kawānanakoa, Abigail Kekaulike 198, 202, 203, 216
Kawānanakoa, David 111, 152, *153*, 154, *155*, 175, 195, 198, 204, 212
Kawānanakoa, David Kalākaua 154, 175, 195, 198–199
Kawānanakoa, Lydia Liliʻuokalani 154, 199
Kawānanakoa, Nuʻuanu 184

240　　　　　　　　　　　　Index

Kawānanakoa Tomb 199, *200*, 201; proposal 198; requirement for Archeology Inventory Survey 203; size comparison 201
Keali'iahonui 53–55, 65, 70, 210, 216, 221
Keaupuni 71
Keaupuni vs. *Fred Ogden* 71
Keaweamahi 25, 51, 207
Keaweawe'ulaokalani I 38, 48
Keaweawe'ulaokalani II 48
Ke'eaumoku, George Cox *23*, 25
Ke'eaumoku Pāpa'iahiahi 5, 25, 36
Ke'elikōlani 68, 74, 85, 88, 94, 96, 99, 100, 102–103, *106*, *107*, 108, *109*, 110, 112–115, 186, 188–190, 194, 211
Keka'aniau, Elizabeth 32, 153, 155, 170–171
Kekaulike 108, 110, *111*, 112, 125, 195, 202, 211, 216
Kekāuluohi 19, 37, 43, 50, *51*, 95, 182, 184, 205, 216
Kekau'ōnohi 43, 53–56, 63, 65, 70–71, 180
Kekūāiwa, Moses 51–53, 61, 63–4, 71, 186–187, 189, 209, 210, 215
Kekūanāo'a, Mataio 38, 40, 58, 62, 64, 69, 74, 80, *85*, 86–87, 106, 188–189, 210
Kekuokalani *see* Kaeo, Peter Young
Kekuokalani, Peter Young *see* Kaeo, Peter Young
Keliiahonui, Edward Abel 126–127, 195, 211
Keli'imaikai 2
Keohokālole 57, *84*, 87–88, 93, 100, 121, 127, 159, 194–195
Keōpūolani 13, 21, *22*, 23, *24*, 25, 30–31, 34, 36, 42–43, 58, 61, 115, 180, 188, 215
Keōua 8–9, 17, 21, 69, 109, 112, 114, 151, 154, 158, 177–178
Keōua Hale 109, 112, 114
Kīna'u 37–38, *44*, 45–6, 48, 50, 58, 74, 80, 85, 112, 180, 182, 184, 186–189
Kīna'u, John William Pitt 68–69, 70, 106, 186, 188–189
King, James Anderson 139
Klieger, P. Christian 38, 48
Knights of Pythias 94, 96, 102–104, 120, 123, 133, 156
Koeckemann, Herman 104, 112
Kōnia 38, 43, 50, *64*, 71, 112, 186, 188–189, 207
Koula Cemetery 152
Kuhina Nui 36, 38, 40–41, 44–45, 48, 50–52, 54, 62, 65, 67, 77, 80, 85, 105, 112
Kūhiō *see* Kalaniana'ole, Jonah Kūhiō
Kūnuiākea, Albert 72, 104, 147–148, *149*, 150–153, 156, 159, 173, 191
Kūnuiākea, Mary 148, 151–152
Kupihea, David Malo 151–152

La'anui 37, 170
La Mothe, John 167, 170
Lanikeha 206–207
Lee, William L. 197
Leleiohoku 43, 50

Leleiohoku, William Pitt 51–52, 56, 64, 68, 88, 106, 209–210, 215
Leleiohoku Guard 110
Lewis, Henry 57, 207
Liholiho *see* Kamehameha II
Likelike 8, *9*, 21, 207
Likelike, Miriam 13–14, 57, 87, 96, 102, 108, 110, 112, 117, 120–121, *122*, 123, 125–126, 139, 156–157, 194, 211
Liliha 4, 38, 43, *46*, 47, 70, 95, 180
Lili'uokalani 31, 51, 63, 86, 96, 101–102, 112–113, 120–123, 133, 138–140, 149, 154, 156, 157, *159*, 160, *161*, *162*, *163*, 166, 169, 172, 176, 192–195, 202, 212, 215
Liliuokalani Educational Society 123, 133, 137
Līloa 177–178, 186, 196, 207, 213
Lincoln, Abraham 63
Littell, S. Harrington 172
Loeau, Jane 94–95
London Missionary Society 13, 31
Loomis, Elisha 8
Lot Kamehameha *see* Kamehameha V
Lui-Kwan, Ivan M. 203–204
Lunalilo, William Charles 50–51, 94, *95*, 96–100, 104, 110, 125, 127, 156, 186–187, 206, 211
Lunalilo Mausoleum 184, 197, 205, *206*, 207
lying in state 1, 3, 10, 13, 19, 20, 25, 28, 29, 32, 33, 39, 44, 60, 75, 89, 92, 95, 100–101, 107, 115–116, 121–122, 126, 129–130, 136, 147–149, 153, 156, 158–159, 161, 167, 171, 173, 175
Lyons, Lorenzo 122

Maheha, Abigail 70–72
Maigret, Louis 81
Maioho, William 196, 202
Marin, Don Francisco de Paula 5, 21
Masonic Lodge Le Progres 137
Maui 5, 17, 21, 24–25, 27, 30, 36, 38, 42, 46–48, 56–57, 70, 83, 102, 109, 114, 177, 180, 207, 213
Mauna 'Ala 41, 48, 51, 55, 57, 87, 105, 120, 124, 139, 158, 169–171, 174–177, 180, 183–184, *185*, 186–187, 189, 191, 193, 195, 197–205, 207, 213, 216
missionaries 3, 6, 8–9, 12–14, 19, 21, 23–24, 26, 28, 34, 36, 40, 43, 45, 50, 76, 80, 88, 131, 162, 183, 202, 207
Missionary Herald 9, 19, 20, 27, 76, 78, 82, 115
Moehonua, William 74, 84, 88, 102
Moku'ula 31, 38, 47–48, 177, 180
Moku'ula: Maui's Sacred Isle 38, 48
Mott-Smith, Ernest A. 143, 157
music: Aloha Oe 166, 172, 176; Chopin's Funeral March 94, 172; Hawai'i Pono'i 166, 172; Largo 166; Star-Spangled Banner 166; *see also* hymns

Naea, George 70, 103, 115, 191, 196–197, 206–207

Nāhiʻenaʻena 24, 35, 41, *42*, 43, 51–52, 58–59, 129, 160, 180, 189
Naihe 25, 195, 197
Nāmāhāna 25, 35–39, 181
Namaile 70
Nāmākēhā 69–70, 143, 187, 191, 198, 207
Namokuelua 5, 56, 187, 207
Napoleon, Nanette 202
Neumann, Paul 139
New Haven, Connecticut 9
NorthStar Memorial Group 213
Nunu 196, 198
Nuʻuanu Cemetery 171–172

Oʻahu 9, 17, 21–23, 27–28, 30, 33, 36, 38, 46, 48, 52, 62, 77, 79, 81–82, 84–86, 90–91, 94, 102, 105, 108–109, 113–114, 117, 127, 170, 187, 202
Oʻahu Cemetery 171
Oahu Cemetery: Burial Ground & Historic Site 202
Oahu College 62, 77, 133, 141, 144
obsequies 1, 9, 12–14, 18, 25, 39, 41, 48, 52, 57, 58–59, 61, 63, 72, 74–76, 78, 82–83, 87–88, 91, 93, 98–99, 106, 110, 117, 121, 125, 127, 130, 136, 139–140, 147, 154, 156, 158, 160, 169, 171, 175–176, 207, 209, 210, 212
Odd Fellows 62–63, 77, 86, 94, 96, 104, 113, 120, 123, 133, 137, 156
Office for Hawaiian Affairs 202
Olohana *see* Young, John
Order of Procession 14, 34, 42, 52–55, 61–62, 65–67, 76–79, 82, 84, 86, 89–90, 93, 96, 97, 99, 102–105, 108, 110–111, 113, 117, 123, 126, 133, 137, 139, 141, 143–145, 149, 151–154, 157, 164, 168, 175, 210–212
Our Lady of Peace Cathedral 150, 152
Owana, Theresa 151, 155, 170

Paʻaʻāina 57, 207
Pākī 50, 52–53, 56, *63*, 64, 74, 112, 186, 188–189
pall 40, 59, 91, 115, 122, 148, 160
pall bearers 40, 66–67, 77, 79, 81, 84, 87, 90, 94, 96, 99, 102, 104, 108, 117, 122–123, 125, 127, 133, 137, 142, 144, 148, 154, 164, 169
Parke, W.C. 102
Parker, David 190
Parker, Henry Hodges 80, 88, 96, 97, 108, 110, 140–141, 158, 162, 166
Parker, Maria Maiopili Piikoi 169
Parker, Samuel 154
Parker, W. 91
pāʻū 19, 59, 129, 160, 217
Pauahi 85, 106, 189, 207
Pauahi, Bernice 38, 63–64, 74, 96, 99, 106, 112, *113*, 114–115, 157–158, 160, 188, 190, 198, 201, 207, 211, 215
Peabody, Lucy K. 148, 151, 152
Pellion, Alphonse 8–9
Poola 102, 104, 108, 110, 112–113, 117, 123, 134, 145, 151, 154, 164, 169

Poʻomaikelani 138–139, 195, 202, 212
Pope, Ida 130
Pratt, Frank S. 170
Prince Albert Edward Kauikeaouli Leiopapa a Kamehameha *see* Prince of Hawaiʻi
Prince of Hawaiʻi 72, *73*, 74, 80–82, 86–87, 89–90, 92, 115, 125, 143, 186, 188
Puritan Way of Death 1
Puuloa, Ewa 54

Queen's Health Systems 204
Quinn, Daniel S. 201–202

rain 26, 172
Resterick, Henry B. 149, 161–162, 190
Rice, Mary Sophia Hyde 131
Richards, William 24
Robertson, James W. 77, 133, 136, 142
Roman Catholic 14, 77–79, 81–82, 87, 89–90, 94, 96, 102, 104, 108, 111–113, 117, 123, 133, 141, 146, 148, 150–153, 156
Roman Catholic Cathederal *see* Our Lady of Peace Cathedral
Roman Catholic Cemetery 151
Rooke, Emma *see* Emma Kaleleonalani
Rooke, George 149
Rooke, Grace KamaʻikuʻI *see* Young, Grace Kamaʻikuʻi
Rooke, Thomas Charles Byde 56, 66, *67*, 68, 115, 191, 198
Rooke House 104, 116
Roosevelt, Franklin Delano 173–174
Ropert, Gulstan F. 146
Royal Hawaiian Band 117, 123, 127, 133, 136–137, 166, 169, 172
Royal Mausoleum *see* Mauna ʻAla
Royal Mausoleum State Monument 201–202
Royal Tomb at Pohukaina 35, 40–41, 50, 66, 70, 81, 177, 180, *181*, 182–183, 197
Ruth *see* Keʻelikōlani

St. Andrew's Cathedral 138, 157, 162, 172
St. Andrew's Priory 117, 133, 143–144, 204
St. Louis College 123, 133, 141, 148, 164, 169
San Antonio Beneficente Society 148
San Francisco 83, 97, 129–131, 173, 210–212
sermon 8–9, 19, 29, 80, 88, 97, 135, 175, 207
Smith, William Owen 192
Sociedade Lusitana Beneficente 144, 146
Stainback, Ingram M. 173–174
Staley, Thomas Nettleship 75, 79, 81–82, 186
Stannard, David E. 1
State Historical Preservation Division 202–203
Stevenson, Robert Louis 140
throne room 75, 121–122, 132, 136, 147–149, 152, 161, 166–167

Thurston, Asa 12, 27–28
Thurston, Lucy 12

Trinity Church, San Francisco 128, 130
Twain, Mark 17, 80, 82

Umi 213
undertaker 77, 79, 81, 84, 86, 89–90, 93, 99, 102, 104, 109, 111, 113, 117, 123, 127, 129, 165, 209–213

Waikīkī 125, 143, 156, 211
wailing 6, 8, 12, 15, 18, 21–23, 28, 46, 59, 69, 93, 108, 115, 132, 215
Waine'e Cemetery 31, 47–48, 180
Waiola Cemetery 47, 56, 180
Washington Place 121, 136, 158, 160
Whiting, William Austin 139
Wilcox 264
Wilcox, Kaohi Kapumahana 151
Wilcox, Keoua 151
Wilcox, Robert 150, 152, 166
Wilcox, Theresa Owana *see* Owana, Theresa
Wilcox, W.S. 151
Williams, Charles E. 123, 209, 211

Williams, E.A. 212
Williams, Henry H. 212–213
Willis, Alfred 139
Wilson, Woodrow 160
Woods, Frank J. 171–172
Wreck of the Glide 39–40
Wyllie, Robert Crichton 32, 51, 56, 77, 79, 182, 185, 187, 191, 198, 210
Wyllie Tomb 177, 190, 196–197, 199, 201

Young, Fanny Kekelaokalani 55, 57, 72, 94, 103, 105, 207, 211
Young, Grace Kama'iku'i 55, *67*, 72, 82–83, 115, 191, 197–198
Young, Jane Lahilahi 55, 72, 105, 147–148, 150, 191, 197–198
Young, John 5, 41, 50, 55–57, 65–66, 72, 74, 82, 103–104, 158, 177, 181, 184, 187, 191, 207
Young, John 2nd *see* Ana, Keoni
Young, Robert 207
Young Burial Site 201

www.ingramcontent.com/pod-product-compliance
Lightning Source LLC
Chambersburg PA
CBHW051218300426
44116CB00006B/621